MW01251762

"Information through Innovation"

TOOL KIT
ACCESS 2.0
FOR WINDOWS

Tim Duffy
Illinois State University

TOOL KIT
ACCESS 2.0
FOR WINDOWS

boyd & fraser publishing company

I(T)P   An International Thomson Publishing Company

Danvers ▪ Albany ▪ Bonn ▪ Boston ▪ Cincinnati ▪ Detroit ▪ London
Madrid ▪ Melbourne ▪ Mexico City ▪ New York ▪ Paris ▪ San Francisco
Singapore ▪ Tokyo ▪ Toronto ▪ Washington

Publishing Process Director: Carol Crowell
Production Editors: Barb Colter, Jean Bermingham
Copy Editor: Elizabeth von Radics
Production: Gary Palmatier, Ideas to Images
Text Designer: Juan Vargas
Manufacturing Coordinator: Lisa Flanagan
Compositor: Ideas to Images

I(T)P The ITP™ logo is a trademark under license.

Printed in the United States of America

1 2 3 4 5 6 7 8 9 10 BN 9 8 7 6 5

For more information, contact boyd & fraser publishing company:

boyd & fraser publishing company
One Corporate Place ▪ Ferncroft Village
Danvers, Massachusetts 01923
USA

International Thomson Editores
Campos Eliseos 385, Piso 7
Col. Polanco
11560 México D.F. México

International Thomson Publishing Europe
Berkshire House 168-173
High Holborn
London, WC1V7AA
England

International Thomson Publishing GmbH
Königswinterer Strasse 418
53227 Bonn
Germany

International Thomson Publishing Asia
221 Henderson Road
#05-10 Henderson Building
Singapore 0315

Thomas Nelson Australia
102 Dodds Street
South Melbourne 3205
Victoria, Australia

Nelson Canada
1120 Birchmount Road
Scarborough, Ontario
Canada M1K 5G4

International Thomson Publishing Japan
Hirakawacho Kyowa Building, 3F
2-2-1 Hirakawacho
Chiyoda-ku, Tokyo 102
Japan

ISBN 0-534-30247-5

To Wendy and Michael

CONTENTS

Preface   xii

Chapter 1

Introduction to Databases and Access 2.0 for Windows   DB.2

Terminology   DB.4
Designing Fields   DB.4
Introduction to Access 2.0 for Windows   DB.5
Limitations of Access 2.0 for Windows   DB.5
Access 2.0 for Windows Modes   DB.5
Starting Access 2.0 for Windows   DB.6
The Access Window   DB.6
The Help Facility   DB.11
Cue Cards and Wizards   DB.18
Leaving Access   DB.19
Communicating with Access   DB.19
Creating and Using a Database   DB.19
Creating an Access Table   DB.22
Access SpeedMenus   DB.29
Displaying and Changing Data   DB.30
Navigating Through Records   DB.30
Activating the Database   DB.32
Adding Records to the Table   DB.33
Editing Records in a Table   DB.34
Printing a Report   DB.36
Chapter Review   DB.38
Key Terms and Concepts   DB.39
Chapter Quiz   DB.39
Computer Exercises   DB.41

Chapter 2

Manipulating Files and Records, Sorting, and Indexing   DB.44

Preparing for This Chapter   DB.46
Datasheet Window   DB.46
Cursor Movement   DB.47
Gridlines   DB.48
Changing Field Display Width   DB.48
Changing Row Height   DB.52
Moving a Field   DB.54
Hiding Fields   DB.54
Locking a Field   DB.57

Adding New Records   DB.58

**Table-Manipulation Commands and
Searching Unordered Tables   DB.58**

Record Pointer   DB.58

Locating Records Using Find   DB.60

Arrangement Commands   DB.65

Sort Command   DB.65

Index Command   DB.70

Filter for Selected Records   DB.76

Chapter Review   DB.78

Key Terms and Concepts   DB.79

Chapter Quiz   DB.79

Computer Exercises   DB.81

Chapter 3

**Modifying a Table Structure, Replacing and
Deleting Records, and an Introduction to Reports   DB.84**

Modifying a Structure   DB.86

Adding a Field to the Record Structure   DB.86

Controlling Data Entry and Display   DB.89

Replace Command   DB.100

Deleting Records   DB.101

Introduction to the Report Feature   DB.101

Building a Report Using Report Wizards   DB.103

The Report Design Window   DB.108

Designing Your Own Report   DB.112

Chapter Review   DB.122

Key Terms and Concepts   DB.123

Chapter Quiz   DB.123

Computer Exercises   DB.125

Chapter 4

Access Print Features   DB.128

Advanced Report Features   DB.130

Subtotals   DB.130

Multiple-Line Reports   DB.139

Embedding Calculations Within a Report Template   DB.151

Printing Labels   DB.158

Hands-On Exercise: Creating Mailing Labels   DB.158

Using Access for a Merge Operation   DB.163

Hands-On Exercise: Executing a Merge Operation   DB.165

Graphing Data in a Report   DB.169

Hands-On Exercise: Graphing the Amount Due by Zip Code   DB.169

Chapter Review   DB.172

Key Terms and Concepts   DB.173

Chapter Quiz   DB.173

Computer Exercises   DB.175

Chapter 5

The Query Feature of Access   DB.178

Queries   DB.180

Access Dynasets   DB.180

The Table Used by Query   DB.182

Creating a Query Specification   DB.182

Query Calculations on Groups of Records   DB.199

Performing Table Maintenance Via Queries   DB.204

Creating Backups and Other Tables   DB.204

Including Only Selected Fields   DB.208

Viewing Data by Linking Tables   DB.210

Including Calculations   DB.218

Performing a Table Update Using a Query   DB.222

Chapter Review   DB.227

Key Terms and Concepts   DB.228

Chapter Quiz   DB.228

Computer Exercises   DB.230

Chapter 6

Creating Input Forms and Macros   DB.234

Forms   DB.236

Creating a Form Using the Form Wizards   DB.240

Creating a Custom Data-Entry Form   DB.245

Adding Graphics   DB.255

Using the Form   DB.259

Macros   DB.261

Creating Macros for Form Controls   DB.263

Creating a Macro That Uses the Macro Datasheets   DB.270

Chapter Review   DB.273

Key Terms and Concepts   DB.274

Chapter Quiz   DB.274

Computer Exercises   DB.276

Appendix

Access 2.0 for Windows Command Summary   DB.277

Glossary   DB.285

Index   DB.297

··
PREFACE

PURPOSE

Each text in *The Software Tool Kit* series provides a complete introduction that teaches software competency, getting students up and running in today's most popular software applications. This series is designed for anyone using a computer at home or work.

······················
DISTINGUISHING FEATURES

Hands-On Tutorials   Throughout, these books present skills and then immediately reinforce them through hands-on tutorials. Keyboard icons and second-color text in the tutorials guide you step by step through each process. These tutorials are identified by a computer icon in the margin.

In-Depth Projects   At the end of most chapters are computer exercises that pull together the skills featured within the chapter and provide students an opportunity for in-depth work.

Command Summaries and Glossaries   Each chapter contains its own summary of the commands presented within that chapter. Each complete module also offers an extensive glossary and an appendix that summarizes commonly used functions and commands. The command summaries are excellent quick-reference tools.

Hints/Hazards Boxes   These boxes give you tips and information about potential traps you may encounter when using a particular software tool.

Concise, Clear Writing Style   This series presents technical information in a clear, concise, and simple manner, enabling you to grasp the contents quickly and apply your new skills more readily.

Ultimate Flexibility   An instructor can use this series in a variety of ways—to supplement lecturing or for independent learning, using as many or as few exercises as time permits.

Any of the modules in *The Software Tool Kit* series can be custom bound, providing maximum flexibility to teachers. Each adopter can select those modules that fit his or her particular curriculum and have them bound to order. For further information, or to order your custom-bound text, contact your local boyd & fraser/ITP representative.

SERIES SCOPE

Texts in *The Software Tool Kit* series include:

DOS-based	Windows-based
dBASE IV, Version 2.0	*Microsoft Office*
dBASE IV, Version 1.1	*dBASE 5.0 for Windows*
dBASE III PLUS	*Lotus 1-2-3, Release 5.0 for Windows*
DOS 6.2	*Access 2.0 for Windows*
DOS 6.0	*Excel 5.0 for Windows*
DOS 5.0	*Word 6.0 for Windows*
Lotus 1-2-3, Release 3.4 for DOS	*Paradox 5.0 for Windows*
Lotus 1-2-3, Release 2.4 for DOS	*PowerPoint 4.0 for Windows*
Lotus 1-2-3, Release 2.3 for DOS	*WordPerfect 6.1 for Windows*
Lotus 1-2-3, Release 2.2 for DOS	*WordPerfect 6.0 & 6.0a for Windows*
Quattro Pro 4.0 for DOS	*WordPerfect 5.2 for Windows*
WordPerfect 6.0 for DOS	*Windows 3.1*
WordPerfect 5.1 for DOS	

Finally, in a single module, *DOS Essentials and Windows 3.1,* an overview of these two operating environments is combined with a very brief introduction to microcomputers. For information on these *Tool Kits,* contact boyd & fraser publishing company. Instructors at two-year or four-year institutions, please call 1-800-423-0563. Instructors at career colleges or proprietary schools, please call 1-800-477-3692.

WORKING IN A HANDS-ON ENVIRONMENT

Each software package covered in this series is treated in enough detail to satisfy the requirements of a computer novice. However, the text assumes that the software has already been configured for your use. If a package has not been configured for a specific machine, please refer to the documentation for that package.

For ease of use, all hands-on exercise commands in the text appear in color. This allows you to quickly identify what keystrokes to enter and to distinguish them from additional exploration about a software feature or command. The computer symbol in the margin indicates a hands-on exercise.

ANCILLARY MATERIALS

An Instructor's Manual is available to each adopter of any book in *The Software Tool Kit* series. The manuals contain:

- lecture outlines

- suggested teaching ideas

- test questions

- an adoption response card through which adopters can obtain an Instructor's Resource Disk containing sample worksheets, text files, and database files and solutions

- transparency masters

NOTES FROM THE AUTHOR

The success of *The Software Tool Kit* series has been gratifying. The kind comments from adopters via letters and personal contact at conventions have been most appreciated. Ideas to improve the text have come from hundreds of users and nonusers in surveys and from focus groups, students, and reviewers.

BOYD & FRASER ONLINE

boyd & fraser is now on the Internet and we would like to answer questions and respond to your comments about this text. Our e-mail address is comments@bf.com. You can access boyd & fraser Online via our World-Wide Web home page, http://www.bf.com/bf.html. boyd & fraser Online offers a variety of resources for instructors and students who are using boyd & fraser products, including mailing lists, newsletters, reviews, software, technical support, job postings, teaching tips, product catalogs, review copy request forms, and links to other valuable and interesting sites on the Net.

ACKNOWLEDGMENTS

I am amazed that eleven years have passed since I started the first edition of *Four Software Tools*. When I began writing, I was totally unaware of the time-consuming efforts needed to produce this level of a textbook. Since then, however, I have developed a sincere appreciation of exactly what is required to make a text a success. This success formula includes family, friends, colleagues, and many individuals in the publishing business.

I remain deeply indebted to my wife, Wendy, who initially encouraged me to write the original version of *Four Software Tools*. Without her encouragement, the original text would never have been finished. Without her continued support, these projects would be impossible to accomplish.

I also want to express sincere appreciation to the reviewers of this manuscript as well as to reviewers of prior manuscripts: Jill Betts, Tyler Junior College; William Farley, Lee College; Sandy Hagman, Forsyth Technical Community College; Luis Hernandez, Mesa Community College; Terri M. Lockett, Lee College; Anita Millspaugh, Mt. San Antonio College; John Morrison, International Business College; Leonard Presby, William Paterson State College; Sandra D. Rodgers, Henderson State University; Ginny C. Ross, Georgia Southwestern College; John Russell, Lee College; Helmut Thiess, Towson State University; Mary Allyn Webster, University of Florida; George Whitson, University of Texas at Tyler; Susan Wiemers, Lamar University; Barbara Minnich, Indiana State University; Jackie Artmayer, Oklahoma City Community College; Marie McCooey, Bryant Business School; Linda Bird, Software Solutions; Kathleen Anderson, Empire College; Sonny Stires, Palomar College; and George Novotny, Ferris State University.

The production staff plays an important role in making or breaking a publishing project. I would like to especially congratulate Gary Palmatier, Robaire Ream, and Elizabeth von Radics of Ideas to Images for making this process as painless as possible. Their attention to meeting schedule requirements, their making certain that changes were made properly, and their professional manner are very much appreciated. Elizabeth, Gary, and Robaire continue to be the very best production staff that I have worked with during eleven years of writing. Their professionalism remains among the highest in the publishing industry.

I would also like to thank Carol Crowell, publishing process director at boyd & fraser. Carol has worked extremely hard to smooth the way for my arrival at boyd & fraser. I greatly appreciate her hard work in marketing my existing titles as well as preparing for the new *Tool Kit* series. I enjoyed Carol and Dan's introduction to the low-fat "Philly sandwich."

I would also like to thank Jim Edwards of boyd & fraser. Jim, too, was instrumental in making my arrival at boyd & fraser enjoyable and nonstressful. I enjoyed the "kick off" dinner that Jim took part in arranging shortly after I joined the company, during which I met and talked with a number of boyd & fraser/ITP representatives.

Barb Colter, the developmental editor, also deserves a sincere word of gratitude. Her efforts to keep the project on deadline as well as to maintain internal consistency between and among software modules were most appreciated.

An overlooked ingredient in the success of many textbooks is the publisher's sales staff. I remain firmly convinced that Thomson International's sales staff is one of the best in the business.

An acknowledgment is not complete without including my son, Michael. Michael continues to make any writing project a challenge. His sudden appearances beside the computer for a hug and a cuddle in Dad's lap are much appreciated. It is harder and harder to reserve large blocks of writing time when requests are made to accompany Michael to the backyard for a game of catch, to go for a bike ride, or to play a game of pool.

Tim Duffy

Illinois State University

TOOL KIT
ACCESS 2.0
FOR WINDOWS

Chapter 1 **Introduction to Databases and Access 2.0 for Windows** DB.2

Chapter 2 **Manipulating Files and Records, Sorting, and Indexing** DB.44

Chapter 3 **Modifying a Table Structure, Replacing and Deleting Records, and an Introduction to Reports** DB.84

Chapter 4 **Access Print Features** DB.128

Chapter 5 **The Query Feature of Access** DB.178

Chapter 6 **Creating Input Forms and Macros** DB.234

Appendix **Access 2.0 for Windows Command Summary** DB.277

Glossary DB.285

Index DB.297

1

INTRODUCTION
TO DATABASES
AND ACCESS 2.0 FOR
WINDOWS

CHAPTER OBJECTIVES

After completing this chapter, you should be able to

- **List some of the basic concepts of a database**
- **Plan a table**
- **List the limitations of Access**
- **Use the Access 2.0 for Windows menu structure**
- **Know the parts of the Access window**
- **Use the Access menu options**
- **Issue commands to Access**
- **Create Access tables**
- **Add and edit data**

The concept behind a database is simple. A database is like a file cabinet. Just as a file cabinet stores information, so does a database. Just as the folders in a file cabinet are arranged to hold data in some useful order, so are the records in a database. Searching a database for certain information is like searching in a file cabinet. Just as you can change the order of the folders in a file cabinet to suit your convenience, you can also change the order of things in a database.

TERMINOLOGY

A **database** is a set of information related to a specific application. In the context of Access 2.0, "database" can be viewed as a large repository (like a file cabinet) in which tables, reports, queries, and other objects are stored. When Access creates a database, it places all application-related objects in a file with an .MDB filename extension.

A **table** is the storage entity for a database. It is made up of records that contain data about a single thing, such as a person or a sales transaction.

A **record** is a unit within the table. Each record in a table contains related information about an entity. An entity can be the details of a single business transaction, all of the summary payroll data related to a single employee, or a single customer's name and address and accumulated sales history.

A **field** is a smaller unit within a record that contains a fact about the entity. In a customer record, for instance, one field might contain the customer's last name; another field might contain his or her street address.

Information from one or more fields is used to define **keys**, which are used to order, identify, and retrieve the records in the database. Several keys are commonly used. The **primary key** is the unique identifier for a particular record, most often a customer number or Social Security number. When a database is in primary-key order, the records may appear in the table in order by the contents of the field used to build the primary key, but no two records can have the same key value. A **secondary key** can also be defined by information from one or more other fields within the database. This key is used to arrange the database in some other order. For instance, a user might create a secondary key from the first- and last-name fields. A secondary key differs from a primary key in that it allows multiple occurrences of the same value.

The **table structure** is a set of instructions regarding the arrangement of information within each record, the type of characters (numeric or alphanumeric, for example) used to store each field, and the number of characters required by each field. Once structured, the table can be managed, and the computer can be instructed to do such things as add new records, change existing records, sort and arrange records in a new order, search for and retrieve specific types of records, print data, and delete data.

DESIGNING FIELDS

It is very important to remember two things when designing the fields of a database. First, fields should isolate those pieces of data that you may need to use as keys to sort and rearrange records. Second, whereas humans can often identify separate pieces of information within a field, computers generally cannot. For instance, consider the following four lines from a customer address table.

```
Gerald B. Dixon
1526 N. Main
Bloomington, IL 61703
(309) 367-8934
```

How many fields should it take to store these lines in a record? It is possible to store the customer's name in one field. However, this way it would be impossible for the computer to sort records by last name, because it wouldn't know that Gerald is a first name and Dixon a last name. Nor, for instance, could the computer readily distinguish an address from a telephone number. Thus, designers and users of database tables must take care to lay out fields and enter data in rigid, predictable patterns. The computer can therefore process information in the table solely on the basis of what field the information is in, without any understanding of the meaning of the data. In practice, the above customer information requires eight fields:

```
First Name        Address        Zip
Middle Initial    City           Phone
Last Name         State
```

The name is divided into three fields so records can be sorted by last name and the first name can be used independently of the middle initial. Divisions in the address line let you rearrange records within the database by city, state, or zip code.

Well-designed records provide great flexibility when you choose secondary keys. With the preceding fields, for instance, to produce a report in order by customer name, you could create a key based on first and last name. By changing the keys to last name and city or state, you could produce another report in order by customer name and location.

••••••••••••••••••••••
INTRODUCTION TO ACCESS 2.0 FOR WINDOWS

The Access 2.0 package is one of the best-selling relational database packages for Windows on the market. The current version of Access (Access 2.0 for Windows) evolved from Access, a program designed specifically for the Microsoft Windows environment. Since its introduction, Microsoft has continued to improve Access, and Access 2.0 is the result.

LIMITATIONS OF ACCESS 2.0 FOR WINDOWS

Anyone who wants to use Access 2.0 for Windows should be aware of the following hardware limitations: (1) It requires a computer with an 80386, 80486, or Pentium processor (the later the model and the more MHz rating of the CPU, the better it will run) with a hard disk drive with at least 20 megabytes (20MB) of available disk storage; (2) the system should have 6MB of RAM (8 are recommended); (3) MS-DOS version 3.1 or later, and Windows 3.1 or later; and (4) a mouse as a pointing device.

ACCESS 2.0 FOR WINDOWS MODES

Access 2.0 provides two different modes. The first is an easy-to-use **menu-driven** interface that lets you issue commands without an in-depth understanding of Access. **Program mode** (also referred to as Batch mode), lets you store instructions in an Access Basic program file and execute all of them with one command. This book concentrates on using Access from the menu.

Figure 1.1

The program icon for starting Access 2.0 for Windows.

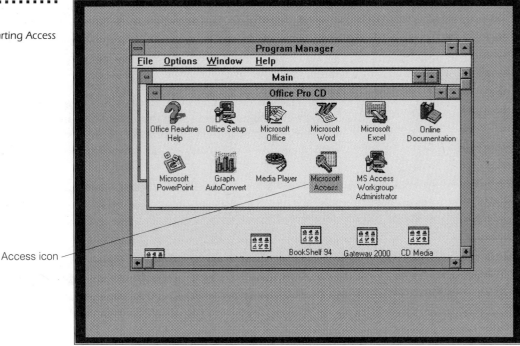

Access icon

STARTING ACCESS 2.0 FOR WINDOWS

Because Access 2.0 for Windows is so large and is Windows-based, it can be run only on a computer containing a hard disk. Starting Access 2.0 requires that you first boot your computer (if it is currently off) and then start Windows. You now double-click the Access icon or the Office Pro Windows group icon. Once the appropriate window appears, you can double-click the Microsoft Access program icon to start Access 2.0 (Figure 1.1).

THE ACCESS WINDOW

Once you have started Access 2.0 for Windows, a copyright screen briefly appears, showing who purchased the package, the company at which this person works, and the version number of the package. This screen disappears after a few seconds, and the Access window is displayed (Figure 1.2). If the screen shown in Figure 1.3 appears, double-click the control-menu button of the MS Access Cue Cards title bar.

Your Access window may not look exactly like Figure 1.2. You may, for instance, have to click the maximize button to get the window to occupy the entire screen.

Title Bar   The **title bar** indicates that you are in Microsoft Access. The control-menu, minimize, and restore buttons are also part of this entity.

Menu Bar (F10)   The line beneath the title bar, the **menu bar**, contains the names of two menus. Activate the menu bar by pressing the F10 function key or Alt key and selecting the menu item by pressing the underlined character. You can also click a menu item using the mouse. Once a menu item is selected, a pull-down menu appears (Figure 1.4). When a pull-down menu appears on an Access screen, you can select options in one of four ways:

Figure 1.2

The Access window.

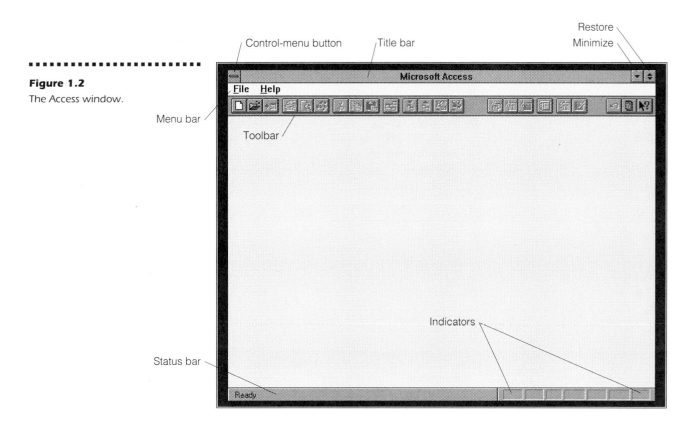

Figure 1.3

The Cue Cards window that
may appear.

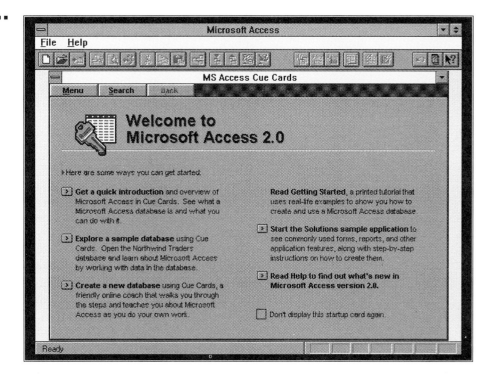

Figure 1.4

The File menu from the menu bar.

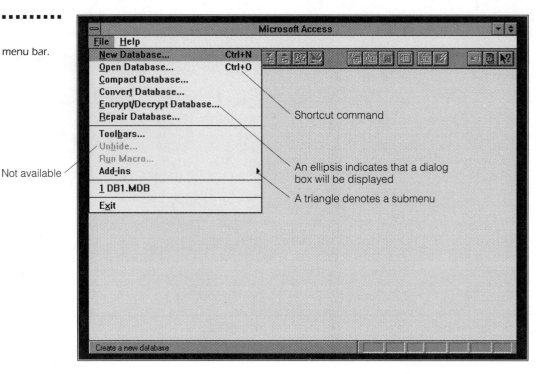

- Move the highlight using the up- or down-arrow keys to choose the desired option from the menu and then press Enter to execute that option.
- Type the underlined character of the menu option.
- Click the desired entry using the mouse. You can position the cursor or use the mouse to select only those options that are in dark black video onscreen. An option that appears in low-intensity video (dimmed) is not available for execution and cannot be reached by using cursor-positioning commands or by entering the underlined character of that menu option.
- Use the shortcut command that appears following the menu item. This command can also be issued without using the Access menu structure.

Once a menu is activated, you can also move horizontally from one menu option to another across the menu bar by pressing the right- or left-arrow key. When you are moving horizontally, you cannot press the first (underlined) character of a desired menu option to choose that option.

Once a menu option is selected, another menu may appear onscreen (this is denoted by the triangle following the menu option). For instance, if you select the Add-ins option from the File menu, a submenu like the one in Figure 1.5 appears. Users frequently make mistakes using menu-driven packages and suddenly find themselves in a menu or submenu that is completely unexpected. If this happens, press Esc to clear the submenu and return to the prior menu.

When an ellipsis appears after a menu item, this signals that a dialog box will appear onscreen. The Open Database dialog box is shown in Figure 1.6. There's a more extensive discussion of dialog boxes later in this chapter.

Figure 1.5

The submenu that appears after you select the Add-ins option from the File menu.

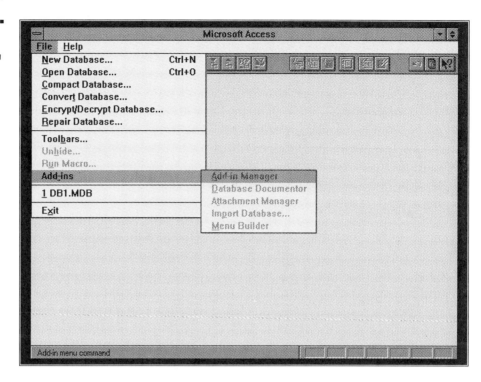

Figure 1.6

The dialog box for the Open Database option of the File menu.

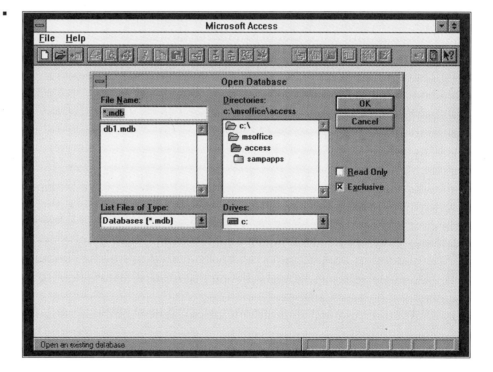

Toolbar   The **toolbar** permits you to click on buttons (see Table 1.1) instead of issuing commands via the Access menu structure. The buttons on the toolbar vary with the Access features that are active. The buttons will be discussed as they are covered in the text.

Table 1.1   Datasheet Toolbar Buttons

Button	Name	Function
	New Database	Opens a pop-up window from which you can choose a new database to create.
	Open Database	Displays the Open Database dialog box, which you use to activate the desired database.
	Attach Table	Attaches a table from another database to the current table.
	Print	Prints the active document.
	Print Preview	Shows how a report, form, datasheet, or module will appear when printed.
	Code	Displays an Access Basic form module or report module where you can view, edit, create, or run procedures.
	Cut	Cuts selected text/data and moves it to the Windows Clipboard.
	Copy	Copies selected text/data to the Windows Clipboard.
	Paste	Pastes the contents of the Windows Clipboard at the cursor location.
	Relationships	Displays this window to view or edit existing relationships or to define new ones between tables and queries.
	Import	Imports data from a text file, spreadsheet, or database table into an Access table.
	Export	Copies information from an Access table into another Microsoft application.
	Merge It	Starts or switches to Microsoft Word Merge Wizard.
	MS Excel	Saves the contents of the current object to an Excel worksheet and starts Excel.
	New Query	Creates a query for the table or object currently open.
	New Form	Creates a form based on the active table or query.
	New Report	Creates a report based on the active table or query.
	Database Window	Displays the database window.
	AutoForm	Creates a form that displays all fields and records of the selected table or query.
	AutoReport	Creates a report that displays all fields and records of the selected table or query.
	Cue Cards	Displays the Cue Cards main menu.
	Help	Invokes on-line help for the next item that you click.

SpeedMenus   Access for Windows makes use of **SpeedMenus**, which are various pop-up menus that appear when you right-click particular objects throughout the program. You can use these menus to quickly perform different operations on the object in question. For example, if you right-click a table name, the SpeedMenu shown in Figure 1.7 appears onscreen.

Figure 1.7
The SpeedMenu for a table.

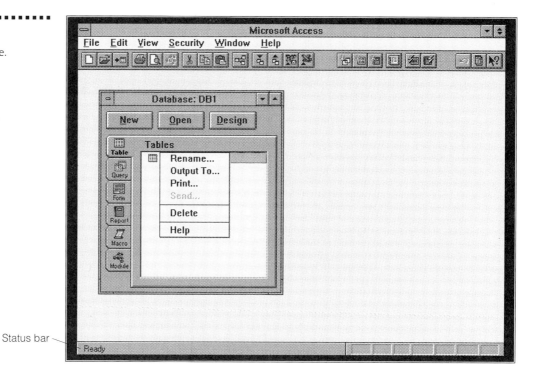

Status bar

Status Bar   The **status bar** appears at the bottom of the screen (Figure 1.7). It displays helpful information while you are using Access. For example, it indicates what a specific menu item is for or gives suggestions about what your next step should be. It also displays an explanation of the task to be accomplished by pointing to a specific button on the toolbar.

In the right-hand portion of the status bar are various squares. Among other things, these are indicators for such things as the Num Lock and Caps Lock keys.

Help, Contents or F1   **THE HELP FACILITY**

Help is available by selecting any item in the Access window or the Access menu structure and then pressing F1 to issue the **Help command**. For instance, if you want help about the Open Database option of the File menu, you would select that item and press F1. A help screen displays a description of what that action accomplishes (Figure 1.8). Once you have read the help screen, double-click the control-menu button to return to the location you were at before Help was invoked.

You can also obtain help about a command, button, or any other entity by clicking the Help button on the toolbar (the pointer now includes a big question mark), and then clicking the entity about which you want information.

For example, to obtain information about the Print Preview feature, you click the Help button on the toolbar and then click the Print Preview button on the toolbar to obtain information (Figure 1.9).

You may also request general help using the Access menu structure when you are not exactly certain about the command for which you need more information. In such a case, the command sequence Help, Contents generates a Help menu like the one in Figure 1.10. Once this command is issued, click the icon for the topic about which you want more information, then select from the

Figure 1.8

The help screen for the Open Database option of the File menu.

Help buttons

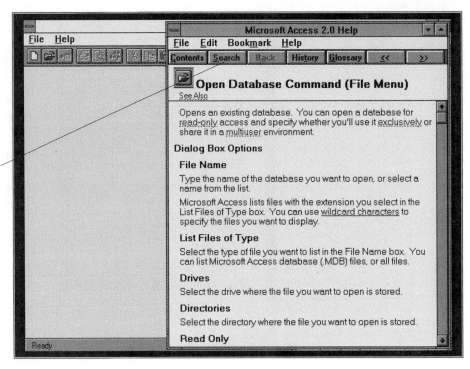

Figure 1.9

The help screen for the Print Preview command, activated by clicking the Help button followed by the Print Preview button on the toolbar.

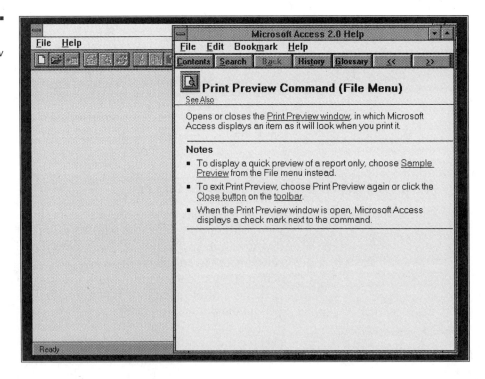

options that are displayed. Figure 1.11 shows options that appear when the Cue Cards option is selected in the help window.

When you are in the various help screens, the help buttons at the top (Figure 1.10) allow you to navigate the various help screens that appear in the help window. Click Contents to get the Help Contents screen, Search to enter

Figure 1.10

The help window for the Help, Contents command entered from the Access menu.

Help buttons

Help topic icons

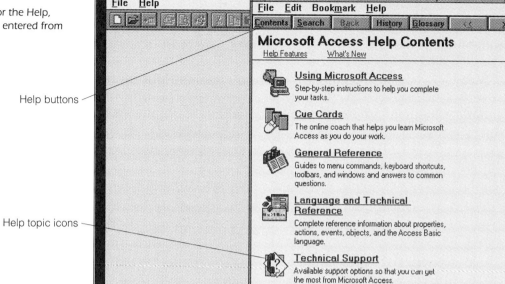

Figure 1.11

The Cue Cards help window obtained from the Help Contents window.

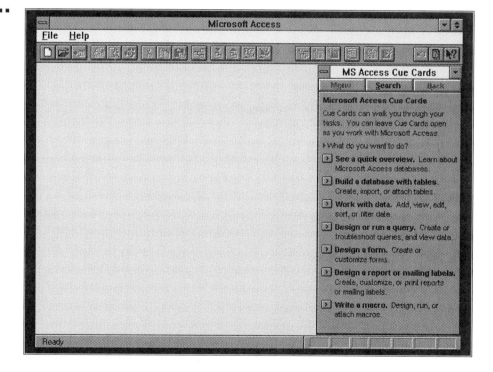

the first letters of a particular command or task that you wish to accomplish, Back for the previous screen, History to get a listing of all help screens that you have displayed, and Glossary to obtain an alphabetical listing of commands.

Once you have obtained a help screen for a command, the command buttons [<<] and [>>] appear next to the help buttons. You can click the [<<]

button to get the previous command in the alphabetical listing or the [>>] button to get the next command.

If you find information about a command or topic that you wish to print, issue the command sequence File, Print Topic, and that information will be sent to the Print Manager for printing.

 Hands-On Exercise: Obtaining Help Information

Begin from the Access window.

1. Get the help screen for the Open Database command of the File menu and info about the New Form button on the toolbar.

File	Open the File menu.
Open Database...	Use the down-arrow key to select this option.
F1	Invoke the Help feature (Figure 1.8).
▭	Double-click the control menu-button of the help window to leave Help.
▶?	Click to display the large question mark with the pointer (see Table 1.1).
▯	Click to activate the Help feature for the New command (File menu).
▼	Click the down arrow of the vertical scroll bar until the New Form icon and information about it appears (Figure 1.12).

■ ■

Figure 1.12

The help window for the New Form icon on the toolbar.

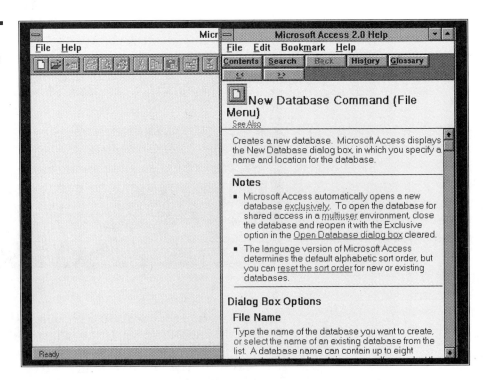

2. Search for the Find command.

Search   Click to get a list of all commands. The Search window now appears onscreen (Figure 1.13).

Type `fin`   The commands that start with these letters appear onscreen (Figure 1.14).

Figure 1.13
The Search window of the Help feature.

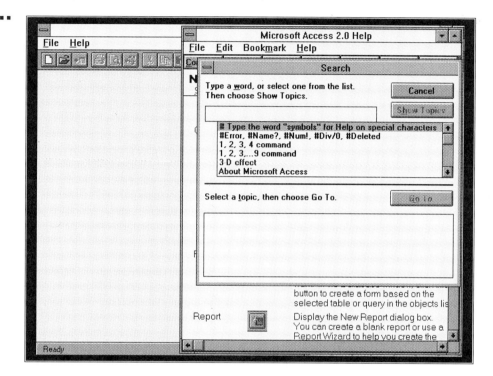

Search text

Figure 1.14
The list of commands that start with the letters "fin".

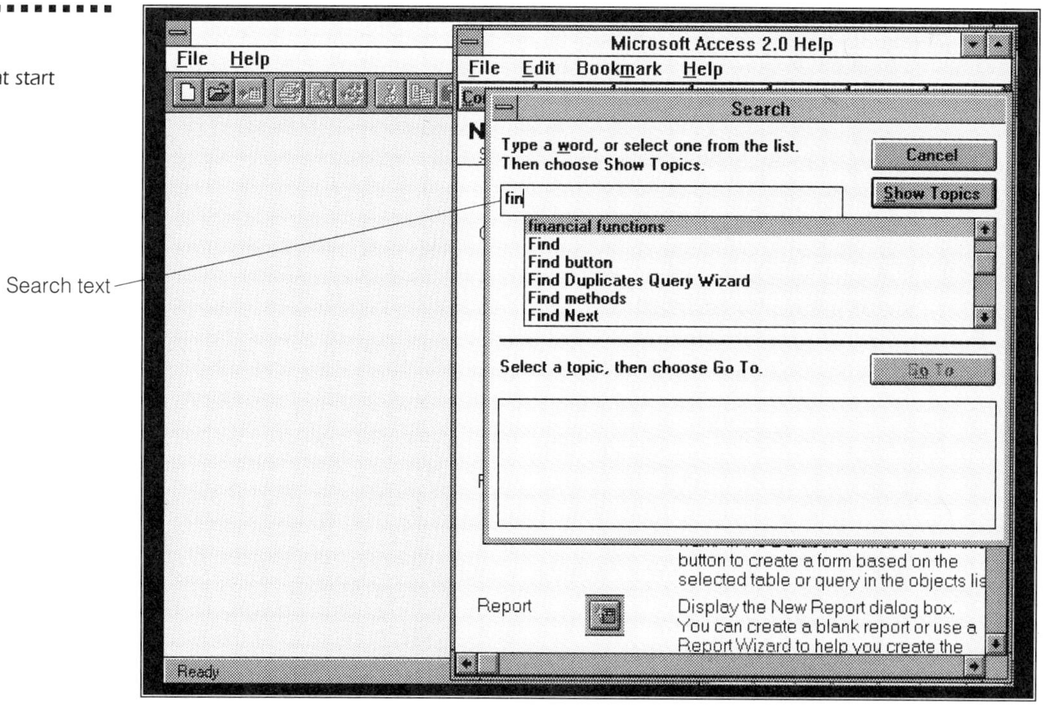

■ ■

Figure 1.15

The help window for the Find command.

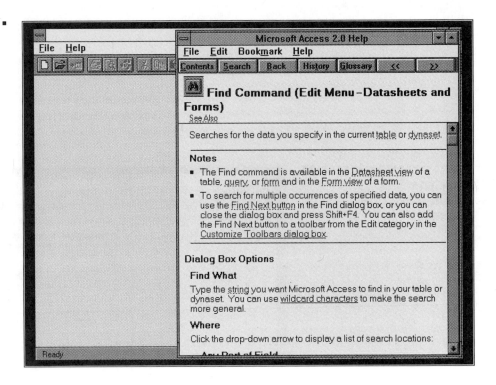

Find	Double-click to select this topic.
Go To	Click to access the help screen (Figure 1.15). Click below the scroll box to see subsequent help screens.
	Double-click the control-menu button of the help window to leave Help.

HINTS/HAZARDS   You can also easily change Help to an inactive window by clicking the mouse anywhere outside the help window. This makes the Access window active.

3. Obtain help via the Help menu.

<u>H</u>elp	Open the Help menu.
<u>C</u>ontents	Click to invoke the Access Help Contents screen (Figure 1.10).
📖	Click for general reference information.
<u>Keyboard Shortcuts</u>	The screen shown in Figure 1.16 appears.
<u>Editing Keys</u>	Click this option. The screen shown in Figure 1.17 appears.

Figure 1.16

The available Keyboard Shortcuts help alternatives.

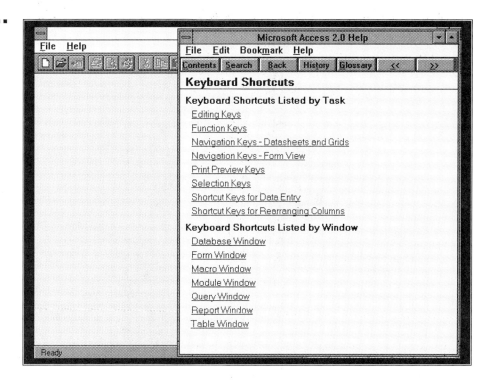

Figure 1.17

The help window for the editing keys.

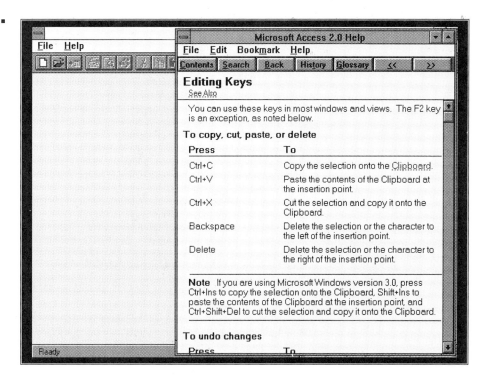

4. Print the contents of a help screen.

<u>F</u>ile   Open the File menu on the Help menu bar.

<u>P</u>rint Topic   Click to obtain a printout of the Editing Keys help screen.

Figure 1.18

The help screen for the File, Convert Database command sequence.

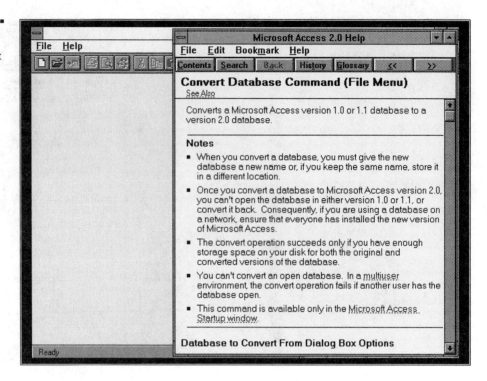

Click	Click the mouse outside the Help window.

5. Practice getting context-sensitive help while you are in an Access pull-down menu.

File	Open the File menu.
↓ (3 times)	Highlight the Convert Database command.
F1	Activate the Help feature for this menu option. A screen that looks like Figure 1.18 appears.
Click	Click the mouse outside the help window.

CUE CARDS AND WIZARDS

Access provides two other kinds of special help—Cue Cards and wizards.

Cue Cards   Access **Cue Cards** are special help screens that provide text-based information on how to perform a specific task. They can be made up of multiple screens (Cue Cards) that step you through a specific task. You can access this feature by issuing the command Help, Cue Cards. The help screen like that shown in Figure 1.11 appears, allowing you to choose the appropriate topic.

Wizards   Access **wizards** provide interactive help. Rather than just providing information about a task like Cue Cards do, wizards ask you questions about the task to be performed and then do most of the work for you. As you start performing various tasks, Access prompts you about whether or not you want to use a wizard.

File, Exit or   **LEAVING ACCESS**

At the end of an Access session, you must properly exit to Windows, using either the File, Exit command sequence or by double-clicking the control-menu button of the Access title bar. To exit Access, issue the following commands.

File	Open the File menu.
Exit	Return to Windows.

■■■■■■■■■■■■■■■■■■■■■
COMMUNICATING WITH ACCESS

This section introduces the Access commands for setting the default drive and defining a table, as well as those for adding records and making changes to that table.

CREATING AND USING A DATABASE

As mentioned previously, Access places in a database each table that is created. It also places each separate report or query in this database. A database is an Access convention that allows Access to track all files that are related to a specific application. For example, all files related to a payroll application can be stored in a database called PAYROLL, and all files related to a personnel application can be stored in a database called PERSONNL. A database for an application lets you more efficiently track only those objects (tables, queries, reports, and so forth) that you use for a specific data-handling task. Only those objects that belong to the invoked database are displayed in the Access window for a specific database application.

To facilitate handling and tracking files in this book, examples are in a database called SALES.

If you want to create your own database, issue the commands File, New Database. Then specify the name of the database (the default is DB1.MDB) and the location, if it is different from the current location specified in the directories and drive boxes of the New Database dialog box.

 Hands-On Exercise: Activating the SALES Database

In the following steps, you will indicate that the database to be activated resides on drive A (or wherever your teacher says) and then activate the SALES database.

File	Open the File menu.
Open Database...	Click to invoke the Open Database dialog box, as shown in Figure 1.19.
⬇	Click the scroll arrow of the Drives list box to view a listing of available disk drives (Figure 1.20).
⬆	Click the scroll arrow of the Drives list box to view drive A.

Figure 1.19

The Open Database dialog box.

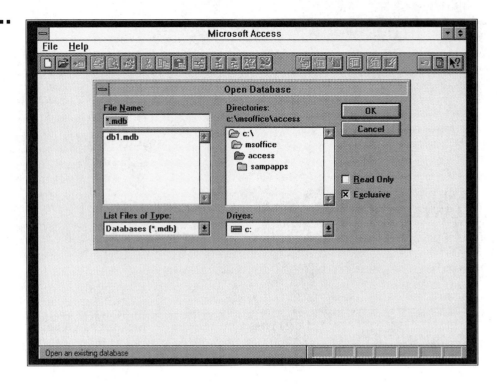

Figure 1.20

The Drives list box of the Open Database dialog box.

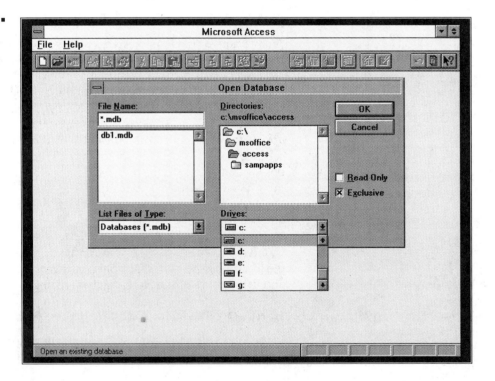

a: Click to change the drive. The databases on drive A now
                appear in the dialog box (Figure 1.21).

sales.mdb   Double-click to activate this database. The window
                shown in Figure 1.22 now appears.

Figure 1.21

The listing of databases on drive A.

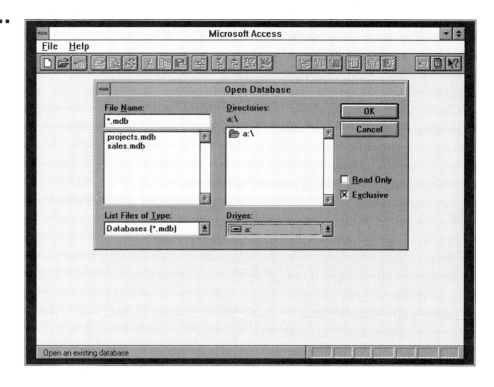

Figure 1.22

The database window with the listing of tables found in the SALES database.

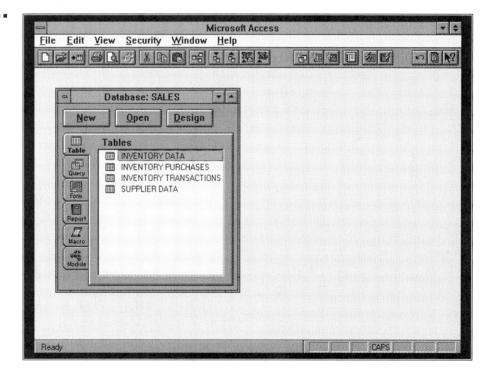

CREATING AN ACCESS TABLE

Before Access can use a table, you must provide the table name and information about its data fields (name, data type, and length) in a structure. Once the structure is created, you can enter data in the table. Use the following rules to create this structure.

Naming Conventions Access **naming conventions** include table names and field names. Access allows you to use up to 64 characters. These can include letters, numbers, spaces, and special characters except the period (.), exclamation mark (!), backquote (`), and brackets ([ ]). You are also prohibited from using leading spaces and control characters.

- A table name follows Access's naming conventions. Do not give the table a filename extension.
- A field name also follows Access's naming conventions. The **data type** to be stored in a field determines the type of field: text, number, yes/no, memo, date/time, currency, counter, and OLE object.
  - A **text field** holds any alphanumeric character (number, letter, or special character).
  - A **number field** is restricted to the plus or minus signs (+ or –), numerals, and the decimal point(.); the decimal point must be counted as part of the field length. This data type is used anytime you want to perform calculations using the contents of the field.
  - A **yes/no field** will be marked Y (yes) or N (no) and is always only one position in length. A yes is stored as a –1, whereas a no is stored as a 0.
  - A **memo field** can hold large documents (up to 64,000 bytes or characters of data). Memo fields can be used when you want to store narrative descriptive information about the entity being represented by the record. For instance, you might want to make annotations about a customer's hobbies, children's names, likes and dislikes, and so forth.
  - A **date/time field** contains eight positions and automatically has the slashes (/) in the correct locations; an empty date field appears as _/_/_.
  - A **currency field** is used for money-related data to be used in calculations. It does a better job of rounding for dollars and cents than a number field. Once the currency data type has been specified, you usually have to indicate how the data is to be displayed and stored in the Fields Properties box for this field.
  - A **counter field** is used if you want to number the records as they appear in a table, query, and so forth. This type of field cannot be updated.
  - An **OLE object field** can be used to store objects from other Windows applications that support object linking and embedding (OLE). When you display a record that contains an OLE field, you can view the OLE object (graphic image, graph, worksheet, and so forth) by double-clicking the field. Windows then launches the parent application against the OLE object.

Let's review the SALES database application. The previously mentioned 12 data items along with some additional fields will be used to compose a data record for each customer:

Customer ID	State
Salutation	Zip
First Name	Phone

```
Middle Initial          Amount Owed
Last Name               Payment Date
Address                 Credit Status
City                    Comments
```

The customer ID, salutation, credit status, and comments fields have been added to the record. The customer ID will act as a unique identifier for each record. The salutation will be used for generating written correspondence, if necessary, with the customer. The credit status will have a Y for a good credit rating and an N for a bad credit rating. The comments field will be used to contain any information that might be pertinent for this customer (likes and dislikes, favorite merchandise, birthdays of children).

After deciding which pieces of information to store, you must decide which type of data is to be stored in each field and how long each field should be. Text data is used for most fields. Why would you want to use text data for the zip field when a zip code is numeric digits? A common rule of thumb is to store data as text data unless it is to be used in calculations. Also, text data is easier to include in indexing.

The phone field is also text data because the area code appears between parentheses, and a hyphen appears between the exchange and the number in that exchange. The amount owed, the only numeric field, has two positions to the right of the decimal point. The payment date is a date field, the comments field is a memo field, and credit status is a yes/no field. Table 1.2 shows the breakdown of field names, data types, and field lengths.

It is important not to use too many fields in a record or to define fields that are too large to hold the data. The size of the fields determines how much space they will take on disk. Unused field positions are filled with blanks. Reserving too much room for a field wastes disk storage space.

Field Properties   Besides giving the field name and data type when you are defining the fields of a record, you also want to determine the optimal field

Table 1.2   Breakdown for the CUSTOMER DATA Table

Field Name	Data Type	Field Length
CUSTOMER ID NUMBER	Text	5
SALUTATION	Text	5
FIRST NAME	Text	10
MIDDLE INITIAL	Text	1
LAST NAME	Text	12
ADDRESS	Text	25
CITY	Text	15
STATE	Text	2
ZIP	Text	10
PHONE	Text	13
AMOUNT DUE	Currency	
DATE OF LAST PAYMENT	Date/Time	
CREDIT STATUS	Yes/No	1
COMMENTS	Memo	10

Figure 1.23

The selection box for the data type and the Field Properties box.

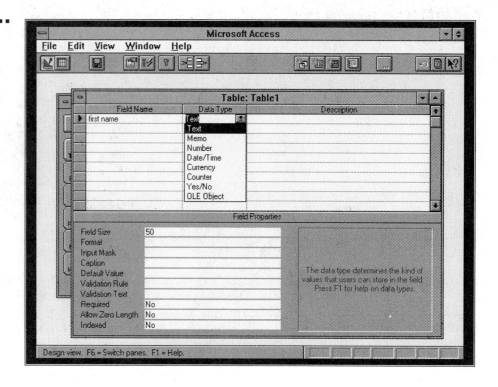

length as well as possibly control how the data is to be entered. Field length, alignment, fill characters, color, and other features are controlled via the **Field Properties box** for each field (Figure 1.23).

Creating the Structure   Creating the CUSTOMER DATA table structure with the above fields requires activating the SALES database and then using the New option of the database window. Build the structure of the table using the following steps.

File	Open the File menu.
Open Database...	Click to invoke the Open Database dialog box

You now have to indicate where the database resides. This may involve selecting a different drive or directory. For example, you might have to double-click the C:\ for a listing of directories on that drive and then click the appropriate directory. The following shows how to indicate to Access that the database resides on drive A.

↓	Click the scroll arrow of the Drives list box to view a listing of available disk drives.
↑	Click the scroll arrow of the Drives list box to view drive A.
a:	Click to change the drive. The databases on drive A now appear in the dialog box.
sales.mdb	Double-click to activate this database. The database window shown in Figure 1.22 appears.

The buttons along the left side of the window allow you to indicate which tool you wish to activate. Access defaults to the Table tool.

Figure 1.24

The New Table dialog box allows you to determine how the table structure is to be built.

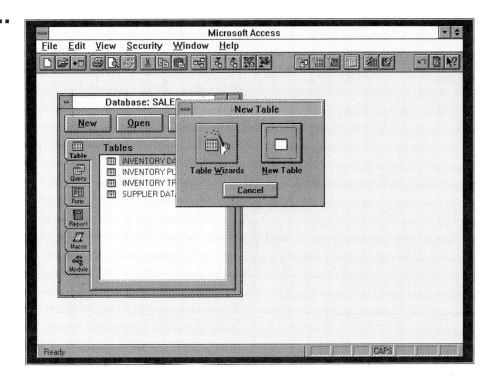

The buttons across the top allow you to indicate the task that you wish to perform for the specified tool.

     Click to define a new table. The New Table dialog box appears, asking you if you want to use a wizard or build the table yourself (Figure 1.24).

 New Table   Click the New Table button to indicate that you want to design the table. The Table Design window now appears. (Figure 1.25). Notice that the default name for the table is Table1.

This screen provides the necessary tools for describing to Access the structure of the table you wish to build. The status bar at the bottom of the window contains several pieces of information about the task being performed. The table name is Table 1. This name will be used by Access until you finish and name the structure. The ▶ indicates that you are ready to describe the first field to Access. The box in the lower-right portion of the Table Design window provides a description of what is to be entered in a cell of the field description row. For each field, you enter the field name, data type, and description, if any.

Information about the field size and any other specifications are entered in the Field Properties box. It is probably a good idea to maximize the Table Design window so that all of this box can be seen without using scroll bars.

The field size can be changed easily using the mouse. This involves clicking and dragging over the current number in the Field Size cell. The number should now appear in reverse video. Once this is accomplished, enter the new field size. The new number replaces the old number.

The Currency data type automatically formats the number in currency format. To view other available formatting options, click in the Format cell of the Field Properties box. An arrow icon will appear. Click the arrow to display the list box (Figure 1.26).

Figure 1.25

The Table Design window allows you enter the structure of the new table.

Denotes field being defined

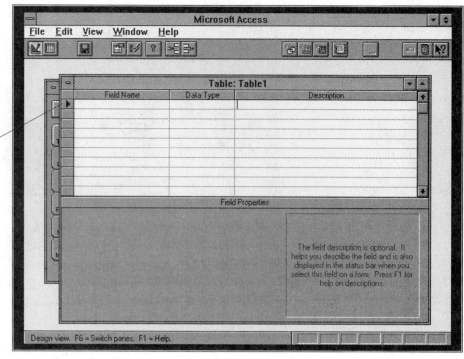

Figure 1.26

The different formatting options for a currency data type.

Currency options

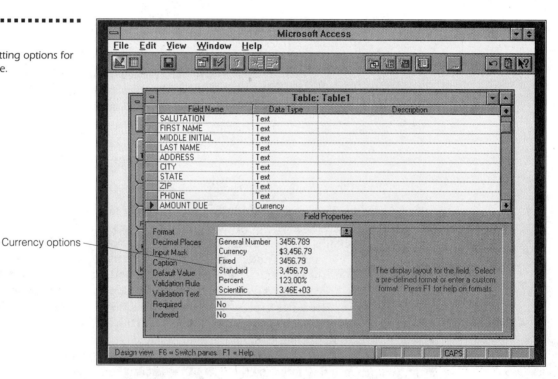

Figure 1.27

The completed record structure for
the table.

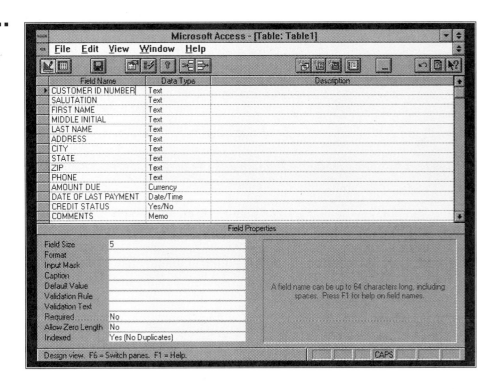

Once the structure is created, it should look like Figure 1.27. To describe
each field in the structure, use the following steps.

 Hands-On Exercise: Defining the Table Structure

1. Define the first field.

▲	Maximize the Table Design window.
Type **CUSTOMER ID NUMBER**	Name the field.
Tab	Execute the command and accept the Text default field type.
Click and drag	Select the 50 in the Field Size cell of the Field Properties box. The 50 should now be in reverse video.
Type **5**	Enter the field width.
Click	Position the pointer to the next field name in the structure and click.

2. Define the second field.

Type **SALUTATION**	Name the field.
Tab	Execute the command and accept the Character default field type. For a field containing another data type, you must click the down-arrow icon, activating the field data type selection box, and then click the appropriate data type.

Click and drag	Select the 50 in the Field Size cell of the Field Properties box.
Type **10**	Enter the field width.
Click	Position the pointer to the next field name in the structure and click.

Continue entering the field definitions by referring to the list of fields in Table 1.2.

Notes on Creating a Structure   Access provides several conventions for creating a structure:

- Correcting errors is a straightforward process. Use the up- and down-arrow keys to position to the correct line, Tab and Shift + Tab to move the cursor horizontally to the desired field, and then reenter the data.
- If you inadvertently forget to enter a field, position beneath its desired location and click the Insert Row button on the toolbar of the Table Design window.

When you have finished entering the field descriptions, the cursor is in the comments field. To terminate the structure definition and save the table structure, enter the following commands.

🖫	Click this button on the toolbar to invoke the Save As dialog box (Figure 1.28) with Table1 as the default.
Type **CUSTOMER DATA**	Enter the name of the table to be created.
OK	Click to save the structure to disk.

Figure 1.28

The Save As dialog box allows you to save the table structure to disk.

Save button

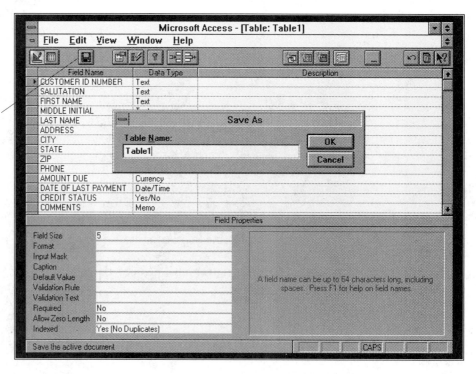

Click this button of the Table Design window.

  Double-click the control-menu button of the Table Design window. You are now returned to the Database:SALES window.

ACCESS SPEEDMENUS

Access SpeedMenus are activated by pressing the right mouse button (Figure 1.29). The SpeedMenu selections displayed are dependent upon the type of object/entity that is active. Invoking a SpeedMenu against a table gives you the following options:

Rename...   Allows you to change the table name.

Output To...   Allows you to create files that can be read by an application such as Excel or a program capable of accepting text data as input.

Print...   Allows you to print a table with each field in a cell.

Send...   Allows you to transmit records to another location.

Delete   Allows you to delete the table from the database.

Help   Invokes the Help facility.

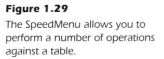

Figure 1.29

The SpeedMenu allows you to perform a number of operations against a table.

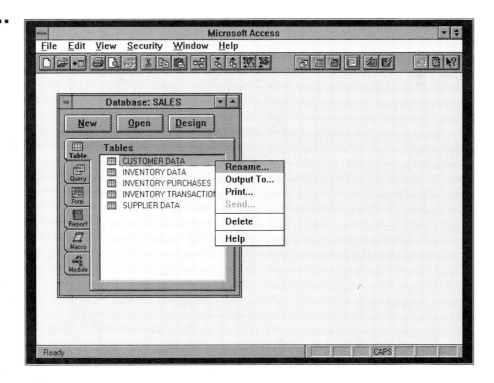

DISPLAYING AND CHANGING DATA

The **Datasheet window** facilitates data entry, enabling you to add or edit data in a table (Figure 1.30). It displays the field names across the top of the screen and the fields in columns.

NAVIGATING THROUGH RECORDS

The Datasheet window provides control over progressing from one record to the next via the group of buttons at the bottom of the window (Figure 1.30). These buttons are made to look similar to the forward and reverse buttons of a tape player.

Hands-On Exercise: Entering Data in a Table

1. Activate the SALES database if necessary, otherwise, go to step 2.

2. Activate the Datasheet window for the CUSTOMER DATA table.

CUSTOMER DATA   Double-click this option from the list of tables and display the Datasheet window.

3. Maximize the screen.

    Click to maximize the Datasheet window.

A blank record form now appears onscreen, with the menu bar at the top of the screen (Figure 1.30). The title bar shows the table name, and the current record number is at the bottom of the datasheet. Each field name appears as a column heading. Fill in the appropriate blanks. When you reach the end of a field, press Enter, and the cursor automatically advances to the next field. When the last field

Figure 1.30

The Datasheet window for adding records to a table.

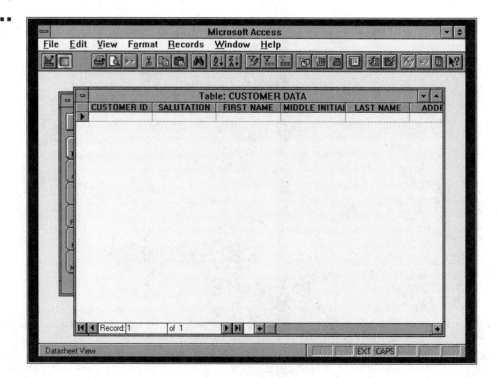

is filled and Enter is pressed, a new blank form appears. Now enter the six records below (don't worry about entering information in the comments field):

Record#	CUSTOMER ID NUMBER	SALU-TATION	FIRST NAME	MIDDLE INITIAL	LAST NAME	ADDRESS	CITY	STATE	ZIP	PHONE	AMOUNT DUE	DATE OF LAST PAYMENT	CREDIT STATUS	COMMENTS
1	40267	Mr.	James	G	Bain	1227 W. Market	Peoria	IL	61601	(309) 685-2025	195.00	12/12/95	-1	memo
2	17634	Ms.	Denise	J	Henderson	6102 Henderson	Framingham	MA	51728	(213) 224-3474	250.00	12/05/95	-1	memo
3	36784	Mr.	Randall	C	Harp	1055 N. Chestnut	Yonkers	NY	10157	(412) 210-4938	750.00	09/08/95	-1	memo
4	75097	Mr.	Harold	D	Messamore	1215 Arcadia	Bloomington	IL	61701	(309) 662-1753	25.00	12/20/95	-1	memo
5	27823	Mr.	John	K	Finnis	4352 S. Main	Normal	IL	61761	(309) 452-7651	150.00	12/11/95	-1	memo
6	40275	Ms.	Donna	L	Bain	1227 W. Market	Peoria	IL	61601	(309) 685-2025	75.00	12/17/95	-1	memo

Notice that as you enter information in the customer ID field, a pencil appears to the left of the record (Figure 1.31). This indicates that this record has not been saved. The asterisk (*) indicates that Access has already made room for the next record. As you continue to enter information in fields, Access automatically moves everything to the right to display any blank fields that will also need to have data entered. Once you position to the next record, Access automatically stores that record to the table on disk. The pencil alerts you that the record has not been saved.

When you enter numeric information, Access automatically right-justifies the digits in the field when you press Enter. If the number does not have decimal positions, do not enter a decimal point; Access automatically places a decimal point in the appropriate location.

When the datasheet has been filled with the data for the first record, it should look like Figure 1.32.

As each record is entered, Access places a new, empty row onscreen and increments the record number at the bottom of the window. When you have finished entering all six records, issue the following commands. Make certain, however, that the pencil icon does not appear in the left margin of the datasheet.

Figure 1.31

The pencil indicates that this record has not been saved to disk.

Denotes a record not yet saved

Next record ready

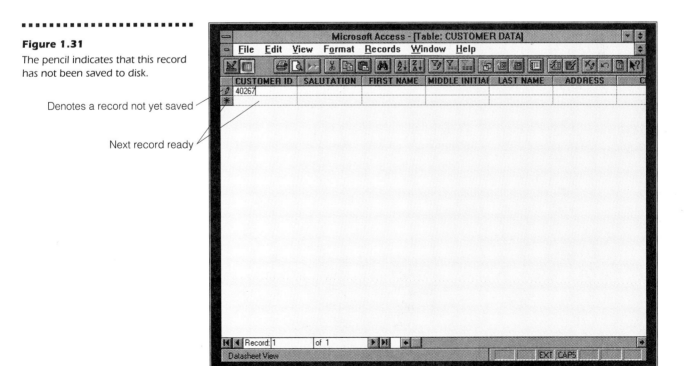

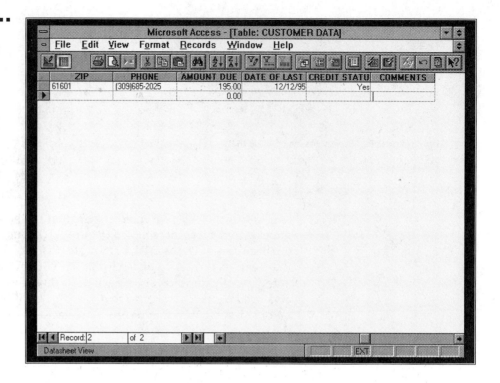

Figure 1.32

Filled-in form for the first record of the CUSTOMER DATA table.

Click this button of the Datasheet window.

Double-click the control-menu button.

HINTS/HAZARDS   If you are inadvertently forced out of the datasheet and returned to the database window, double-click the CUSTOMER DATA table.

If you note errors in a record, you can correct them using editing conventions. A record is saved to the table anytime PgUp or PgDn is pressed when you are filling in a form. You can also use these keys to view the records in the table to ensure that there are no errors.

ACTIVATING THE DATABASE

You have now created the CUSTOMER DATA table and entered six records in it. If you are still in Access and have not activated any other table, to add records to the CUSTOMER DATA table just double-click that table name.

If you quit Access or have saved and closed the table and later want to add records to the CUSTOMER DATA table, you must reenter Access and perform some or all of the following steps.

1. Open the database.

2. Activate the table.

Once a table has been activated and the Datasheet window is onscreen, you can look at the structure of the table by clicking the Design View button on the toolbar. This displays the structure of the table. Once you have obtained the needed information, click the Datasheet View button to return to the Datasheet window.

ADDING RECORDS TO THE TABLE

Use the same steps as indicated earlier to add records to the table. You can edit as well as add records to a table in the Datasheet window. Table 1.3 contains a number of positioning commands for moving within a table and within a screen.

You can now add records to the end of the table by positioning to the row with the asterisk (*) in the left-hand border.

When you have finished adding new records, return to the database window.

Add the following records to the CUSTOMER DATA table using the Datasheet window.

Record#	CUSTOMER ID NUMBER	SALU-TATION	FIRST NAME	MIDDLE INITIAL	LAST NAME	ADDRESS	CITY	STATE	ZIP	PHONE	AMOUNT DUE	DATE OF LAST PAYMENT	CREDIT STATUS	COMMENTS
7	58404	Dr.	Michael	D	Keiser	1784 N. Hansen	Champaign	IL	61729	(217) 234-4956	500.00	11/28/94	-1	memo
8	94219	Mrs.	Kim	F	Schulz	322 W. Normal Ave.	Normal	IL	61761	(309) 452-7362	125.00	11/15/95	-1	memo
9	63198	Dr.	Ann	D	Sokol	927 Anchor Dr.	Washington	IL	61604	(309)299-9521	253.00	12/10/95	-1	memo
10	27245	Mr.	Robert	Y	Tuttle	5529 N. Harmon	Bloomington	IL	61701	(309)663-8322	150.00	12/14/95	-1	memo
11	38724	Mr.	Neal	T	Ringg	221 W. McClure	Peoria	IL	61603	(309)685-9875	400.00	10/19/95	-1	memo
12	41833	Mr.	Andrew	F	Garcia	1523 W. Grove	Bloomington	IL	61701	(309)662-9437	75.00	12/10/94	-1	memo
13	67392	Ms.	Dongmei	T	Yen	553 N. Main	Normal	IL	61761	(309)452-3948	35.00	08/19/95	-1	memo
14	89301	Ms.	Juanita	T	Juarez	1527 Barton Dr.	Normal	IL	61761	(309)452-0928	275.00	12/01/95	-1	memo
15	95388	Mr.	John	N	Schulz	322 W. Normal Ave.	Normal	IL	61761	(309)452-7362	25.00	12/05/95	-1	memo

Table 1.3   Positioning Commands in the Datasheet Window

Key(s) or Button	Action
[◄◄]	Moves to the first record.
[►►]	Moves to the last record.
Home	Moves to the first column.
End	Moves to the last column.
Tab or Enter	Moves to the next column.
Shift + Tab	Moves to the previous column.
↑ or ◄	Moves to the previous record.
↓ or ►	Moves to the next record.
Ctrl + Home or [◄◄]	Moves to the first record, first column.
Ctrl + End	Moves to the last record, last column.
[►►]	Moves to the beginning of the last record.
Pg Up	Moves to up 26 rows.
Pg Dn	Moves to down 26 rows.

EDITING RECORDS IN A TABLE

There should be 15 records in the table. Examine each record for errors. Notice that in record 11 (Figure 1.33) the last name is spelled incorrectly (there should be only one "g"). Correct this, using the following commands:

1. Activate the desired database and the CUSTOMER DATA table.

2. Maximize the screen

   [▲]   Maximize the data-entry screen.

3. Correct the error.

   Ringg   Click the mouse on this field contents to the right of the second "g."

   [Backspace]   Press the Backspace key once to delete the second "g."

4. Resize the Datasheet window.

   [▲▼]   Click the restore button of the Datasheet window.

5. Close the table.

   [—]   Double-click the control-menu button of the Datasheet window.

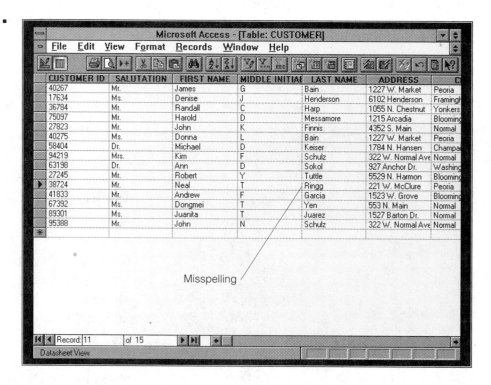

Figure 1.33

The CUSTOMER DATA table displayed in the Datasheet window. Note the misspelled Ringg in record 11.

Table 1.4   Field Editing Commands

Key(s)	Action
F2	Switches from navigation mode to edit mode when using the cursor keys to move among fields/records.
→	Moves right one character.
←	Moves left one character.
Ctrl + →	Moves right one word.
Ctrl + ←	Moves left one word.
Home	Moves to the beginning of the field.
End	Moves to the end of the field.
Ctrl + End	Moves to the end of a multiple-line field.
Ctrl + Home	Moves to the beginning of a multiple-line field.
Ctrl + C	Copies to the Clipboard.
Ctrl + V	Pastes contents of Clipboard at the insertion point.
Ctrl + X	Cuts and copies to the Clipboard.

Access 2.0 for Windows also has a number of commands that you can use for editing text within a field of data. These commands are summarized in Table 1.4.

HINTS/HAZARDS

If you want to delete or replace the contents of a cell rather than just change it, use the cursor keys to position to the field (it should be in reverse video), and then press the Del key. The current contents are gone. To replace the contents of a field, position to that field (contents in reverse video). Any data that you enter replaces the highlighted data in the field.

Entering Data in a Memo Field The CUSTOMER DATA table has a structure that includes a comments field with a data type of memo. None of the records has yet used this field. A memo field is a field that belongs to a different (memo) file and can store and link text-oriented data with a database record. Using a different file in this way is necessary, because every record in a database table will not necessarily require this text-oriented data, which uses vast amounts of record space.

Suppose you want to add information to Denise Henderson's record using the comments field. Position the cursor to the correct row using the appropriate positioning command and then position to the comments field. To open the text editor for a memo field, issue the **Zoom command** (Shift + F2).

Figure 1.34

The Zoom dialog box for entering a memo.

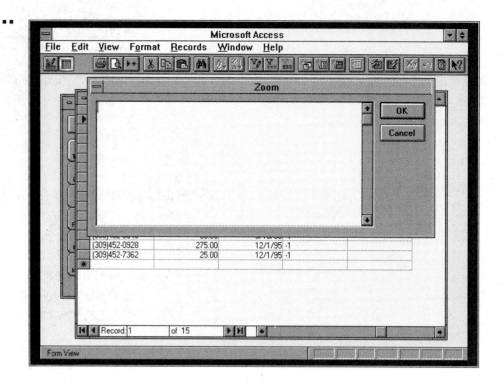

 Hands-On Exercise: Entering Data in a Memo Field

1. Activate the table.

CUSTOMER DATA   Double-click the CUSTOMER DATA table in the table list.

2. Make an entry in a memo field.

↓   Position to the second record.

End   Position to the COMMENTS field.

Shift + F2   Issue the Zoom command. The Zoom dialog box shown in Figure 1.34 now appears. Enter the following comments:

```
Denise has several hobbies. One that is of special interest is sky
diving. Over the last few years she has made enough jumps to reach
instructor status. She also enjoys driving sports cars. At this time
she owns a Mitsubishi Eclipse.
```

Your screen should now look like Figure 1.35.

OK   Click to save the text to the COMMENTS field.

PRINTING A REPORT   Access allows you to quickly generate a printout of records in a table. You accomplish this by issuing the following commands while the CUSTOMER DATA table is onscreen.

Figure 1.35

The completed dialog box.

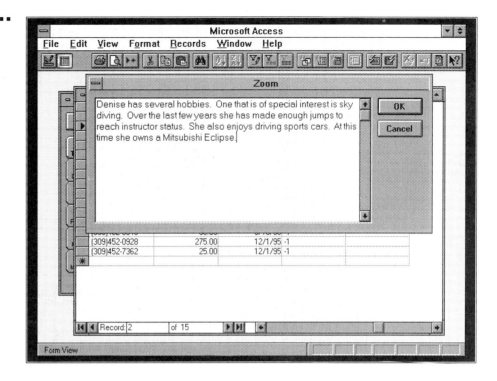

 Hands-On Exercise: Printing the Table

 Click this button on the toolbar to invoke the Print dialog box (Figure 1.36). Make certain that the All radio button is selected.

Figure 1.36

The Print dialog box for printing a data table.

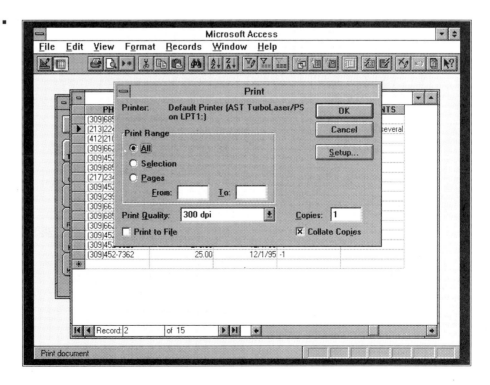

Figure 1.37

The CUSTOMER DATA table in Print Preview.

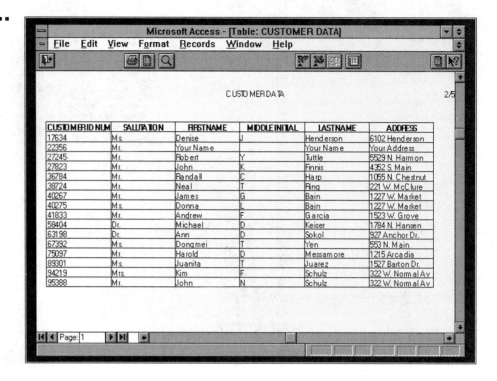

OK   Print the report.

Since the report is so wide, it extends over three pages of paper. Figure 1.37 shows how the report will print (the Print Preview button clicked against the table).

The report starts at the beginning of the table and lists all records. For readability, Access lists the field names above the data and continues printing records. It displays the field names as the first line of the report. If a line is too long, it is printed on the second sheet of paper. All fields are surrounded by a grid.

As Access prints the report, it places the name of the table and the date at the top of each page. It places a page number at the bottom of each page.

CHAPTER REVIEW

The term "database" is synonymous with "receptacle" for holding data tables, forms, queries, and so forth. A table consists of records that hold information about some type of business entity or transaction. Each record contains pieces of data, called fields, that relate to the transaction.

When designing the format of the table to hold data, you must design it to handle future processing needs. This may mean separating name fields into last-name, first-name, and middle-initial fields so the computer can arrange the records in alphabetical order by last name.

Microsoft Access 2.0 for Windows is a combination menu-driven and command-driven software package. It must be run from Windows on a hard disk drive.

Before creating an Access table, you must plan the field name, field length, and type of data to be used for each field and place this information in the structure of the table. The structure is built by clicking the New button of the database window with the list of tables displayed. Once the table structure is built, you can add records to the table or edit existing records by using the Datasheet window.

Displaying records is accomplished using the Datasheet window. The field names appear at the top of the window; the records and fields appear in a grid. Various Access commands using the Ctrl key as well as cursor-movement keys on the numeric keypad can position the cursor and move from one record to the next within a table.

The SpeedMenu or the Print button on the toolbar can be used to generate a quick report containing a grid. If the records are long, the report will spill over several pages.

KEY TERMS AND CONCEPTS

counter field	OLE object field
Cue Cards	primary key
currency field	Program mode
database	record
Datasheet window	secondary key
data type	SpeedMenu
date/time field	status bar
field	table
Field Properties box	table structure
Help command	text field
key	title bar
memo field	toolbar
menu bar	wizards
menu-driven	yes/no field
naming conventions	Zoom command
number field	

CHAPTER QUIZ

Multiple Choice

1. Which of the following is a true statement about Microsoft Access 2.0 for Windows?
   a. The package can be run from diskette.
   b. It can be run using an 8088 IBM PC.
   c. It can be run from the DOS C> prompt.
   d. All of the above statements are false.

2. Which of the following lets you place records in a database table?
   a. Catalog
   b. Datasheet window
   c. Append
   d. Add Records

3. Access buttons are found in the:
   a. speedbar
   b. toolbar
   c. SpeedMenu
   d. all of the above
   e. none of the above

4. Which of the following features/commands lets you make a change to an existing database?
   a. File, Table
   b. File, New Database
   c. File, Open Database
   d. none of the above

5. Which of the following are valid data types for use with Access 2.0?
   a. text
   b. number
   c. memo
   d. date/time
   e. currency
   f. all of the above

True/False

6. The Access 2.0 for Windows package is menu-driven.

7. Access 2.0 for Windows places all entities related to an application in a database.

8. When exiting Access, it is advisable to use the File, Exit command sequence to avoid data loss or file corruption.

9. The Access package makes use of the arrow keys as well as other commands in the Datasheet window for cursor movement.

10. The toolbar buttons let you move forward and backward in a table.

Answers

1. d   2. b   3. b   4. c   5. f   6. t   7. t   8. t   9. t   10. f

Exercises

1. Define or describe each of the following:
   a. database table
   b. menu-driven
   c. table structure

2. The entity used to hold tables, queries, reports, and so forth about a record-keeping application is called a _____.

3. The _____ contains buttons that can be clicked instead of issuing commands via the menu structure.

4. You can invoke the Help feature by pressing the _____ function key.

5. Before you turn off the computer, you must exit to _____ to avoid data loss.

6. Press the _____ key to exit from a submenu or Help.

7. The _____ _____ contains the description of the task to be performed by a toolbar button.

8. An Access field name can have up to _____ characters.

9. Use the _____ button of the database window to describe a record to Access.

10. A table is made available to Access by double-clicking the table name in the _____ window.

11. The _____ at the bottom of the Datasheet window gives the physical location (record number) of a record in a table.

12. Double-click the _____ _____ button to exit Access and return to Windows.

13. The design of a table (field names and data type) is called the table _____.

14. Use the _____ command of the SpeedMenu to change the name of an existing database table.

15. A _____ allows you to keep related files together.

16. Access automatically places a _____ filename extension on a database file.

17. When you are editing the contents of a field, you can erase the field's contents by pressing the _____ key when the field is in reverse video.

18. A memo field is placed in a file with the _____ + _____ (Zoom) command sequence.

19. When editing a table field, you can move to the right a word at a time with the _____ + _____ key sequence.

20. When in the datasheet, you can move to the right a field/column at a time by pressing the _____ or _____ key.

COMPUTER EXERCISES

Before you can begin the exercises, you must activate the PROJECTS database using the following instructions:

File   Open the File menu.

Open Database...   Click to invoke the Open Database dialog box.

You now have to indicate where the database resides. This may involve selecting a different drive or directory. For example, you might have to double-click the C:\ for a listing of directories on that drive and then click the appropriate directory. The following shows how to indicate to Access that the database resides on drive A.

⬇	Click the scroll arrow of the Drives list box to view a listing of available disk drives.
⬆	Click the scroll arrow of the Drives list box to view drive A.
a:	Click to change the drive. The databases on drive A now appear in the dialog box.
projects.mdb	Double-click this database to activate.

1. Create a table called PAYMAST. It should have the following structure:

Field	Field Name	Type	Width	
1	EMPLOYEE ID	Text	4	Primary key
2	DEPARTMENT	Text	2	
3	FIRST NAME	Text	10	
4	INIT	Text	1	
5	LAST NAME	Text	12	
6	PAY RATE	Currency	Standard	
7	YTD GROSS	Currency	Standard	

2. Enter the following records in the PAYMAST table.

Record#	EMPLOYEE ID	DEPARTMENT	FIRST NAME	INIT	LAST NAME	PAY RATE	YTD GROSS
1	1232	10	Arthur	D	Winnakor	10.50	12560.00
2	9234	15	Mildred	T	Klassen	12.75	15960.00
3	4873	10	Martin	D	Wilhelm	8.75	9450.00
4	2956	15	Monica	D	Wilson	9.50	7694.00
5	9643	10	Stephanie	D	Grapchek	7.75	8964.00

3. Display the contents of the PAYMAST table using the Datasheet window.

4. Add the records below to the PAYMAST table.

Record#	EMPLOYEE ID	DEPARTMENT	FIRST NAME	INIT	LAST NAME	PAY RATE	YTD GROSS
6	7650	10	Willard	D	Farnsworth	8.75	1200.00
7	7645	10	Margery	T	Fitzgibbons	9.75	3570.00
8	6594	15	Tomas	D	Ruiz	7.75	2975.00
9	9346	20	Alan	D	Chapin	9.50	6750.00
10	6295	20	Alfred	D	Benjamin	5.75	2375.00
11	3957	20	William	D	Rich	8.50	3460.00
12	4075	20					

5. Correct any errors in PAYMAST. Also use the Datasheet window to place your name in the name fields for record 12.

6. Use the SpeedMenu to print the PAYMAST table.

7. Invoke the CLUB table. Use the Datasheet window to examine the table.

2

MANIPULATING
FILES AND RECORDS,
SORTING, AND
INDEXING

CHAPTER OBJECTIVES

After completing this chapter, you should be able to

- **Use the Datasheet window**

- **Enter commands using the Access menu structure**

- **Use a number of data-manipulation commands**

- **Find records in a table**

- **Sort records in a file**

- **Index records in a file**

- **Delete unwanted index files**

- **Use a filter to sort and extract selected records**

This chapter reinforces the use of the Datasheet window and a number of file-manipulation commands. It also shows how to sort files, create indexes, and locate records in a table. These commands are covered using the Access menus.

PREPARING FOR THIS CHAPTER

To prepare for the examples and exercises in this chapter, you must reset the default drive (if necessary) and activate the database using the following commands. Hereafter, in subsequent chapters you will only be directed to perform these tasks, if needed. The keystrokes will not be listed.

File	Open the File menu.
Open Database...	Click to invoke the Open Database dialog box.

You now have to indicate where the database resides. This may involve selecting a different drive or directory. For example, you might have to double-click the C:\ to receive a listing of directories on that drive and then click the appropriate directory (you would, of course, then omit the remaining steps below). The following shows how to indicate to Access that the database resides on drive A.

⬇	Click the scroll arrow of the Drives list box to view a listing of available disk drives.
⬆	Click the scroll arrow of the Drives list box to view drive A.
a:	Click to change the drive. The databases on drive A now appear in the dialog box.
sales.mdb	Double-click to activate this database.

DATASHEET WINDOW

The **Datasheet window** is Access's main method of displaying the records of an invoked (active) table. You can use this window to make any desired changes to a table. Many Access commands display their results using the Datasheet window. It is therefore important that you understand how various commands work with this screen. The usual method of invoking this screen is by double-clicking the desired table in the list displayed in the database window.

Make certain you have used the steps at the beginning of this chapter to activate the SALES database. Invoke the CUSTOMER DATA table using the following commands.

1. Invoke the CUSTOMER DATA table.

 CUSTOMER DATA   Double-click this table in the database window. Your screen should look like Figure 2.1.

2. Maximize the Datasheet window.

    Click to maximize the Datasheet window (Figure 2.2).

Figure 2.1

The invoked CUSTOMER DATA table displayed in the Datasheet window.

Figure 2.2

The maximized Datasheet window with the CUSTOMER DATA table.

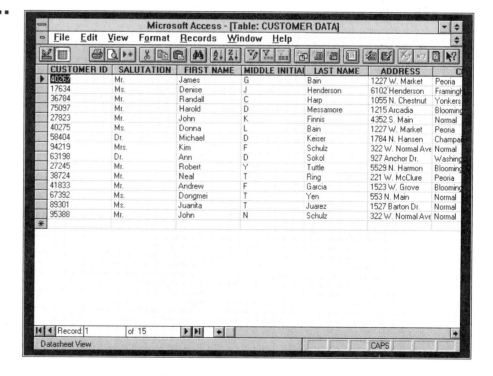

CURSOR MOVEMENT

Once the Datasheet window appears (Figure 2.1), you can use the F2 function key to shift between display and edit modes. In display mode you can use any of the cursor-movement commands shown in Table 1.3 to move through the table.

Figure 2.3

The CUSTOMER DATA table without gridlines.

GRIDLINES

Access automatically includes **gridlines** around each cell of the table displayed in the Datasheet window. For most people, these gridlines increase the readability of the table by helping the eye track along the appropriate line/record. For others, however, these gridlines can prove to be distracting. If you want to get rid of the gridlines, issue the following commands.

F<u>o</u>rmat	Open the Format menu.
<u>G</u>ridlines	Click to eliminate the gridlines. Your Datasheet window should now look like Figure 2.3.

The gridlines should have disappeared. If you issue the Print command to print the table, the printed table along with column headings will be the only portions of the report to be included within printed lines. Now, restore the gridlines by reissuing the above commands.

CHANGING FIELD DISPLAY WIDTH

When in the Datasheet window, you may want to resize one or more columns so additional fields can appear onscreen. Do this either by using the mouse to drag a column's right border to the desired location or by selecting the entire column and entering a new column width in the **Column Width** dialog box. When you resize a column or field onscreen, only the display is altered. The table remains unchanged. The field that is resized is the field at the cursor location.

The above discussion makes use of the mouse to resize a column in one of two ways: dragging or selecting.

Dragging The width of a column can be changed by placing the cursor on the right-hand border of the field name cell in the table heading. The cursor

Figure 2.4

The middle-initial column selected.

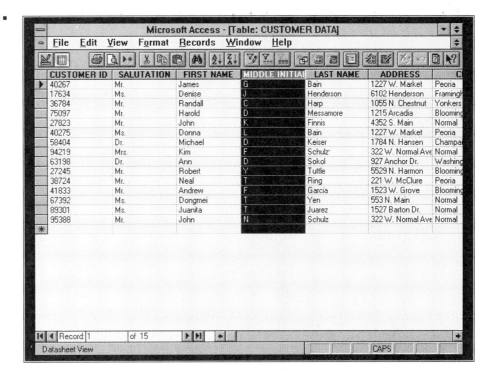

then changes into a bar with right- and left-hand arrows (⟷). You can now drag the cell border to the right to increase column width or to the left to decrease column width.

Pointing   You can use the pointing method by placing the pointer anywhere in the field name cell. Position the pointer in the middle-initial field name cell. The pointer turns into a large down arrow (↓). When you click the mouse, the entire column is selected and is displayed in reverse video (Figure 2.4). Once the column is selected, you can issue the follwing commands.

F**o**rmat	Open the Format menu.
Column Width...	Click to invoke the Column Width dialog box (Figure 2.5). You can enter the new column width or let Access reset the width via the Best Fit button (you are better off trying to reset it yourself—Access doesn't do a very good job of guessing). Figure 2.6 shows the column width set to 2.

You can also select multiple columns at one time and reset their widths either by holding down the Shift key and clicking the beginning and ending columns, or by dragging the pointer across the field names at the top of the Datasheet window. Figure 2.7 shows the salutation through address columns selected.

If you try to close the Datasheet window to return to the database window, Access does not automatically save changes that you have made to the appearance of the table like it does when you change the contents of a record. When you double-click the control-menu button of the Datasheet window, Access displays a dialog box like that shown in Figure 2.8, asking you whether you want to save the changes to the table in the database. Many times you just want to make temporary changes to the table for use in the Datasheet window and, therefore, do not want to save those changes to the table itself.

Figure 2.5

The Column Width dialog box.

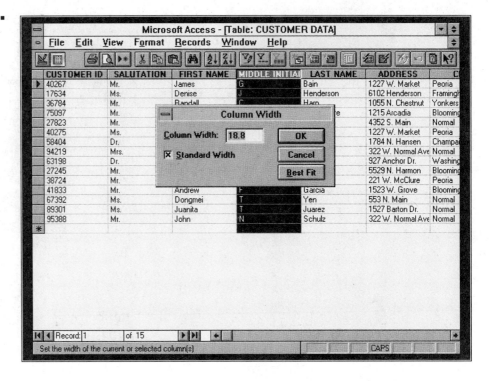

Figure 2.6

The middle-initial column set to a width of 2.

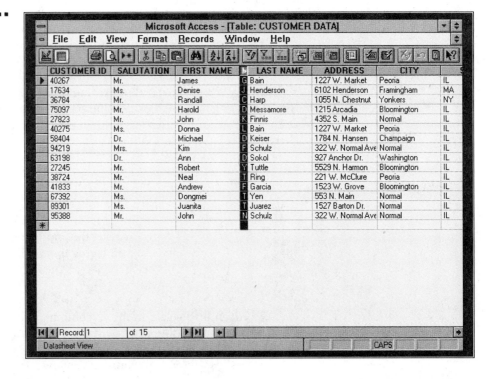

Suppose you want to resize the address field. After positioning the cursor to that field, enter the following instructions:

  Hands-On Exercise: Resizing the Address Field

ADDRESS   Click the ADDRESS field name at the top of the datasheet when you see the large down arrow in that cell. The address column should now be selected.

Figure 2.7

The adjacent salutation through address fields selected.

Figure 2.8

The dialog box prompting you about saving changes to the database table.

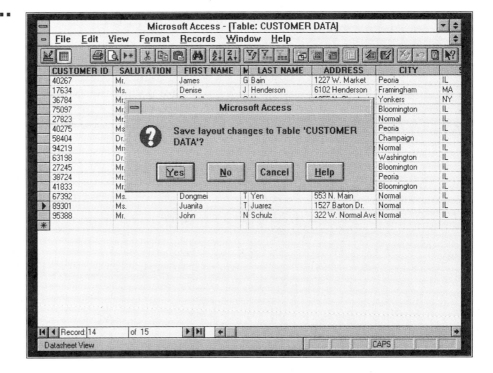

Format	Open the Format menu.
Column Width...	Click to invoke the Column Width dialog box (Figure 2.5).
Type **21**	Enter the new column width.
Enter	Make the change. Your screen should now look like Figure 2.9).

Figure 2.9

The resized address field of the CUSTOMER DATA table.

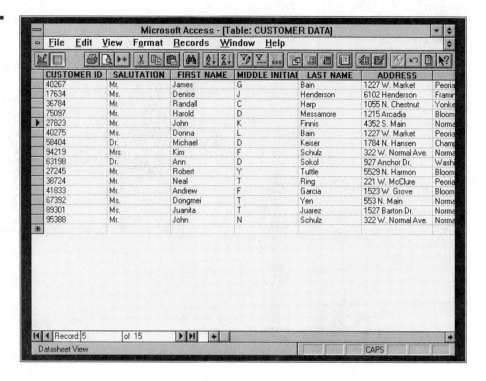

CHANGING ROW HEIGHT

You can select a record or change the height of table records/rows in much the same way you changed the width of a field/column. These processes involve using the gray border column to the left of the records in the Datasheet window.

To select a record, position the pointer in the appropriate box of the gray border column; the pointer turns into a fat right arrow (➜). Click the mouse, and the record will appear in reverse video (Figure 2.10). You can then issue the

Figure 2.10

The CUSTOMER DATA table with a selected row.

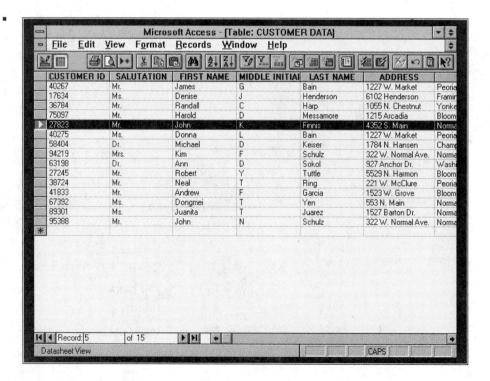

....

Figure 2.11
The Row Height dialog box.

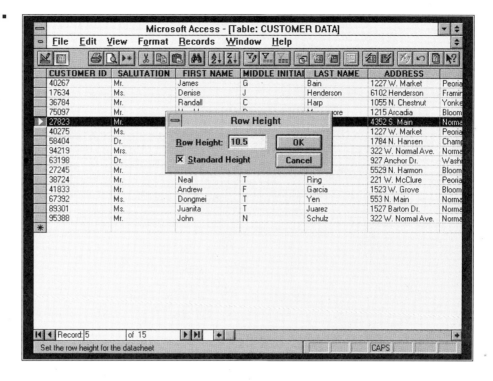

....

Figure 2.12
The CUSTOMER DATA table with the resized rows.

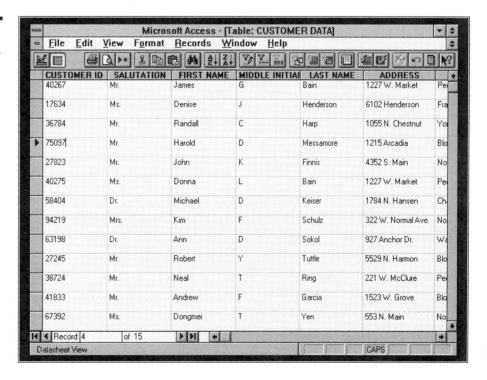

Format, **Row Height** command to display the Row Height dialog box (Figure 2.11) and enter the new row height. Access then displays the resized table rows in the Datasheet window (Figure 2.12).

You can also change the height of the lines used by Access to display records. This allows you, for example, to give the impression that Access is using double-spacing to display the records, making the table easier to read for many individuals. This is accomplished by placing the pointer on one of the upper or lower lines of the border-column boxes and, when you see it turn into a horizontal bar with up and down arrows (⬍) drag it down to the desired location.

HINTS/HAZARDS   Be careful when you are resizing the records by dragging. If you move the pointer up rather than down, you can make the table records seem to disappear by setting the height to 0. In such a situation, position the pointer to any line left in the table and increase the record display by dragging downward.

MOVING A FIELD

Access 2.0 for Windows allows you to move entire fields from one location in the table to another. This is accomplished by moving the mouse pointer from the table lines to the heading line of the table. Use the method shown previously for selecting the column. Now, position the pointer in the selected column's field name and press and hold the left mouse button (a square should now appear beneath the pointer). Drag the pointer to the desired location (a thin black line appears between the columns as the field is dragged to the desired location). Once the field is in the appropriate location, release the mouse button. The field should now be moved.

 Hands-On Exercise: Moving the Middle-Initial Field

MIDDLE INITIAL	Position the pointer in the middle-initial heading. The pointer should turn into a big down arrow.
Click	Click to select the column.
Click and hold	Position the mouse to the middle-initial heading again and click. A square appears below the pointer arrow, indicating that you can move this column.
Drag	Drag the middle-initial field to the right until a dark line appears between the last-name and address columns.
Release	Release the mouse button. The column should now be moved (Figure 2.13).

HIDING FIELDS

Access also allows you to hide fields so that you can group desired fields on one screen to make the table more readable. This is accomplished by selecting a column or columns and then issuing the Format, **Hide Columns** command. The fields can later be restored using Format, **Show Columns**.

 Hands-On Exercise: Hiding Columns

Suppose you wanted to hide the salutation and middle-initial fields so that identifying information about a customer is available on one screen. This is accomplished by issuing the following commands.

Figure 2.13

The Datasheet window with the middle-initial field moved to a new location.

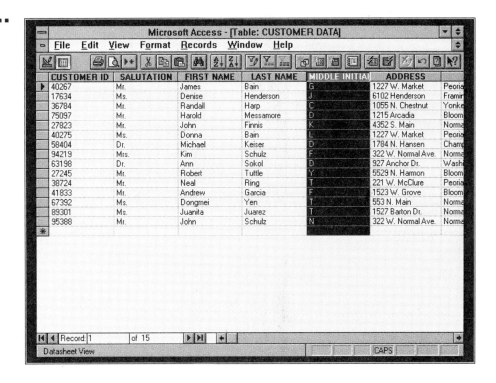

1. Hide the salutation field.

SALUTATION	Position the pointer in the heading cell for the salutation field and wait for the pointer to become a fat down arrow.
Click	Click to select the column.
Format	Open the Format menu.
Hide Columns	Click to hide the salutation column.

2. Hide the middle-initial field.

MIDDLE INITIAL	Position the pointer in the heading cell for the middle-initial field and wait for the pointer to become a fat down arrow.
Click	Click to select the column.
Format	Open the Format menu.
Hide Columns	Click to hide the middle-initial column. Your Datasheet window should look like Figure 2.14.

3. Restore the columns to the Datasheet window.

Format	Open the Format menu.
Show Columns	Click to invoke the Show Columns dialog box (Figure 2.15). Fields (listed in alphabetical order) that are included in the current datasheet are marked with a check.

Figure 2.14
The CUSTOMER DATA table with the columns hidden.

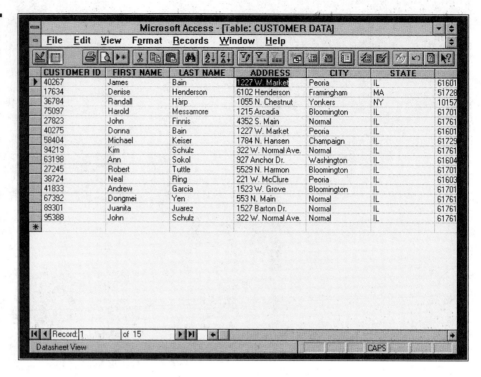

Figure 2.15
The Show Columns dialog box.

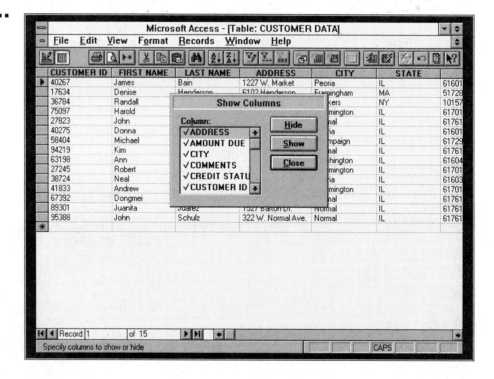

	Click the scroll arrow to view the MIDDLE INITIAL entry.
MIDDLE INITIAL	Double-click to place back into the table.

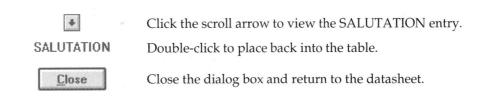

⬇	Click the scroll arrow to view the SALUTATION entry.
SALUTATION	Double-click to place back into the table.
Close	Close the dialog box and return to the datasheet.

LOCKING A FIELD

One problem with displaying records is that sometimes some of the identifying data is shifted off the screen when you view other parts of a record. If you want to make certain that some identifying fields of each record always appear on the screen, you use the **Freeze Columns** option of the Format menu.

 Hands-On Exercise: Locking Fields

1. Hide the salutation column.

SALUTATION	Position the pointer in the heading cell for the salutation field and wait for the pointer to become a fat down arrow.
Click	Click to select the column.
Format	Open the Format menu.
Hide Columns	Click to hide the salutation column.

2. Lock the customer ID, first-name, and last-name fields.

CUSTOMER ID NUMBER	Position the pointer to the CUSTOMER ID NUMBER field name. The cursor should change to a big down arrow.
Click and drag	Click the mouse and drag to the last-name field. All three of the columns should now be selected.
Format	Open the Format menu.
Freeze Columns	Click to freeze the first three columns.
➡	Click the right arrow of the horizontal scroll bar at the bottom of the Datasheet window to display the amount due field. You can see that the frozen fields remain as you move to the right (Figure 2.16).

3. Close the CUSTOMER DATA table.

⬍	Click the restore button of the Datasheet window to return it to its smaller size.
⬜	Double-click the control-menu button of the Datasheet window. Access now asks what you want to do with the changes.
Type N	Do not save the changes to the database table.

Figure 2.16

The Datasheet window with the first three columns frozen for continuous display.

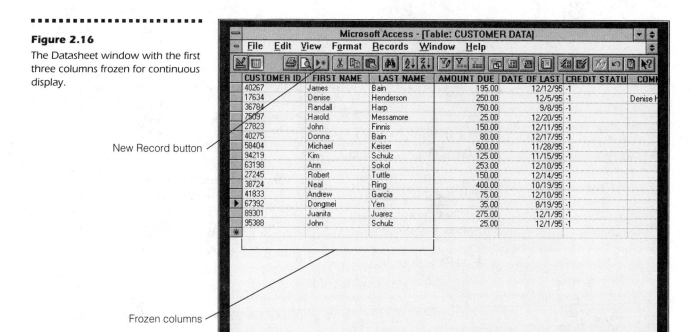

New Record button

Frozen columns

ADDING NEW RECORDS

If you want to add new records to a table in the Datasheet window, position the pointer to the last row (the one with the asterisk in the gray border column). You can also click the New Record button on the toolbar, and Access will insert the new record line in the table. Now start adding data to the field cells. As you position to the next or previous record, the new data is automatically saved to the table.

TABLE-MANIPULATION COMMANDS AND SEARCHING UNORDERED TABLES

This section introduces a number of Access table-manipulation commands that can be accessed from the menu bar once a table has been invoked. In addition, we discuss locating records in unordered tables.

RECORD POINTER

Recall from chapter 1 that Access uses a **record pointer** to keep track of where it is within a table. The record number that appears in the speedbar when you are in the Datasheet window is the current location of the pointer. Many commands result in this pointer moving from one location (record) in a table to another.

The following examples using the CUSTOMER DATA table illustrate Access's tracking of the pointer. Activate the SALES database.

 Hands-On Exercise: Pointer Manipulation

CUSTOMER DATA   Double-click the CUSTOMER DATA table in the database window. The Datasheet window should appear.

Figure 2.17

The Record entry of the speedbar shows the pointer location in the table.

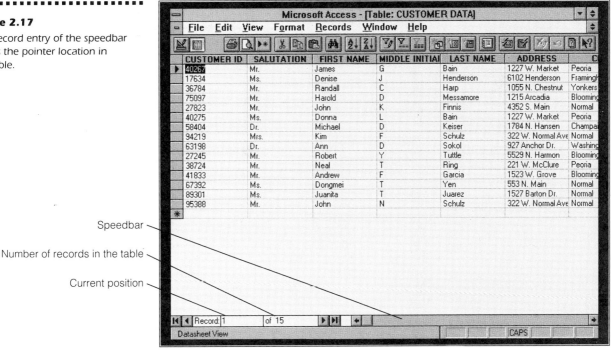

Speedbar

Number of records in the table

Current position

    Maximize the Datasheet window.

Your screen should now resemble Figure 2.17. Notice that the speedbar contains the entry "Record 1 of 15". This is the current position of the pointer. You can position the pointer to other records by using the up- or down-arrow keys. Press the down arrow three times. Notice that the Record entry in the speedbar now has the value "4 of 15", indicating that the pointer is now positioned to record 4.

Using arrow keys to position the pointer is adequate when your tables contain only a few records. If you had several thousand records in a table, however, such pointer-positioning commands would take far too long. A faster way to move the pointer within a table is to use the **Go To submenu** of the **Records menu** (Figure 2.18). The First option positions the pointer at the beginning of the table. The Last option positions the pointer at the end of the table. (These two options, as well as Next and Previous, of course have corresponding buttons on the speedbar.) The New option positions to the row containing the asterisk (*).

Hands-On Exercise: Using the Navigation Buttons

Move among the records using the buttons on the speedbar at the bottom of the Datasheet window.

Click to position to the last record. Notice that the Record entry shows "15 of 15". This is the same as issuing the command sequence Records, Go To, Last.

Click to position to the first record. Notice that the Record entry shows "1 of 15". This is the same as entering the command sequence Records, Go To, First.

(3 times)   Click to position the pointer to record 4 (of 15).

Figure 2.18

The Go To submenu provides one method that allows you to position to a desired record.

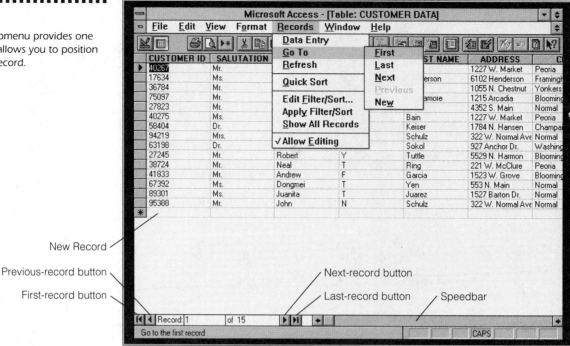

LOCATING RECORDS USING FIND

Positioning to a record is a straightforward task using the Go To submenu or the navigation buttons. What happens, however, when you do not know the record number? In such situations, Access lets you enter the characteristics of the desired record and then positions to the record that meets those specifications via the **Find dialog box**. In performing this operation, you specify the field to be searched as well as the characters to search for. Access then compares those with the contents of this field for each record. The search starts with the first record *or* the current record and ends with the last record. To locate a record using this technique, you must select the field to be searched and enter the characters being sought.

HINTS/HAZARDS

You can activate the Find dialog box by any of the following methods:

- Using the shortcut command Ctrl + F.
- Issuing the command sequence Edit, Find.
- Clicking the Find button on the toolbar.

The Find dialog box is accessed by selecting the Find button on the toolbar (Figure 2.19). The text to be searched for is entered in the Find What text box. The field to be searched defaults to the field in which the cursor resides. The following options in the dialog box can also be used to control the search.

The Where selection box contains the options shown in Figure 2.20, which are discussed in the following paragraphs.

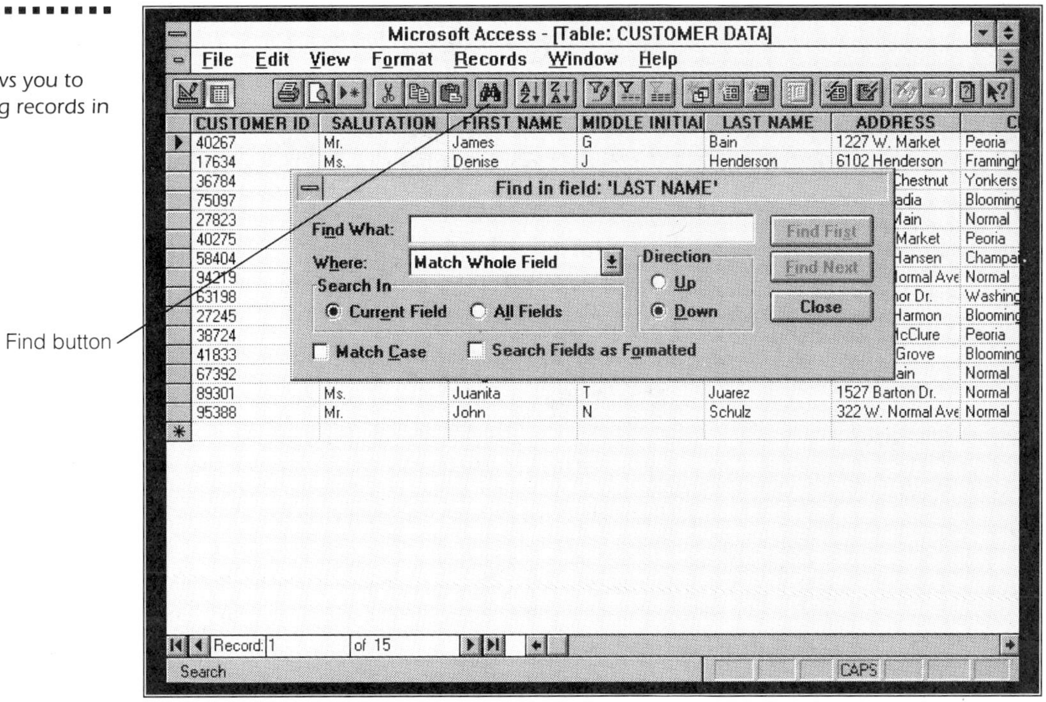

Figure 2.19

The Find dialog box allows you to specify criteria for locating records in a table.

Find button

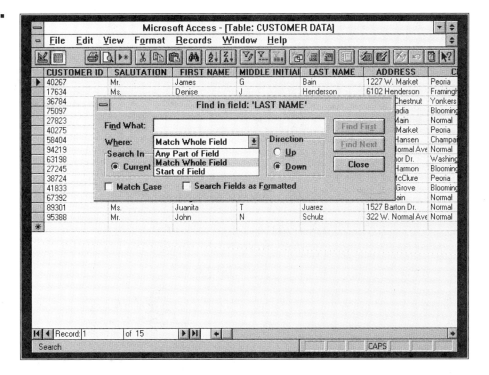

Figure 2.20

The options of the Where selection box determine how a field is to be searched.

Any Part of Field   This option finds records where the search text matches any part of the selected field.

Match Whole Field   This option is the default and finds records where the selected field matches and is the same length as the specified search text.

Start of Field   This option finds records where the selected field begins with the specified search text.

The Search In box controls which fields of the table are to be used in the search.

Current Field   This radio button indicates that you want to include only the specified field.

All Fields   This radio button specifies that all fields of the table are to be included in the search process.

The Direction box controls the direction in which the search is to take place: forward (down) or backward (up) in the table.

Match Case   This checkbox finds records that match the case of the search text exactly. If, for example, you specify "Access" as your search text, the program will ignore records that contain the strings "access" or "ACCESS".

Search Fields as Formatted   This option finds data based on its display format. Searches using this method are usually slower than a text-based search.

The Find First command button finds the first occurrence of the search string, whereas the Find Next button finds subsequent occurrences of the search string. After the first item is located, the Close button is used to return to the datasheet and view the located record. To find subsequent occurrences, you can use the shortcut command (Ctrl + F) or click the Find button and then select the Find Next command button.

HINTS/HAZARDS   You can save some time by first positioning the cursor in the field of the record that you want to search or by selecting the entire column, as you did in the discussion of previous commands used in this chapter.

Find the record with a first-name field that has the contents "Ann". When you initiate a search, the cursor should be in the field that you wish to search (in this search, the cursor is automatically in the customer ID field, so you must move it to the first-name field):

Hands-On Exercise: Using the Find Command

1. Activate the CUSTOMER DATA table. Click the first-name field of the first record.

2. Find the record with the first-name field contents of "Ann".

Click	Click the first-name field of the first record.
🔍	Click the Find button on the toolbar to invoke the Find dialog box (Figure 2.19).
Type **Ann**	Enter the search criteria. Since the pointer is already at the beginning of the table, you want the Down and the Current Field defaults.
Find First	Click the command button to find the first record with the match. Notice that the record indicator now specifies "9 of 15", indicting that a match as been found on record 9.

Figure 2.21

Record 9 contains a match of "Ann" in the first-name field.

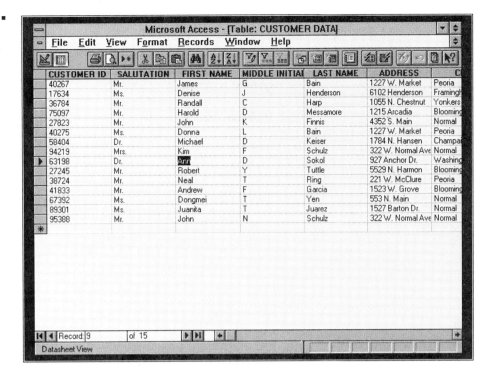

Figure 2.22

The alert dialog box that appears when no record meets the criteria or when the end of the table has been reached (after the last match).

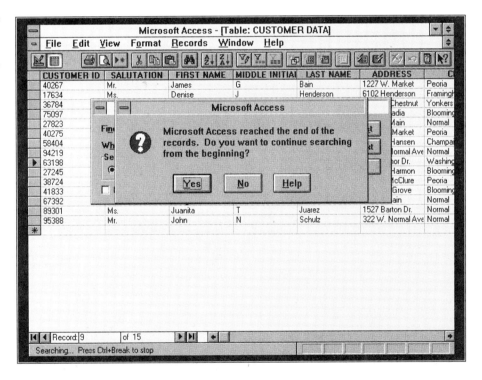

View the record that has generated the match (Figure 2.21).

In a successful search, the record number that matches the search criteria appears at the bottom of the Access window. If the search fails, an alert dialog box (Figure 2.22) indicates that the value was not found.

When specifying search criteria, you can also use the **wildcards** * and ? in exactly the same fashion as you do in DOS. The ? specifies one position, and the * specifies any remaining characters. For example, to use * for locating any records with the contents "Bloomington" in the city field, use the following commands.

 Hands-On Exercise: Using a Wildcard in a Search Operation

1. Use the shortcut command to start the search.

    CITY   Click the CITY column name.

    [icon]   Invoke the Find dialog box.

2. Find any record that has Bloomington in the city field.

    Type **Blo**   Enter the search criteria (the city field should be highlighted).

    [↓]   Click the down arrow of the Where selection box.

    Any Part of Field   Click to find this character string anywhere in the city field.

    [Find First]   Click to find the first occurrence. You should get a "hit" on record 4 of 15. The highlight is on the city field of this record.

    [Find Next]   Click to find the next occurrence. You should get a hit on record 10 of 15.

    [Find Next]   Click to find the next occurrence. You should get a hit on record 12 of 15.

    [Find Next]   Click to find the next occurrence. You should get an alert dialog box, indicating that the value was not found.

    Type **N**   Do not continue the search. Access now displays a dialog box indicating that it has reached the end of the file.

    [Enter]   Accept the OK prompt.

    [Close]   Return to the CUSTOMER DATA table.

    [↕]   Click the restore button of the Datasheet window.

    [—]   Double-click the control-menu button of the CUSTOMER DATA table to close the table.

Continuing the Search   Once search criteria have been specified, you can locate other records that meet that criteria by clicking the Find Next command button. Notice that when you get to the end of the table, Access displays two different dialog boxes, both indicating that Access has reached the end of the records.

ARRANGEMENT COMMANDS

The Access package has two commands for rearranging data within a table. The Sort command physically rearranges the contents of a table and creates a new table to hold the rearranged data. The Index command leaves the original table alone but creates another table to rearrange the record numbers.

SORT COMMAND

The **Sort command** physically rearranges records according to values contained in one or more specific fields of each record. To do this, the sort operation rearranges the records of the original table in a different order.

Sorting on One Field   Before sorting a table, you must first activate it. In using the Sort command to sort by one field, determine the key field for sorting by placing the insertion point in a field and clicking or by selecting the column. Then click the Sort Ascending or Sort Descending button on the toolbar. The changes made by the Sort command do not affect the original table unless you issue a Save command. The unsorted CUSTOMER DATA table and the sort buttons are shown in Figure 2.23.

Hands-On Exercise: Sorting the CUSTOMER DATA Table in Order by Last Name

1. Activate the SALES database.

2. Activate the CUSTOMER DATA table.

3. Sort by last name in ascending order.

Figure 2.23

The unsorted CUSTOMER DATA table.

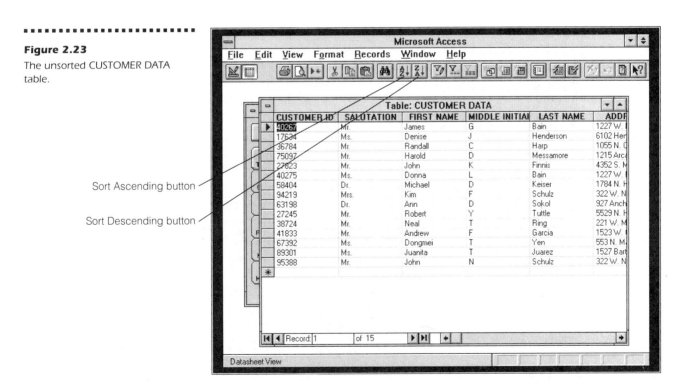

Sort Ascending button

Sort Descending button

■■■■■■■■■■■■■■■■■■■■■■■

Figure 2.24

The CUSTOMER DATA table sorted in ascending order by last name.

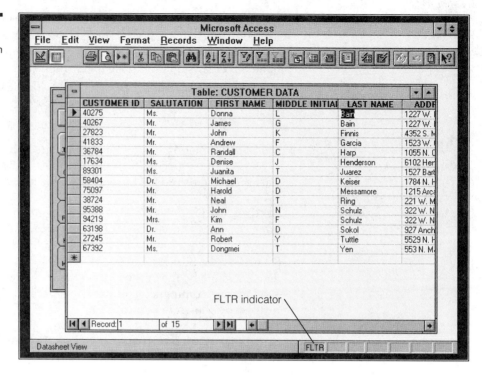

Click	Click the last-name field of any record in the table.

 Click to begin the sort operation. The CUSTOMER DATA table is now sorted in ascending order by the last-name field. The sorted CUSTOMER DATA table now appears in the Datasheet window (Figure 2.24).

When you are performing a sort that involves only one field of a database, the sort process is pretty straightforward. You click the field to be sorted, and then click the icon representing the ascending or descending sort order. Now sort the CUSTOMER DATA table in order by zip code.

4. Sort the table in order by zip code.

5. Sort the table in order by city.

6. Sort the table in order by amount due.

When Access performs a sort, it uses what it calls a **filter** to process the data and rearrange it in the table based on the selected column. You can verify that it has performed this filter process by locating the FLTR indicator in the status bar of Figure 2.24. With a one-field sort, Access automatically applies the selected field to the filter. However, with a multiple-field sort, you must specify the fields to be included in the filter process.

Multiple-Field Sorts   A multiple-field sort must be specified to Access via the Filter dialog box (Figure 2.25). This dialog box can be accessed via the Edit Filter/Sort button on the toolbar or via the command sequence Records, Edit Filter/Sort. The bottom portion of the Filter dialog box allows you to specify the fields to be included in the sort process. The sort is executed by clicking the Apply Filter/Sort button on the toolbar.

Figure 2.25

The Filter dialog box used for defining multiple-field sorts.

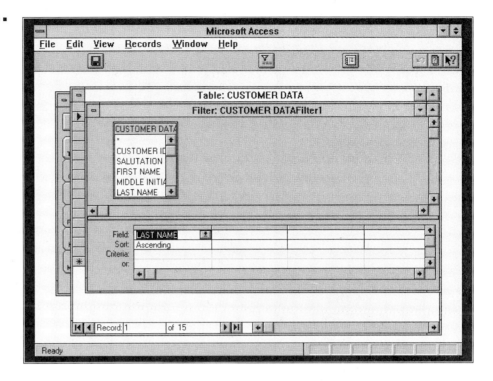

Suppose that you want to sort the CUSTOMER DATA table by last name within zip code. Since the Filter dialog box has the information from the previous sort (amount column), you have to change the first field to be included in the sort. This entails clicking on the AMOUNT DUE field entry and then clicking the down arrow to obtain a listing of table fields (Figure 2.26). In this case, you

Figure 2.26

The list box for selecting a field to be included in the sort.

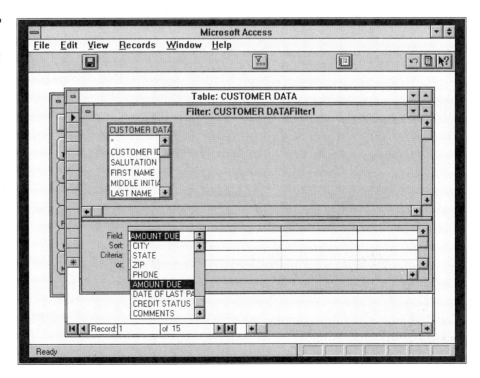

Figure 2.27

The list box for selecting the order in which a column is to be sorted.

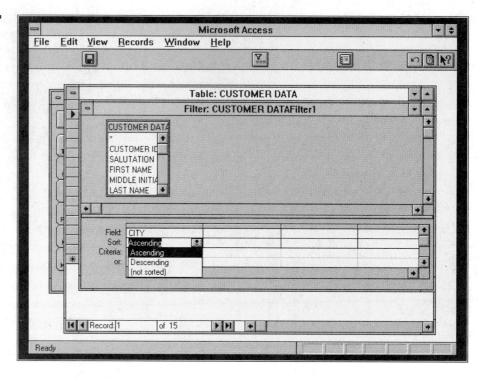

would click on CITY. Access defaults to the ascending sort from the previous sort on the amount field. You now position to the second field entry in that row, click the mouse to activate the field, and then click the down arrow to display the field name list. Select the desired field by clicking with the mouse. Next, you specify the sort order for the new field by positioning the mouse to the second row of the new column and clicking once to activate that field, and a second time on the down arrow to activate the sort order selection box (Figure 2.27). Once all of the fields to be included in the sort and the sort order for each field have been specified, the Apply Filter/Sort button on the toolbar can be clicked to perform the sort operation and return to the Datasheet window.

Hands-On Exercise: Sorting the Table in Order by Name Within City

1. If necessary, activate the CUSTOMER DATA table of the SALES database.

2. Build the sort filter.

    Click to invoke the Filter dialog box (Figure 2.25). If you have followed the previous hands-on exercise with this exercise, the amount field should appear in the filter. If not, click the FIRST NAME entry of the Sort line to activate that entry.

3. Define the first sort field.

    Click the down arrow of the amount field to obtain a selection box of field names (Figure 2.26).

Figure 2.28

The completed Filter dialog box for the sort.

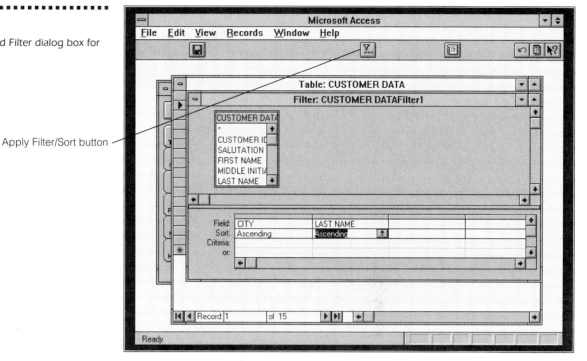

Apply Filter/Sort button

CITY   Click the CITY field name. The CITY value should now appear in the first Field cell. Ascending should appear in the Sort cell beneath it. If it doesn't, click the box, click the down arrow, and then click Ascending.

4. Define the second sort field.

    Click   Click the Field box to the right of the CITY entry to activate it.

    ⬇   Click the down arrow of the new field to obtain a selection box of field names (Figure 2.26).

LAST NAME   Click to include in the Field entry.

    Click   Click the Sort cell beneath the LAST NAME entry to activate the cell.

    ⬇   Click the down arrow of the new field to obtain a selection box of sort orders (Figure 2.27).

Ascending   Click to select ascending order. If you fail to make a selection, Access defaults to (not sorted). Your completed Filter dialog box should look like Figure 2.28.

5. Perform the sort.

          Click the Apply Filter/Sort button on the toolbar to perform the sort and return to the Datasheet window. Your screen should now look like Figure 2.29. (You may have to move the screen to the left using the scroll arrows.)

Figure 2.29

The CUSTOMER DATA table sorted in order by name within city.

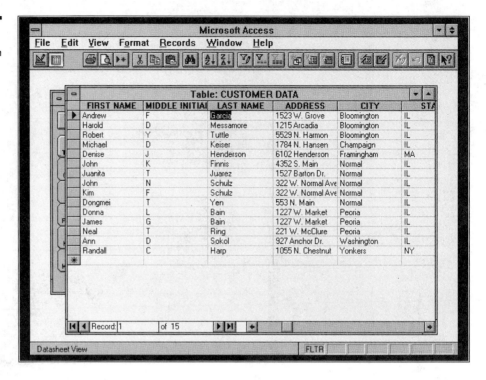

When you are using tables with just a few records, like the exercises in this book, the Sort command makes a lot of sense. When you have tables that contain thousands of records, however, the sort process can take a lot of time, even with a powerful computer. For large tables, ordering records within a table can be accomplished via the next topic.

INDEX COMMAND

The best way to reorder records is to use the **Index command**, which does not rearrange them physically but rather logically, without moving records. This is accomplished by an index table in which each specified field points to the appropriate record in the specified table. The contents of the original table remain unchanged, with the same physical table order and the same record numbers; the new index table holds the logical order of the table.

Indexes are created for a table from the Table Design window. Once the Table Design window appears, you can invoke the Indexes window (Figure 2.30) by clicking the Indexes button on the toolbar. An index can contain multiple fields, each of which will be listed in the Field Name column of the dialog box, along with the sort order for each field.

Primary-Key Index   A **primary-key index** is the unique identifier of a record in a table. Every record within a table must have a different value in the field that has been designated as the primary key. In this application, the customer ID number will be used as the primary key. Once the primary key has been specified, the table will be displayed in that order, unless the table is displayed in order by a secondary key. The Set Primary Key button on the toolbar can be used to create the primary key for a table.

Figure 2.30

The Indexes window used for creating and modifying indexes.

Design View button

Datasheet View button

Indexes button

Set Primary Key button

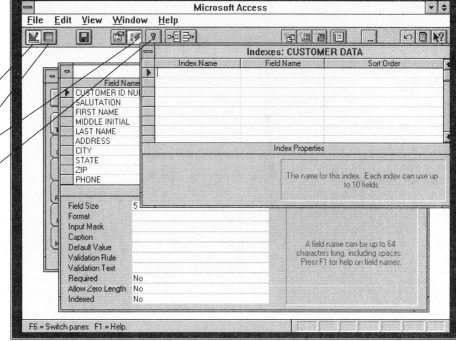

 Hands-On Exercise: Creating the Primary-Key Index

1. Activate the SALES database, if necessary.

2. Activate the CUSTOMER DATA table in the Datasheet window.

3. Activate the Table Design window and create the primary key.

     Click to invoke the Table Design window (Figure 2.31). The customer ID field should be selected. If it isn't, click that field.

     Click to create the primary key. A key icon like that shown in Figure 2.32 should appear to the left of the field name.

4. Return to the Datasheet window.

     Click to invoke a dialog box that indicates that the table must be saved.

     (Or click the OK button) to save the table. Once the table is saved, it is displayed in order by the customer ID number (Figure 2.33). Now whenever a record is added to the table, the table will be displayed in order by customer ID number whenever the table is retrieved.

Single-Field Indexes A table with a **single-field index** is ordered by the contents of one field only. It must be created via the Indexes window.

Figure 2.31

The Table Design window for the CUSTOMER DATA table.

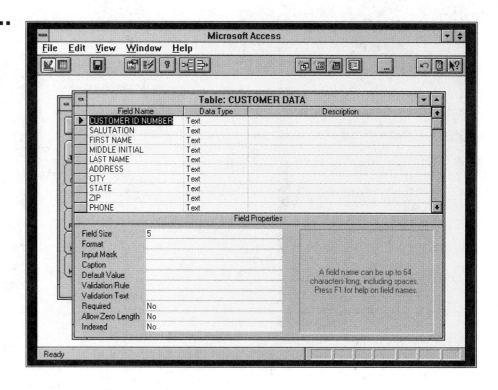

Figure 2.32

The primary-key designator (a key icon) next to the field name.

Primary-key designator

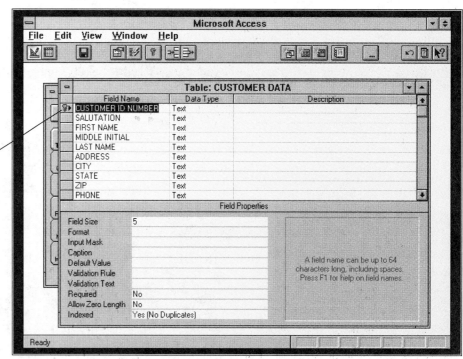

 Hands-On Exercise: Creating the ZIPCUST Index

1. Activate the SALES database, if necessary.

2. Activate the CUSTOMER DATA table in the Datasheet window.

3. Activate the Table Design window and create the primary key.

Figure 2.33

The CUSTOMER DATA table in order by the primary-key field—customer ID number.

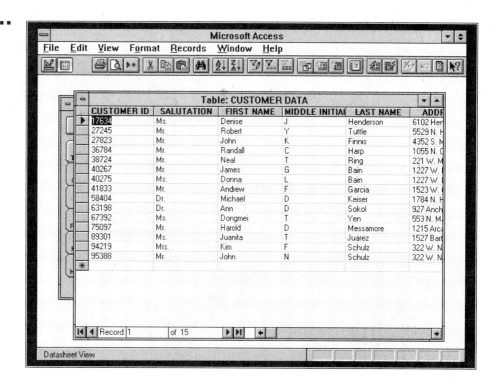

     Click to invoke the Table Design window.

4. Activate the Indexes window and define the index.

   The Indexes window now appears and looks like Figure 2.30 except that the primary key is included.

Click   Click the cell beneath the PrimaryKey entry.

Type **ZIPCUST**   Enter the name of the index.

Click   Click the Field Name cell for ZIPCUST to activate that cell.

     Click to display a listing of field names. Keep clicking until the ZIP field name appears.

ZIP   Click this field name. Your Indexes window should now look like Figure 2.34.

5. Display the table.

     Click to display the table. Access indicates that you must save the table.

OK   Save the table.

     Click the right arrow on the horizontal scroll bar until the ZIP field appears. Notice that the datasheet is still in order by the customer ID number. Creating the index does not affect the display of the table in the Datasheet window.

Figure 2.34

The completed Indexes window for the ZIPCUST index.

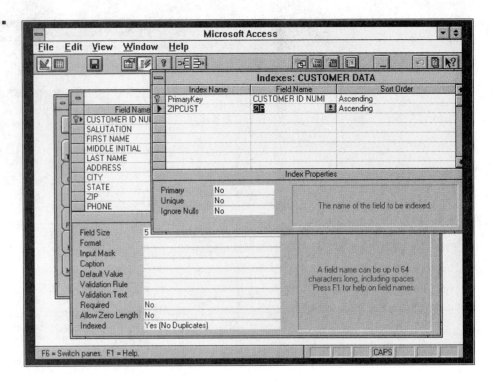

Figure 2.35

Information contained in the ZIPCUST index table: the zip code and the location of each record.

ZIP	Record
10157	00003
51728	00002
61601	00001
61601	00006
61603	00011
61604	00009
61701	00004
61701	00010
61701	00012
61729	00007
61761	00005
61761	00008
61761	00013
61761	00014
61761	00015

The above steps have created an index called ZIPCUST; each record in the ZIPCUST index contains the zip field for a record in the CUSTOMER DATA table and the number of the record with that particular zip-code value (Figure 2.35). When the records are displayed, Access first accesses the ZIPCUST index table, which in turn displays the appropriate record from the CUSTOMER DATA table.

When Access accesses the records from an indexed table, it performs a number of tasks automatically. First, it goes to the ZIPCUST index (see Figure 2.35) and finds zip code 10157. It also finds that record 3 of the CUSTOMER DATA table holds the data for this index entry. Access now accesses record 3 of the CUSTOMER DATA table. It then moves to the second index entry and repeats the process until all index entries have been processed.

Because an index contains only the data from the specified field, it is a small table that can be loaded into RAM and searched quickly to locate records. Access allows you to create up to 32 indexes for a table, and 5 of those can be composed of multiple fields. Each multiple-field index can include up to a maximum of 10 fields. Whenever a change is made to a field that is used in an index, or when records are added or deleted, the indexes are automatically updated by Access to reflect the change. Working with a large database with several indexes open can result in a slower response and can, as a result, slow editing operations. However, this is a small price to pay for the flexibility provided by indexing.

Multiple-Field Indexes What if you want the table to appear in order by more than one field, such as by first name and last name? The Manage Indexes dialog box makes this task easy by letting you **concatenate** (join) fields in creating the index. The result is a **multiple-field index**. The first multiple-field index here will arrange the table alphabetically first name within last name.

To create the LFNAME index, make sure the CUSTOMER DATA table is activated (it already is unless you have just started Access) and issue the following commands.

Hands-On Exercise: Creating the LFNAME Index

1. Activate the SALES database, if necessary.

2. If necessary, activate the CUSTOMER DATA table.

3. Activate the Table Design window and create the index.

![]	Click to invoke the Table Design window.

4. Activate the Indexes window and define the index.

![]	The Indexes window now appears.
Click	Click the cell beneath the ZIPCUST entry.
Type **LFNAME**	Enter the name of the index.
Click	Click the Field Name cell for LFNAME to activate that cell.
![]	Click to display a listing of field names.
LAST NAME	Click the LAST NAME field name.
Click	Click the cell beneath LAST NAME to enter the next field name.
![]	Click to display a listing of field names.
FIRST NAME	Click the FIRST NAME field name. Your Indexes window should now look like Figure 2.36.
![]	Click the control-menu button of the Datasheet window to return to the database window.

Deleting Unwanted Indexes As you are creating indexes, you may find that you have indexes on disk that are no longer needed. Such indexes can be

Figure 2.36

The completed Indexes window for the LFNAME index.

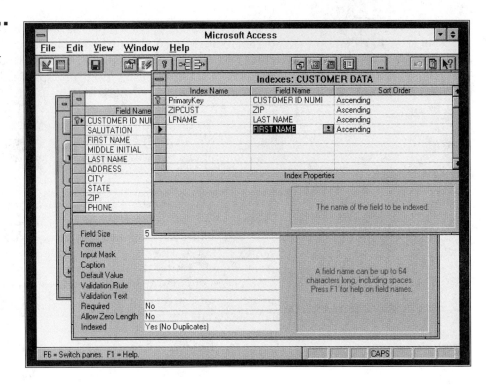

deleted by selecting the index (that line now appears in reverse video) and then using the Del key to delete the line.

FILTER FOR SELECTED RECORDS

Besides using the Access filter to sort records, you can also use it to display only those records that meet certain criteria. If you have an extremely large table, you may not want to include all records in a sort. For example, assume that you are interested only in those records for Normal, IL (zip = 61761), and you want to display and manipulate only those records.

This example creates an alphabetical listing of the CUSTOMER DATA table but includes only those records with 61761 in the zip field.

Hands-On Exercise: Creating a Filter to Display Only 61761 Records in Alphabetical Order

1. If necessary, activate the CUSTOMER DATA table of the SALES database.

2. Build the sort filter.

     Click to invoke the Filter dialog box.

3. Define the first sort field.

     Click the down arrow of the Field cell to obtain a selection box of field names.

     Click the down arrow of the vertical scroll box until the ZIP field appears.

ZIP   Click to place the ZIP value in the first Field cell.

Click   Click the Sort cell beneath the ZIP entry.

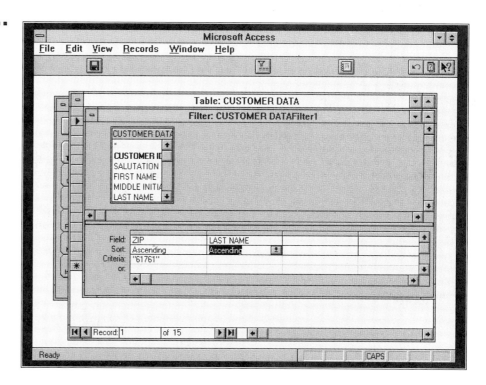   Click the down arrow of the Sort cell to obtain a selection box of sort alternatives.

Ascending   Select ascending order.

4. Enter the selection criteria.

Click   Click the Criteria cell beneath the ZIP entry.

Type **61761**   Enter the selection criteria. Since the desired zip code is in a text cell, Access automatically places the text between double quotation marks.

5. Define the second sort field.

Click   Click the Field box to the right of the ZIP entry to activate it.

    Click the down arrow of the new field to obtain a selection box of field names.

LAST NAME   Click to include in the Field entry.

Click   Click the Sort cell beneath the LAST NAME entry to activate the cell.

    Click the down arrow of the new field to obtain a selection box of sort orders.

Ascending   Click to select ascending order. Your Filter dialog box should look like Figure 2.37.

Figure 2.37

The completed Filter dialog box for the selection.

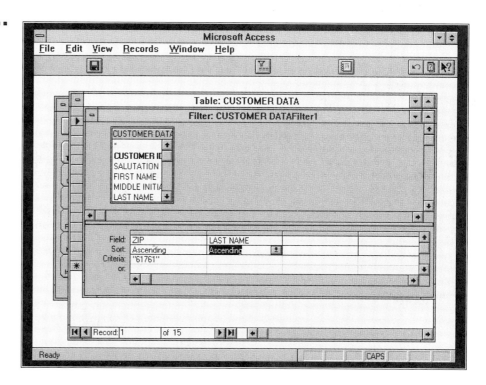

Figure 2.38

The CUSTOMER DATA table containing only those records with a zip code of 61761, sorted in order by name.

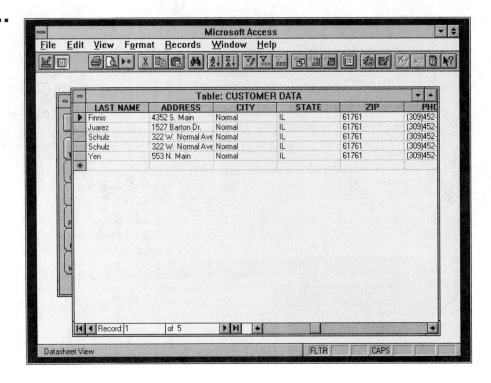

6. Perform the selection sort.

 Click the Apply Filter/Sort button on the toolbar to perform the sort and return to the Datasheet window. Your screen should now look like Figure 2.38. (You may have to move the screen to the left using the scroll arrows.)

7. Close the Datasheet window.

 Double-click the control-menu button of the Datasheet window to return to the database window.

CHAPTER REVIEW

The Datasheet window is Access's method of displaying database tables. The datasheet of Access lets you change column widths, lock fields so they are always displayed, change row height, and move fields. Using the datasheet, you can quickly move through a table in physical record order or by primary-key order and manually make changes to selected records.

The Go To submenu and the speedbar at the bottom of the datsheet provide a number of ways to position the pointer. The Find dialog box lets you search tables.

The Access package provides two ways to order records within a table: the Sort command and the Index command. The Sort command creates tables in which the records are sorted by one or more specified fields. For large tables, the sorting process is time-consuming.

The Index command creates an index whose contents consist of the key field of each record and the location of each record on disk. The database table is left in its original order (the primary-key order), whereas the index is arranged in the desired order. To access a record, Access first goes to the index table to find the location of the desired record, and then goes to the identified location in the database table. An index table can be built using a number of fields and will produce the information in only one pass. For example, the table could be logically arranged in last-name/first-name order with only one command/statement. With indexing, the original table remains in its original order; only the index table is arranged to reflect the changed relationship.

When you are using multiple indexes, you often want changes to be reflected in several different indexes. Access does this automatically anytime you make a change to a field that is involved in an index. Up to 32 indexes can be open at one time.

The Filter dialog box can be used to extract and sort selected records from a table.

KEY TERMS AND CONCEPTS

Column Width command
concatenate
Datasheet window
filter
Find dialog box
Freeze Columns command
Go To submenu
gridlines
Hide Columns command
Index command

multiple-field index
primary-key index
record pointer
Records menu
Row Height command
Show Columns command
single-field index
Sort command
wildcards

CHAPTER QUIZ

Multiple Choice

1. Which of the following statements about sorting is false?
   a. It makes use of an Access filter.
   b. A single-field sort involves only clicking an icon after the field is selected.
   c. A multiple-key sort is impossible.
   d. You are allowed to sort on only one field at a time.
   e. All of the above statements are true.

2. Which of the following statements about indexing is false?
   a. An indexed table appears in order only by the primary key.
   b. The original table is left the same when subsequent indexes are created.
   c. First the index must be accessed and then the database table, if the records are desired in indexed order.
   d. The index holds the contents of each data record.
   e. All of the above statements are true.

3. Which command finds records in a table?
   a. Find
   b. Browse
   c. List
   d. Index
   e. Continue

4. Which of the following tasks is not permitted in the Datasheet window?
   a. change column width
   b. change row height
   c. move a column
   d. change a column/field name
   e. All of the above are permitted.

5. Which navigation button positions to the last record in a table?
   a. ⏮
   b. ◀
   c. ▶
   d. ⏭

True/False

6. You must index a table before using the Find dialog box.

7. Access allows you to move a field in the Datasheet window by dragging it to a new location.

8. The indexed field contains one or more fields in sequential order within the index.

9. You can use the Filter dialog box for both sorting and indexing records.

10. Column width can be changed only via a drag operation.

Answers

1. c, d, e   2. d, e   3. a   4. d   5. d   6. f   7. t   8. t   9. t   10. f

Exercises

1. Define or describe each of the following:
   a. index
   b. multiple-field index
   c. primary key
   d. filter
   e. index table
   f. concatenation

2. Use the _____ command to physically reorder the records within a table and create a new table.

3. You can sort the records in a table in either _____ or _____ order.

4. The Sort command sorts tables using one or more _____.

5. The _____ file contains both the key field contents and the record location.

6. Changing row height in a table can be accomplished via the Row Height dialog box or by _____ a cell border.

7. Selecting a column can be accomplished by placing the pointer in the _____ and clicking the mouse.

8. The process of joining two or more fields to form one index is known as _____.

9. Moving a column is accomplished via a _____ operation.

10. Use the _____ key to delete an index after it has been selected.

11. When several indexes appear in the Indexes window, only the _____ index is used to list records in the Datasheet window.

12. When several indexes are open, a changed field contained in several indexes will result in _____ index(es) being updated.

13. The _____ dialog box is used to find records based on the contents of a field.

14. The _____ command of the Format menu is used to "unfreeze" any frozen fields.

15. A _____ process is performed anytime a sort is executed.

16. You can drag the right _____ of a column to resize a field in the Datasheet window.

17. A new record can be inserted in the datasheet by clicking the _____ button on the toolbar.

18. The _____ and _____ buttons moves the pointer forward or backward in a table one record at a time when you are in the Datasheet window.

19. The record _____ is moved anytime a record-positioning command is used.

20. A _____-field sort must be defined in the Filter dialog box.

COMPUTER EXERCISES

The following exercises require the PAYMAST table, created previously. Remember to activate the PROJECTS database before starting these exercises. Refer to the beginning of this chapter if you do not remember how to perform these tasks.

1. Perform the following tasks on the PAYMAST table.
   a. Sort the table by last name.
   b. Sort the table by gross pay.
   c. Sort the table by employee ID.
   d. Index the table by employee ID (primary key). List the table.
   e. Index the table by last name. List the table.
   f. Sort the table by last name and first name. List the table.
   g. Find all the employees who have a gross pay of 2975.00. Use the Find command to do this.

h. Use the Find command to find all the employees who have a pay rate of 7.75.

2. You are responsible for maintaining the database for a student club to which you belong. This database contains information about each student member. Name and address information as well as interests and graduation data are stored in the table. The database, CLUB, has the following structure:

Field	Field Name	Type	Width
1	ID	Text	4
2	DATE	Text	8
3	LAST	Text	15
4	FIRST	Text	12
5	INIT	Text	1
6	LOCADDR	Text	25
7	LOCCITY	Text	15
8	LOCSTATE	Text	2
9	LCZIP	Text	5
10	LOCPHONE	Text	13
11	HOMADDR	Text	25
12	HOMCITY	Text	15
13	HOMSTATE	Text	2
14	HOMZIP	Text	5
15	HOMPHONE	Text	13
16	YEAR	Text	1
17	GRADDATE	Text	15
18	MAJOR	Text	3
19	CLUBMAJR	Text	1
20	NEW_REN	Text	1
21	MEMB	Text	1
22	PUBL	Text	1
23	SOCIAL	Text	1
24	BUS	Text	1

The fields with the LOC prefix contain data about the local address of the member, whereas the HOM prefix refers to the home data.

The YEAR field contains a number that designates the year in school (1 = freshman, 2 = sophomore, 3 = junior, and 4 = senior).

Your first task is to create the indexes that will be used to list records from the table (name and ID [primary key]). Once the indexes have been created and activated, add yourself as a member.

Use the Datasheet window to display each member's first and last name onscreen, together with his or her graduation date.

3

MODIFYING A TABLE STRUCTURE, REPLACING AND DELETING RECORDS, AND AN INTRODUCTION TO REPORTS

CHAPTER OBJECTIVES

After completing this chapter, you should be able to

- **Change the structure of a table and control data input**
- **Delete records**
- **Generate reports**

This chapter shows you how to change the structure of a table, limit the type of data that can be entered in a field, search and replace fields in a record, and delete records. Finally, it introduces the Report command, which provides control over how a printed report is generated.

· ·

MODIFYING A STRUCTURE

Assume that you decide the existing CUSTOMER DATA table does not provide enough geographic information; you want to add a 1-byte region field (of text data) to each record, after the zip field. To do this, you use the **Insert Row command**.

ADDING A FIELD TO THE RECORD STRUCTURE

Access provides two different ways of invoking the Table Design window.

- Clicking the Design command button of the database window after you have selected the desired table invokes the Table Design window.
- After the Datasheet window for a table is displayed, click the Design View button on the toolbar.

HINTS/HAZARDS

If you are changing the name of several fields of the table structure using the Design command, it is a good idea to save the table after each field has been changed. This allows Access to keep track of which field in the old structure belongs to the changed table in the new structure. If you don't do this, Access does not know where to put the data, and simply erases any fields about which it has doubts.

 Hands-On Exercise: Adding a Field to the CUSTOMER DATA Table

In the following steps you will insert the region field following the zip field in the CUSTOMER DATA table.

1. Activate the SALES database.

2. Select the CUSTOMER DATA table.

CUSTOMER DATA   Double-click the table to activate the Datasheet window.

     Maximize the Datasheet window.

3. Activate the Table Design window.

     Click to invoke the Table Design window (Figure 3.1).

Figure 3.1
The structure for the CUSTOMER DATA table.

Design View button

Insert Row button

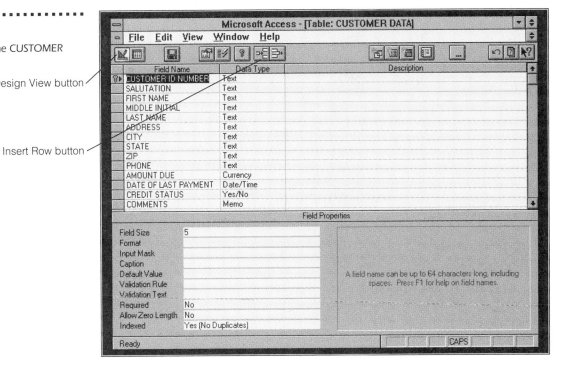

Figure 3.2
The CUSTOMER DATA table with the blank, inserted row for the new field definition.

Inserted field

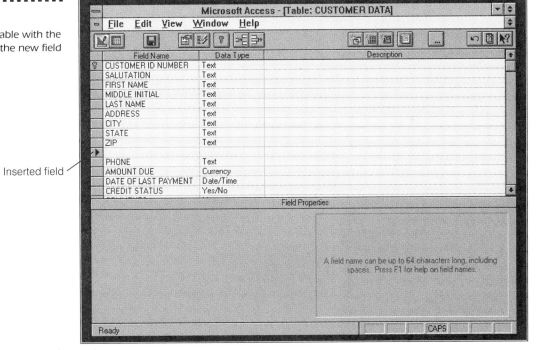

4. Insert the new field.

PHONE   Click the PHONE field.

          Click this button on the toolbar to invoke a blank field definition in the table structure (Figure 3.2).

Figure 3.3

The region field added to the table structure.

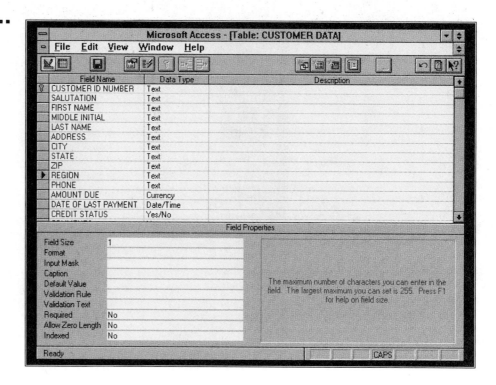

5. Enter the structure characteristics for the new field.

Type **REGION**   Name the field.

[Enter]   Accept the name and the text data type.

6. Enter the field size.

Field Size   Click to the right of the 50 in the Field Size cell of the Field Properties box at the bottom of the Table Design window.

[Backspace] (twice)   Delete 50.

Type **1**   Enter the field width. Your structure should now look like Figure 3.3.

7. Save the structure to disk.

Click to decrease the size of the Table Design window.

Double-click the control-menu button of the Table Design window. A dialog box asks if you want to save your changes to the CUSTOMER DATA table.

Yes   (Or press Enter.) The changes to the structure are now saved to the table on disk. You are returned to the database window.

Figure 3.4

The CUSTOMER DATA table with the inserted region field.

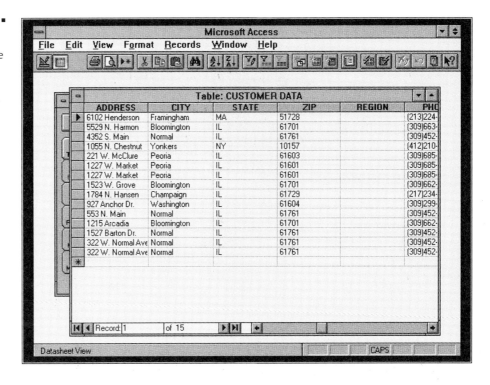

8. Activate the CUSTOMER DATA table.

CUSTOMER DATA   Double-click the table name to invoke the Datasheet window.

Click the scroll arrow on the horizontal scroll bar to view the blank REGION field (Figure 3.4).

CONTROLLING DATA ENTRY AND DISPLAY

You also want to exercise more control over how data is entered into the table and later displayed. Let's assume, for example, that you want to control the range of characters to be entered in the region field, automatically include parentheses and a dash in the phone field and slashes in the date field, and force uppercase characters in the state field. You also want yes/no fields to display values other than -1 and 0 and date fields to show the month name rather than the number. Access allows you to control how data are entered via the Field Properties box of the Table Design window. Access uses the Format, Input Mask, Default Value, Validation Rule, and Validation Text cells of the Field Properties box to control data input and display.

Format   The **Format cell** allows you to use a predefined format for a data type and enables you to design your own display format (we concentrate here on the predefined display formats). Remember from chapter 1 that we used this format for controlling the amount field. The format selected or entered affects only the display of data in a field. It does not affect how you enter data in a field.

Two predefined formats that affect our application are for the yes/no field and the date data types used in the fields for credit status and date of last

Figure 3.5

The predefined formats for the date/time data type.

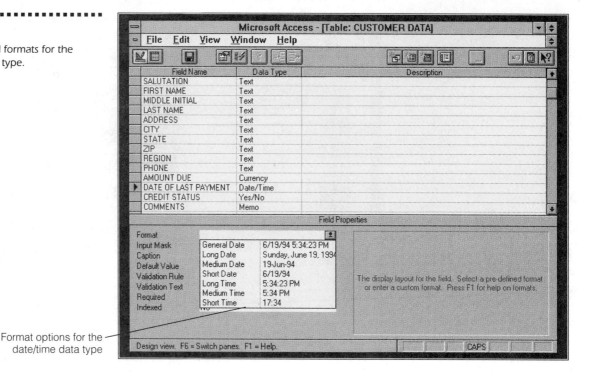

Format options for the date/time data type

Figure 3.6

The predefined formats for the yes/no data type.

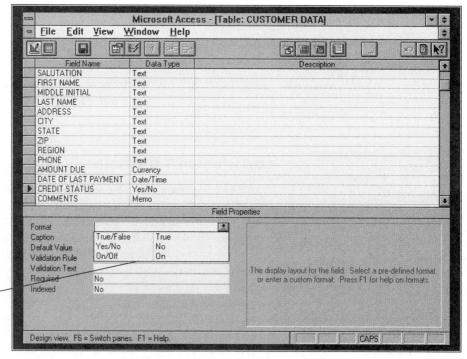

Format options for the yes/no data type

payment. When you are dealing with a field that has a predefined format, a down-arrow icon appears in the Format cell when you click it with the mouse. Clicking the down-arrow icon displays the available predefined formats for that data type.

The predefined field formats for the date/time data type are shown in Figure 3.5; the predefined field formats for the yes/no data type are shown in Figure 3.6.

Table 3.1   Input Mask Characters

Character	Description
0	Requires a digit (0–9) entry; no plus (+) or minus (–) signs allowed.
9	Digit or space entry required; plus and minus signs not allowed.
#	Digit or space entry not required; blank positions are converted to spaces; plus and minus signs are allowed.
L	Letter (A–Z), entry required.
?	Letter (A–Z), entry optional.
A	Letter or digit, entry required.
a	Letter or digit, entry optional.
C	Any character or space, entry optional.
&	Any character or space, entry required.
.,:;-/	Decimal placeholder and thousand, date, and time separators. (The characters depend on the settings in the International section of the Microsoft Windows Control Panel.)
<	Causes all characters that follow to be converted to lowercase.
>	Causes all characters that follow to be converted to uppercase.
!	Causes input mask to fill from right to left, rather than from left to right, when characters on the left side of the input mask are optional. You can include the exclamation point anywhere in the input mask.
\	Causes the character that follows to be displayed as the literal character (for example, \A is displayed as A).

Input Mask   The **Input Mask cell** specifies how data is entered and displayed in the text box. Table 3.1 contains **input mask characters** that can be used to control how data is entered. If you do not want to enter the input mask manually, you can click the **wizard button** in the right-hand portion of the cell, and Access offers to build the mask for you (Figure 3.7) via the **Input Mask Wizard**. Once the Input Mask Wizard appears onscreen, you can select the desired entry.

The Try it text box shows how the field will appear with that particular mask applied. Figure 3.8 shows the use of the Phone Number mask in the Try it text box.

If you enter a mask manually, the mask can contain up to three parts separated by semicolons. A sample mask for the phone number might be entered as

    (000)000-0000!;0;" "

The first part specifies the input mask: [(000)000-0000]. The second part specifies whether Access stores the literal display characters when you enter data. If you use '0' for this part, all literal display characters (for example, the parentheses in the Phone Number mask) are stored with the value in a field of the record. A '1' or blank specifies that only the characters you type into the text box are stored as part of the record.

Figure 3.7

The Input Mask Wizard dialog box allows you to quickly control data entry in a field.

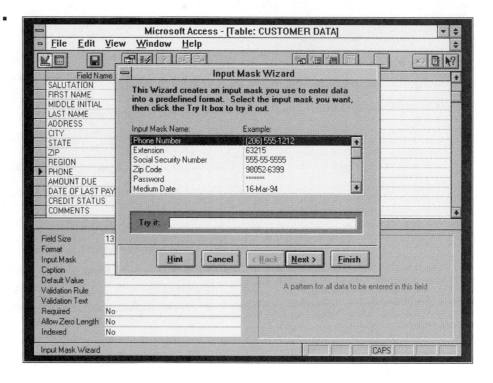

Figure 3.8

The Phone Number mask applied to the Try it text box shows how the data-entry field will appear in the table.

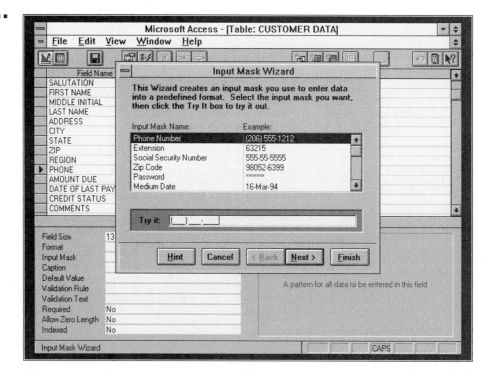

The third part specifies the character (a space) that Access displays for spaces in the input mask.

Default Value   The **Default Value cell,** as the name implies, allows you to specify the default value for a field or control. This default value is entered in a field when a new record is created. For example, in an address field, you might specify the city most likely to occur (Normal, in this application). You can either accept this value or enter a new name/value when adding records to the table.

Figure 3.9

The Expression Builder dialog box invoked by the wizard button that appears to the right of the Validation Rule cell when it is selected.

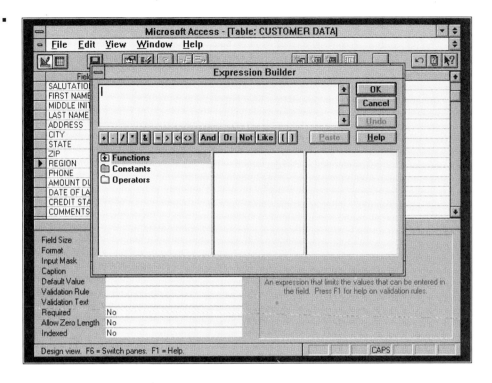

Figure 3.10

An example of an alert dialog box, which appears when the data entered do not conform to the specification in the Validation Rule cell.

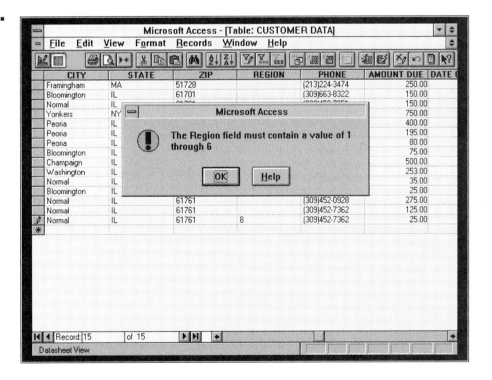

If you are using a numeric field, the entry can be a numeric constant or a formula.

Validation Rule/Validation Text   The **Validation Rule cell** allows you to enter the algebraic or logical expression that is to be evaluated when data are entered for this field. You can enter an algebraic expression manually or use the wizard button to invoke the **expression builder** (Figure 3.9). The **Validation Text cell** specifies text that is part of the alert dialog box that appears (Figure 3.10)

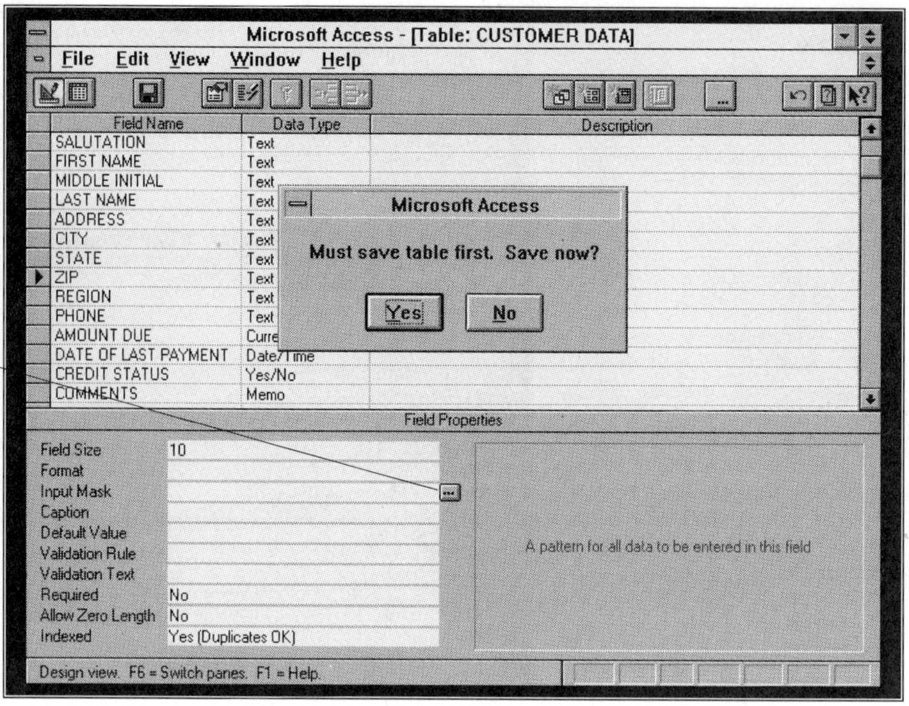

■ ■

Figure 3.11
The Access dialog box requiring you to save the table before making changes to the table via the Field Properties box.

Wizard button

if the data entered in the field do not conform to the expression entered in the Validation Rule cell. The maximum length of the message text is 255 characters.

If the validation rule is omitted, no validation takes place, so it makes no sense to enter anything in the Validation Text cell (no error could trigger the display of the text).

These two entries are typically used in conjunction with one another to make it easier for you to enter valid data in a table cell. You can, for example, use this feature to make certain that a user enters a region field value between 0 and 7. If no value is entered, or the value entered is greater than 6, the error message can be displayed. As the default, Access does not allow a null value (empty field) to be stored in a field. If you do want to allow null values in a field, you must add the **Is Null operator** to the Validation Rule cell entry.

When you are using some of the features discussed above from the Field Properties box, Access requires that you save the table before making any changes by displaying the dialog box shown in Figure 3.11. To continue with the selected process/command, you must press Enter or click the Yes command button.

Hands-On Exercise: Controlling Data Entry in Selected Fields of the CUSTOMER DATA Table

In this hands-on exercise, you will be making the following changes.

- Place "Normal" as the default for the city field.
- Change all state data entered to uppercase.
- Use the Input Mask Wizard to create an input mask for the zip field.
- Create a validation rule which will allow only the values 1 through 6 to appear in the region field. If a value outside that range is attempted, display an appropriate error message to the user.
- Use the Input Mask Wizard to create an input mask for the phone field.

- Use the Format cell to control the display of the date of last payment field and create an input mask for the date slashes.
- Use the Format cell to control the display of the credit status field.

1. Activate the SALES database.

2. Activate the CUSTOMER DATA table and the Table Design window for that table.

CUSTOMER DATA	Double-click the table name.
	Maximize the Datasheet window.
	Invoke the Table Design window to make changes to the table structure.

3. Place "Normal" as the default for the city field.

Data Type	Click the Data Type cell of the CITY field. The Field Properties box for that field now appears at the bottom of the Table Design window.
Default Value	Click this cell of the Field Properties box.
Type **Normal**	Enter the default value.

4. Change the state field data to uppercase.

Data Type	Click the Data Type cell of the STATE field. The Field Properties box for that field now appears at the bottom of the Table Design window.
Input Mask	Click this cell of the Field Properties box.
Type **>LL**	Enter the greater-than symbol (>) to indicate that all letters that follow are to be changed to uppercase. The "LL" entry indicates that two letters must be entered.

5. Use the Input Mask Wizard to create an input mask for the zip field.

Data Type	Click the Data Type cell of the ZIP field. The Field Properties box for that field now appears at the bottom of the Table Design window.
Input Mask	Click this cell of the Field Properties box.
[...]	Invoke the Input Mask Wizard dialog box. Access now prompts you to save the table (Figure 3.11).
Yes	Save the table. The Input Mask Wizard dialog box now appears (Figure 3.7).
Zip Code	Click this entry.
Finish	Click to incorporate the input mask into the Field Properties box (Figure 3.12).

6. Create a validation rule to allow only the values 1 through 6 to appear in the region field. If a value outside that range is attempted, display an appropriate error message to the user.

Figure 3.12

The input mask for the zip field created by the Input Mask Wizard.

Input mask for the zip field

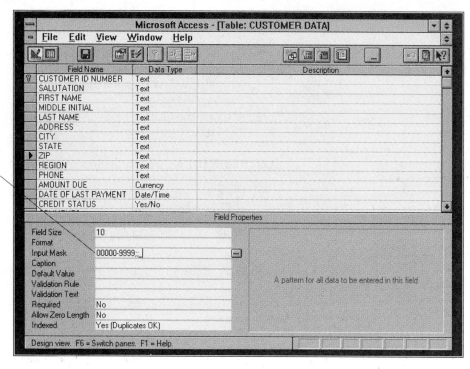

Data Type	Click the Data Type cell of the REGION field. The Field Properties box for that field now appears at the bottom of the Table Design window.
Validation Rule	Click this cell of the Field Properties box.
[...]	Click to invoke the Expression Builder dialog box (Figure 3.9).
Type 1	Enter the first valid value.
Or	Click the Or icon. This now appears as part of the expression in the expression box.
Type 2	Enter the second valid value.
Or	Click the Or icon. This now appears as part of the expression in the expression box. Continue until the values through "6" are entered. Do not click the Or icon after entering the "6". Your finished expression should look like Figure 3.13.
OK	Place this expression in the Validation Rule cell.
Validation Text	Click this cell of the Field Properties box.
Type Only the values 1 through 6 are valid.	Enter the text to be displayed if the region value is not a digit from 1 to 6.

7. Use the Input Mask Wizard to create an input mask for the phone field.

Data Type	Click the Data Type cell of the PHONE field. The Field Properties box for that field now appears at the bottom of the Table Design window.

Figure 3.13

The completed Expression Builder dialog box for entering the validation rule for the region field.

Expression used for validating the region field entries

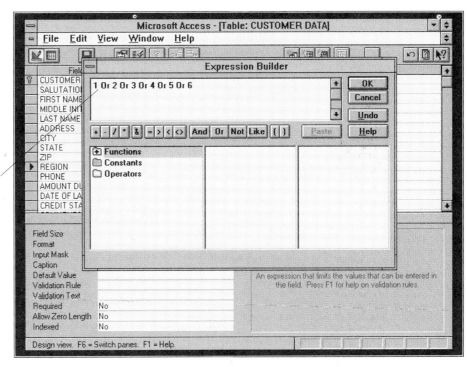

Input Mask	Click this cell of the Field Properties box.
...	Invoke the Input Mask Wizard dialog box. Access now prompts you to save the table (Figure 3.11).
Yes	Save the table. Access now indicates that integrity rules have changed and asks if you want to apply the new rules.
No	Do not apply the rules (all of your existing region fields are currently blank). The Input Mask Wizard dialog box now appears (Figure 3.7).
Phone Number	Click this entry (it should already be selected).
Finish	Click to incorporate the input mask into the Field Properties box.

8. Use the Format cell to control the display of the date of last payment field and create an input mask for the date slashes.

Data Type	Click the Data Type cell of the DATE OF LAST PAYMENT field. The Field Properties box for that field now appears at the bottom of the Table Design window.
Format	Click this cell of the Field Properties box.
▼	Click this icon in the Format cell. The selection box depicted in Figure 3.5 appears.
Medium Date	Click this entry to activate this type of display. This entry now appears in the Format cell.
Input Mask	Click this cell of the Fields Properties box.

⬚	Click this icon in the Input Mask cell. Access now prompts you about saving the table (Figure 3.11).
Yes	Click to invoke the Input Mask Wizard dialog box (Figure 3.7).
Short Date	Click this entry.
Finish	Click to incorporate the input mask.

9. Use the Format cell to control the display of the credit status field.

Data Type	Click the Data Type cell of the CREDIT STATUS field. The Field Properties box for that field now appears at the bottom of the Table Design window.
Format	Click this cell of the Field Properties box.
⬚	Click this button in the Format cell. The selection box depicted in Figure 3.6 now appears.
Yes/No	Click this entry to activate this type of display. This entry now appears in the Format cell.

10. Return to the Datasheet window.

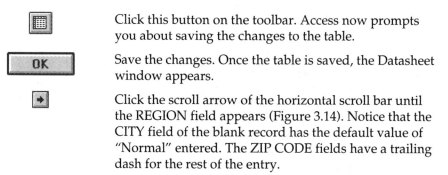

⬚	Click this button on the toolbar. Access now prompts you about saving the changes to the table.
OK	Save the changes. Once the table is saved, the Datasheet window appears.
⬚	Click the scroll arrow of the horizontal scroll bar until the REGION field appears (Figure 3.14). Notice that the CITY field of the blank record has the default value of "Normal" entered. The ZIP CODE fields have a trailing dash for the rest of the entry.

11. Enter the new region numbers depicted in Figure 3.15. Try to enter an invalid number. Once you try to move to another record, an alert dialog box similar to that shown in Figure 3.10 should appear.

12. Enter a new record with your name and address information, using the new data-entry formats and displays.

⬚	Click to enter a record containing your data. Use the value 22356 for your customer ID number. Notice that as you get to the fields with the input masks, those masks do not appear until you start to enter data in that field.

13. Resize the Datasheet window and save the table.

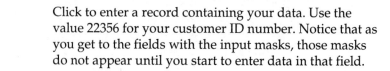

⬚	Click to restore the Datasheet window.
⬚	Double-click the control-menu button to save the table.

Figure 3.14

The datasheet incorporating the recent changes.

LAST NAME	ADDRESS	CITY	STATE	ZIP	REGION	PH
Henderson	6102 Henderson	Framingham	MA	51728-		(213)224
Tuttle	5529 N. Harmon	Bloomington	IL	61701-		(309)663
Finnis	4352 S. Main	Normal	IL	61761-		(309)452
Harp	1055 N. Chestnut	Yonkers	NY	10157-		(412)210
Ring	221 W. McClure	Peoria	IL	61603-		(309)685
Bain	1227 W. Market	Peoria	IL	61601-		(309)685
Bain	1227 W. Market	Peoria	IL	61601-		(309)685
Garcia	1523 W. Grove	Bloomington	IL	61701-		(309)662
Keiser	1784 N. Hansen	Champaign	IL	61729-		(217)234
Sokol	927 Anchor Dr.	Washington	IL	61604-		(309)299
Yen	553 N. Main	Normal	IL	61761-		(309)452
Messamore	1215 Arcadia	Bloomington	IL	61701-		(309)662
Juarez	1527 Barton Dr.	Normal	IL	61761-		(309)452
Schulz	322 W. Normal Ave	Normal	IL	61761-		(309)452
Schulz	322 W. Normal Ave	Normal	IL	61761-		(309)452
		Normal				

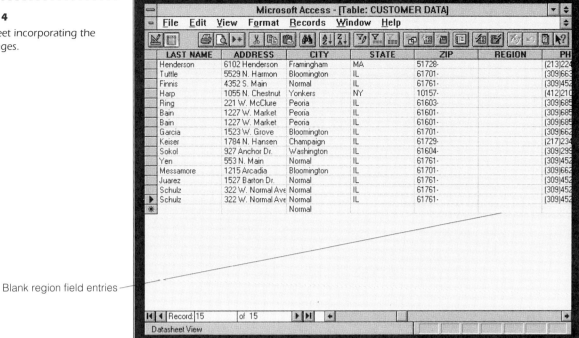

Blank region field entries

Figure 3.15

The table with the new region numbers.

LAST NAME	ADDRESS	CITY	STATE	ZIP	REGION	PH
Henderson	6102 Henderson	Framingham	MA	51728-	5	(213)224
Tuttle	5529 N. Harmon	Bloomington	IL	61701-	2	(309)663
Finnis	4352 S. Main	Normal	IL	61761-	2	(309)452
Harp	1055 N. Chestnut	Yonkers	NY	10157-	4	(412)210
Ring	221 W. McClure	Peoria	IL	61603-	1	(309)685
Bain	1227 W. Market	Peoria	IL	61601-	1	(309)685
Bain	1227 W. Market	Peoria	IL	61601-	1	(309)685
Garcia	1523 W. Grove	Bloomington	IL	61701-	2	(309)662
Keiser	1784 N. Hansen	Champaign	IL	61729-	2	(217)234
Sokol	927 Anchor Dr.	Washington	IL	61604-	3	(309)299
Yen	553 N. Main	Normal	IL	61761-	2	(309)452
Messamore	1215 Arcadia	Bloomington	IL	61701-	2	(309)662
Juarez	1527 Barton Dr.	Normal	IL	61761-	2	(309)452
Schulz	322 W. Normal Ave	Normal	IL	61761-	2	(309)452
Schulz	322 W. Normal Ave	Normal	IL	61761-	2	(309)452
		Normal				

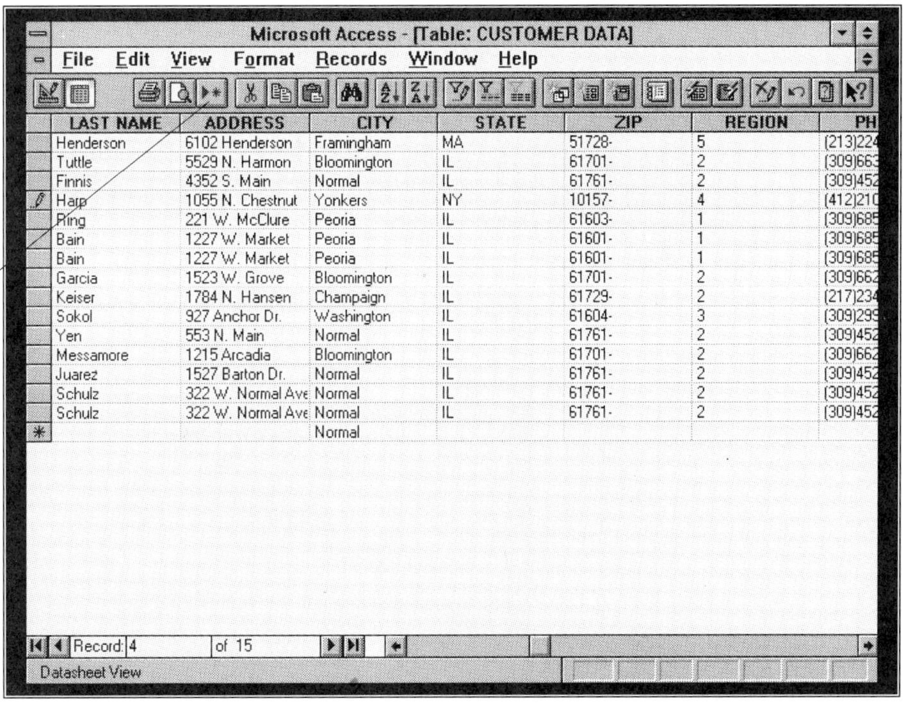

New record button

HINTS/HAZARDS

If you don't like the position of a field in the table structure, you can use a drag procedure to drag that field to the desired location. This involves the following steps.

1. Select the field by placing the cursor in the gray border column and waiting for it to become a fat right arrow.
2. Click. The field row appears in reverse video.
3. Click the border-column box again and drag to the desired location.

REPLACE COMMAND

You already know how to make changes in a record via the Datasheet window. The **Replace command** also makes changes to a specific record or to all records within a table. Unlike the Datasheet window, however, the Replace command does not display a record before it is changed.

The Replace command functions much like a search-and-replace word processing command. Access searches for one character string and, when it finds it, replaces it with another character string.

The Replace command of Access can be executed via the Edit, Replace command sequence or the Ctrl + H shortcut command. Once the Replace command is executed, the **Replace dialog box** appears (Figure 3.16). You type the text you want to locate in the Find What text box, and then enter the replacement text in the Replace With text box. This command is especially useful if, for example, you misspell a frequently entered value for a field. You could easily locate every occurrence of "Blooomington" and replace it with the correct spelling of "Bloomington."

The Replace command works similarly to the Find command covered in chapter 2. You first position the cursor to the desired field/column in the table and then issue the Replace command. You can also select the entire column.

Figure 3.16

The Replace dialog box used in a search-and-replace procedure.

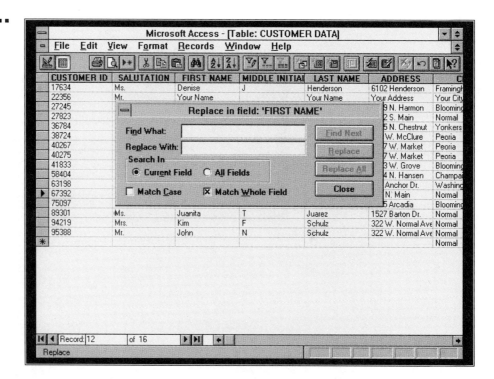

DELETING RECORDS

From time to time, you will want to delete records from a database table. This is a three-step process:

1. Select the record(s) by placing the cursor in the gray border column and clicking the mouse when the pointer turns into a fat right arrow (you can also use a drag operation to include adjacent records).

2. Press the Del key. Access then displays a dialog box like that shown in Figure 3.17, indicating that you have deleted a record.

3. If you select OK, the record is physically removed from the table. If you select Cancel, the record remains.

Figure 3.17

The dialog box prompting you about physically deleting the selected record(s) from the table.

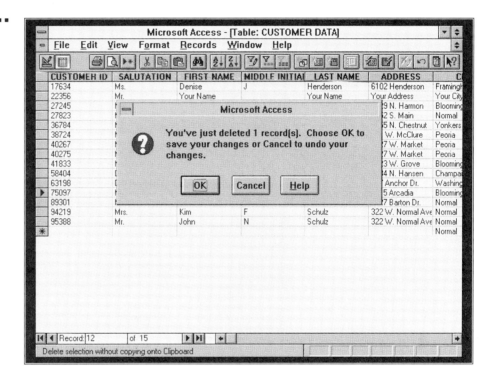

INTRODUCTION TO THE REPORT FEATURE

Having data stored in a table is not worth much by itself; for the data to be useful in practical terms, they must be printed in report form. Chapter 1 introduced a method for simply producing listings of records in a table. This method, however, did not give you much control over how the information appeared on the report.

Access's report-generation feature provides much more flexibility in designing reports. The Report feature builds a **report template** on disk, containing the report format, headings, and fields to be included in the report.

To create the template, respond to various Access prompts about the desired characteristics of the report. These are then placed in the database and available via the **Reports sheet** of the database window. Whenever you want to print a report using these specifications, activate the report template and use it with the database table that was specified when the template was created.

To build a report, click the Report tab of the database window. The Reports sheet (Figure 3.18) of the database window now appears. Click the New button, and the New Report dialog box appears. It is at this point that you click

Figure 3.18

The Reports sheet of the database window is used to build a report or activate an existing report.

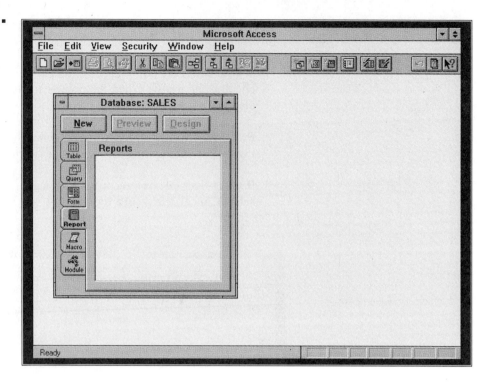

Figure 3.19

The New Report dialog box allows you to determine the table/query to be used as well as how the report is to be created.

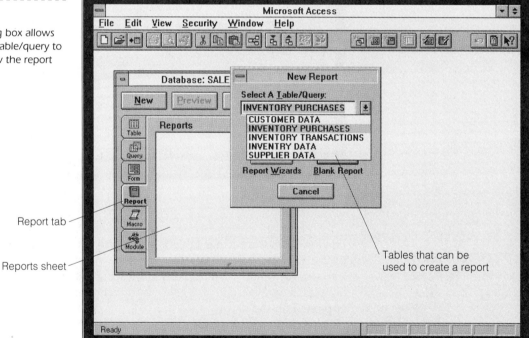

Report tab

Reports sheet

Tables that can be used to create a report

the down arrow of the selection box to display the existing tables/queries in the database that can be used to create the report (Figure 3.19). Click the desired table.

Now you have to decide how you are going to generate the report: using a wizard or designing the report yourself.

BUILDING A REPORT USING REPORT WIZARDS

This example illustrates creating a report using the Access **Report Wizards**. If a table does not have many fields, you can tell Access to put the report together and then make changes to the report template. The following example makes use of the database table INVENTORY PURCHASES.

Hands-On Exercise: Using a Report Wizard to Create the Report

1. Activate the SALES database.

2. Invoke the Reports sheet of the database window.

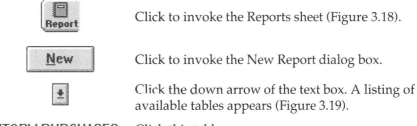

Report	Click to invoke the Reports sheet (Figure 3.18).
New	Click to invoke the New Report dialog box.
↓	Click the down arrow of the text box. A listing of available tables appears (Figure 3.19).
INVENTORY PURCHASES	Click this table.
Report Wizards	Click to invoke the Report Wizards dialog box, which prompts you for the type of report you want (Figure 3.20). Table 3.2 describes each type of report.

Figure 3.20

The Report Wizards dialog box for determining the type of report to be generated.

Report types

Report tab

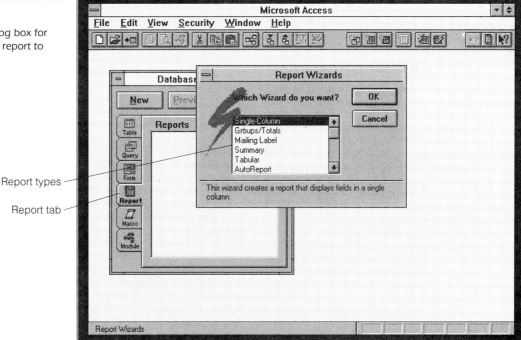

Table 3.2   Report Types of the Report Wizard

Report Type	Characteristics
Single-Column	All table fields are placed in one column as text, and the contents of each field are placed in a text box.
✳Groups/Totals	Table fields are grouped together, and totals are generated for each grouping. This is a common style of report.
Mailing Label	Mailing labels for Avery labels are created. Each group of fields constitutes a cell (label), which will be printed according to the design of the stock labels you are using.
✳Summary	A report made up of totals for groups of records is created.
Tabular	A report is created that has each record on one row. This is similar to the appearance of the Datasheet window display.
AutoReport	A report similar to the Single-Column report is generated. Any intermediate dialog boxes are bypassed, and the report is displayed via Print Preview.

3. Select the report type.

Tabular	Click this report type.
OK	Click to invoke the Tabular Report Wizard dialog box (Figure 3.21). Use this dialog box to specify the fields to be included in the report. Include a selected field by clicking the [>] button, or all fields by clicking the [>>] button. Single fields can be deselected using the [<] button, and all fields using the [<<] button.
>>	Click to include all of the fields. The field names are now copied to the right-hand text box.
Next >	Click to move to the next dialog box. Access now prompts you to determine the order of records in the report (Figure 3.22).

4. Indicate that the report is to appear in ID number order.

IDNUMBER	Select this field.
>	Click to copy the IDNUMBER field to the right-hand text box.
Next >	Access now prompts you for the report style (Figure 3.23).

Figure 3.21

The Tabular Report Wizard dialog box used for specifying which fields to include in the report.

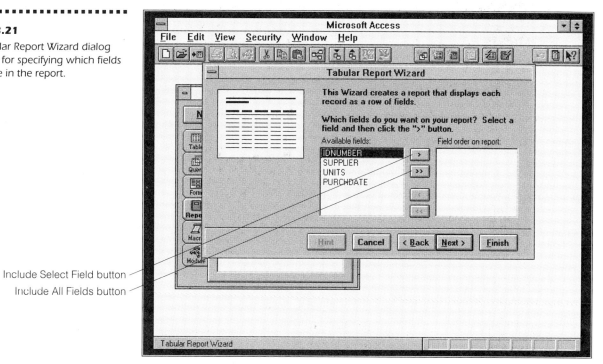

Include Select Field button

Include All Fields button

Figure 3.22

The Tabular Report Wizard dialog box for determining the order of the records within the report.

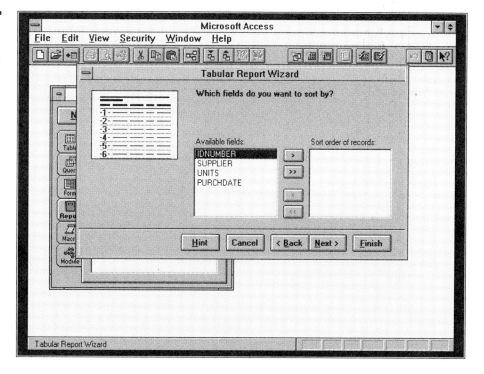

■■■■■■■■■■■■■■■■■■■■■■

Figure 3.23

The dialog box for determining the print quality of the report and other characteristics.

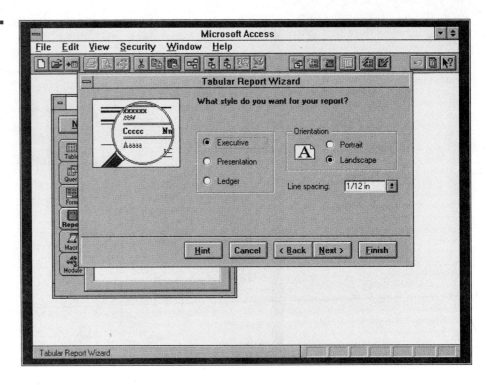

5. Determine the characteristics of the report.

Portrait   Access defaults to the Landscape orientation.
                             Since there are just a few fields to be included, the
                             standard 8.5-by-11-inch style is more desirable than
                             the 11-by-8.5-inch orientation.

         Access now provides you with the option to use a report
                             title that is different from the name of the table
                             (Figure 3.24).

6. View the report.

         Access now spends a fair amount of time preparing
                             the report based on these specifications. When it is
                             finished, it displays the Print Preview window for the
                             generated report.

7. Maximize the Print Preview window.

                             Maximize Print Preview to see the generated report.
                             Your screen should look like Figure 3.25.

8. View the report template.

         Click the Close Window button on the toolbar
                             (Figure 3.25). The Report Design window now shows
                             the specifications that Access used for creating the report
                             (Figure 3.26). The toolbox provides the ability to make a
                             number of changes to a report.

Figure 3.24

The dialog box for changing the title of the report.

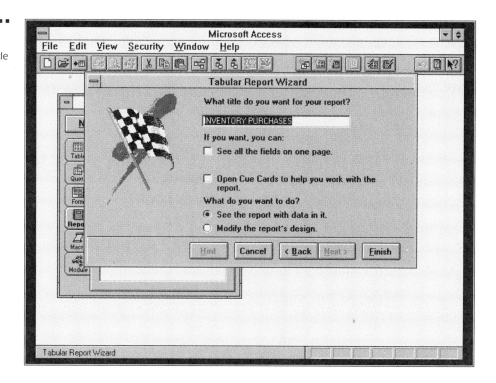

Figure 3.25

The Print Preview window for the generated report.

Close Window button

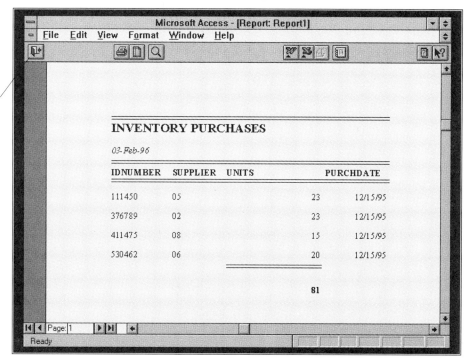

9. Save the report.

   Click the Save button on the toolbar to invoke the Save As dialog box.

Type **Inventory Purchases Report**   Enter the name of the report.

Figure 3.26

The Report Design window with specifications created by the Report Wizard.

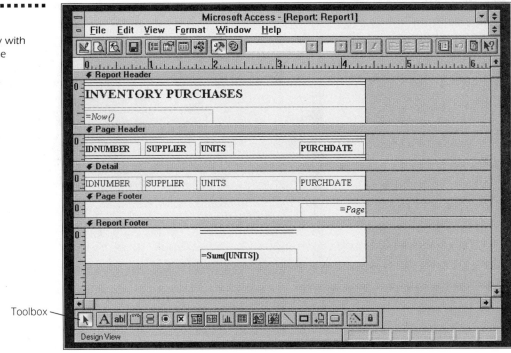

Toolbox

	Save the file.
OK	Save the file.
	Click this button of the Report Design window.
—	Double-click the control-menu button to close the Report Design window and return to the database window. You should now see the report name in the Reports sheet.

THE REPORT DESIGN WINDOW

The **Report Design window** has nine main components (Figure 3.27).

Menu Bar   The menu bar is the standard Windows menu. It contains menu options relevant to the Access Report feature.

Toolbar   The toolbar is the row of buttons directly beneath the menu bar. These buttons let you bypass menu command sequences to do a particular task more quickly. It also lets you adjust the font, size, and style of text in your report. Table 3.3 summarizes the various buttons of the toolbar.

Ruler Ribbon   The **ruler ribbon** appears below the title bar of the Report Design window. As you position objects in the report, their location is shown in a dark shading on the ruler.

Report Layout   The **Design view** is the white, rectangular part of the Report Design window. It is divided into bands (Figure 3.27):

   Report Header   The **Report Header band** contains information that you want to appear only on the first page of the report.

Table 3.3   Report Design Window Toolbar Buttons

Button	Name	Function
	Design View	Displays the report in Design view.
	Print Preview	Displays the document in Print Preview to see how it will look when printed.
	Sample Preview	Displays a quick preview with sample data.
	Save	Saves the report specifications to disk.
	Sorting and Grouping	Adds, deletes, or changes group levels using the Sorting and Grouping dialog box.
	Properties	Opens or closes the Properties sheet for the selected item.
	Field List	Opens or closes a list of fields for the underlying table that can be included in the report or form via a drag operation.
	Code	Opens the Module window to enter SQL statements to further manipulate the database.
	Toolbox	Opens or closes the toolbox used to create controls.
	Palette	Opens or closes the palette used to control the appearance of fields and lines used in a report.
	Bold	Boldfaces text in a selected field.
	Italic	Italicizes text in a selected field.
	Left-Align Text	Left-aligns text within a selected field or control.
	Center-Align Text	Centers text within a selected field or control.
	Right-Align Text	Right-aligns text with a selected field or control.
	Database Window	Shows the database window.
	Undo	Undoes the most recent change.
	Cue Cards	Displays the on-line coach to help you with a specific task.
	Help	Activates context-sensitive Help when you click a specific area of the screen.

Page Header The **Page Header band** defines the area at the top of each page of the report. It contains information such as page numbers, dates, and titles (company name, report name, and column headings).

Group Header The **Group Header band** contains information such as a group name or text that you want to have printed at the beginning of a group of records. This header is added automatically when the group field is defined to Access.

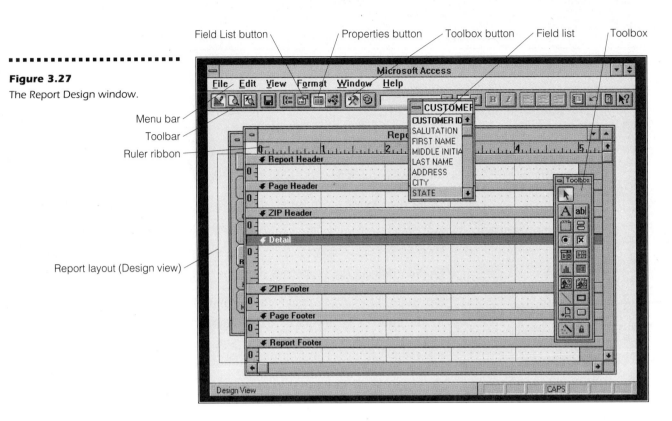

Figure 3.27

The Report Design window.

Detail The **Detail band** contains the actual data from the records in the database. Text boxes that allow you to display fields from records are placed in this band.

Group Footer The **Group Footer band** holds any identifying text and subtotals that have been generated by Access for a group of records.

Page Footer The **Page Footer band** contains the text or data that are placed at the bottom of each page. The page number is automatically placed in this band by Report Wizards.

Report Footer The **Report Footer band** holds text and data that you want to have printed at the bottom of the last page of a report. A grand total number would, for instance, appear in this band.

Toolbox The **toolbox** is a floating palette that is displayed whenever the Design view of a form or report is invoked (Figure 3.27). Clicking one of the toolbox buttons activates that tool, and the pointer then changes to the picture on the button. Table 3.4 indicates the use for each tool.

If the toolbox is in the way of an area of the Report Design window that you want to access, you can either close the toolbox by issuing the commands View, Toolbox or by clicking its control-menu button, or you can drag the toolbox to another location onscreen.

Field List The **field list** (Figure 3.27) displays a list of fields of the underlying table. The field(s) used in creating the primary key appear in bold. Fields can be dragged from the field list to the desired location in the report specification.

This feature can be invoked by clicking on the Field List button on the toolbar or by issuing the View, Field List command sequence. When you are finished with the field list, double-click its control-menu button.

Table 3.4   Toolbox Buttons

Button	Name	Function
	Pointer	Deselects an active tool and returns the pointer to its original shape and function. This is the default when the toolbox is displayed.
	Label	Creates a box that contains constant text.
	Text Box	Creates a box that allows you to display and edit text data.
	Option Group	Creates an adjustable frame that can be used to hold toggle buttons, option buttons, or check boxes. Only one object may be selected and active at a time.
	Toggle Button	Creates a button that changes from on to off when clicked with the mouse. The on equals -1; the off equals 0.
	Option Button	Creates a round button that behaves the same as a toggle button.
	Check Box	Creates a check box that toggles on and off.
	Combo Box	Creates a drop-down combo box with a list from which you can select an item or enter a value in a text box.
	List Box	Creates a drop-down list box from which you can select. A list box is a combo box without the editable text box.
	Graph	Launches the Graph Wizard to create a graph object based on a query or table.
	Subform/Subreport	Adds a subform or subreport to a main form or report. The subform or subreport must exist before this control is used.
	Unbound Object	Adds an OLE object to a form or report.
	Bound Object	Displays the contents of an OLE field if that field contains a graphic object. Otherwise, an icon appears at that location.
	Line	Draws a straight line that can be sized and relocated. The size and color of the line can be controlled via the palette.
	Rectangle	Creates a rectangle that can be sized and relocated. Various display attributes are controlled via the palette.
	Page Break	Causes the printer to start a new page at this location in the report.
	Command Button	Creates a command button that, when selected, triggers an event that can execute an Access macro.
	Control Wizards	Toggles the Control Wizards on or off. These wizards can assist you in creating option groups, list boxes, and combo boxes.
	Tool Lock	Maintains the currently selected tool as the active tool until you select another tool, click the Tool Lock button again, or click the Pointer button. Without the lock, Access reselects the pointer tool after you use a tool.

Figure 3.28

The Properties sheet for the Detail band invoked by double-clicking its border.

Properties button

Properties sheet

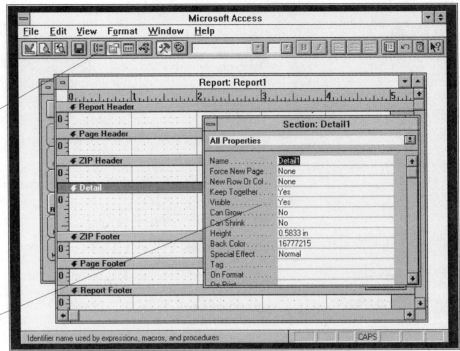

Properties Sheet The **Properties sheet** (Figure 3.28) shows the rules governing how a section or control is being displayed. This feature can be activated in three ways:

- Double-clicking a section or control.
- Selecting a section or control and clicking the Properties button on the toolbar.
- Issuing the View, Properties command sequence.

Palette The **palette** displayed in Figure 3.29 is used to add color and the appearance of depth in your forms and reports, as well as to change the appearance of borders and lines.

Before invoking the palette via the button on the toolbar, you should activate the control or section whose appearance you wish to change.

Scroll Bars The scroll bars let you move to a new location in your report layout. As you build your report, some areas may not be visible. Move to the desired area using the scroll bars.

One advantage of using Design view is that the printed report looks more or less like the onscreen template. This results in few or no surprises when the report is finally printed. If you want to see exactly how the final product will appear, use **Print Preview**, which can be invoked via a toolbar button.

DESIGNING YOUR OWN REPORT

When you are generating reports, the data presented are typically in some type of order. To create the report shown in Figure 3.39, activate the SALES database.

■■■■■■■■■■■■■■■■■■■■■■■■

Figure 3.29

The palette used to control the appearance of a section or control of the report.

Print Preview button

Palette button

Palette

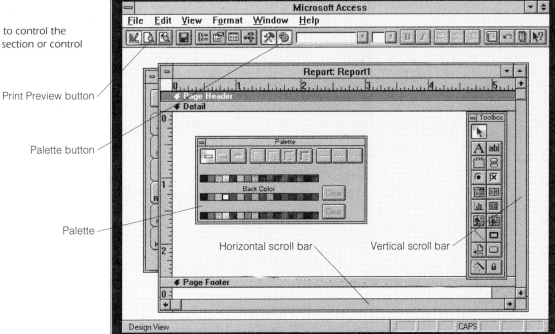

In generating this report, you will create the bulk of the report specifications using the Report Wizards. Issue the following commands.

 Hands-On Exercise: Building a Report

1. Invoke the Reports sheet of the database window.

Report	Click to invoke the Reports sheet.
New	Click to invoke the New Report dialog box.
↓	Click the down arrow of the text box. A listing of available tables appears.
CUSTOMER DATA	Click this table.
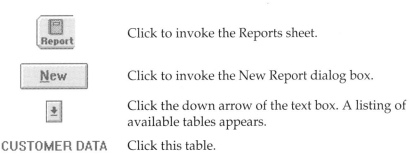 Report Wizards	Click to invoke the Report Wizards dialog box, which prompts you for the type of report you want.

2. Select the report type.

Tabular	Click this report type.
OK	Click to invoke the Tabular Report Wizard dialog box.

3. Specify the fields to be included in the report.

FIRST NAME	Click this field name in the Available fields selection box.

Figure 3.30

The Tabular Report Wizard dialog box for including the desired fields in the report.

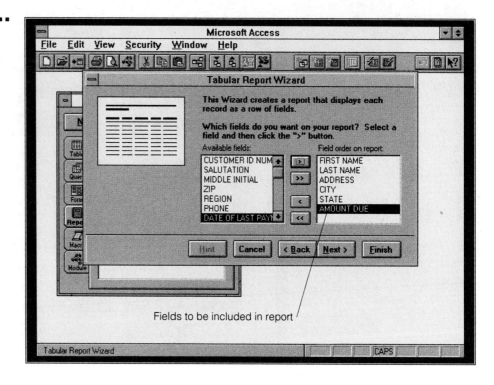

Fields to be included in report

`>`	Click to include the FIRST NAME field.
LAST NAME	Click this field name.
`>`	Click to include the LAST NAME field.
`>` (3 times)	Include the ADDRESS, CITY, and STATE fields in the right-hand text box.
AMOUNT DUE	Click this field name in the Available fields selection box.
`>`	Click to include the AMOUNT DUE field. Your dialog box should now look like Figure 3.30.
`Next >`	Click to move to the next dialog box. Access now prompts you to determine the order of records in the report.

4. Specify the order of the report as alphabetical order by name.

LAST NAME	Click this field name in the Available fields selection box.
`>`	Click to include the LAST NAME field.
FIRST NAME	Click this field name.
`>`	Click to include the FIRST NAME field. Your dialog box should now look like Figure 3.31.
`Next >`	Access now prompts you for the report style.

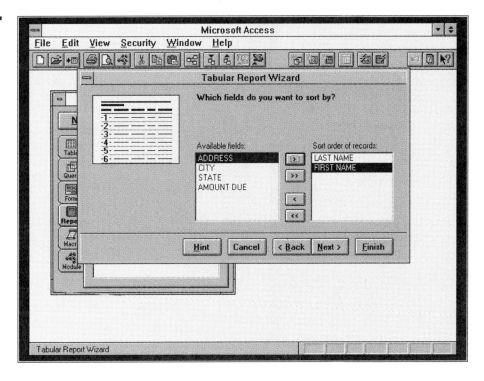

Figure 3.31
The specification for the order of the records in the report.

5. Determine the characteristics of the report.

Portrait   Change the report so that it appears on standard 8.5-by-11-inch paper.

    Access now provides you with the option to use a report title that is different from the name of the table.

Type **CUSTOMER NAME AND ADDRESS REPORT**   Enter the new report title. Your screen should look like Figure 3.32.

6. View the report.

    Access now prepares the report based on these specifications. When finished, it displays the Print Preview window for the generated report.

7. Maximize the Print Preview window.

    Maximize Print Preview to see the generated report. Your screen should look like Figure 3.33. (Use the scroll bars to position in this manner.)

8. View the report template.

    Click the Close Window button on the toolbar. The Report Design window now shows the specifications that Access used for creating the report. Unfortunately, your toolbox is in the way.

Figure 3.32

The specification for the new report title.

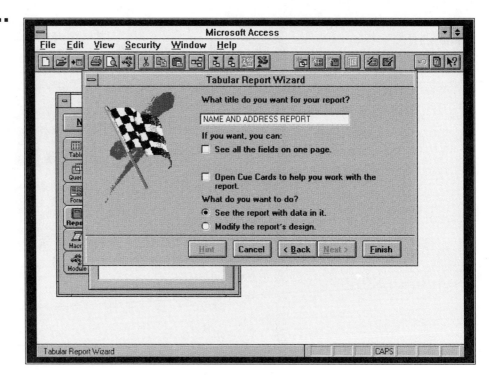

Figure 3.33

The Print Preview window for the generated report.

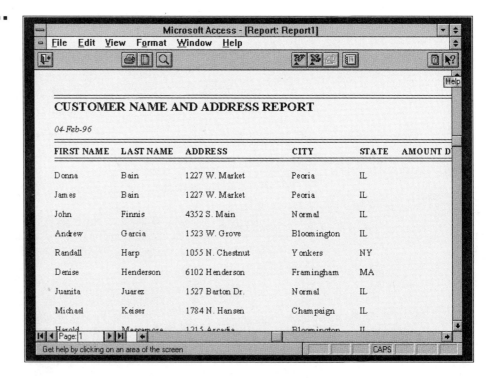

■ ■ ■ ■ ■ ■ ■ ■ ■ ■ ■ ■ ■ ■ ■ ■ ■ ■ ■ ■

Figure 3.34

The Design view with the toolbox at the bottom.

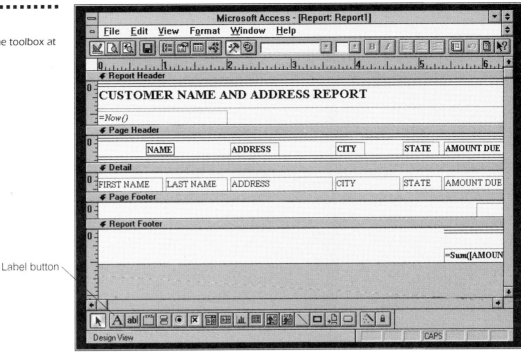

Label button

9. Move the toolbox to the bottom of the window.

> Drag   Click and drag the toolbox to the bottom of the window. Your screen should look like Figure 3.34.

10. Erase the FIRST NAME and LAST NAME field names as column headings of the Page Header band by issuing the following commands for each heading.

> Click   Select the FIRST NAME column heading by clicking. A border with little boxes, called handles, now appears.
>
> Del   Delete the column heading.

11. Enter a new column heading for the name fields.

> [A]   Click the Label button in the toolbox (Figure 3.34). A label icon now appears as the pointer. Position the pointer to the area between the FIRST NAME and LAST NAME fields in the Page Header band and click.
>
> Type NAME   Enter the new column heading. Your screen should now look like Figure 3.35.

12. Change the report header.

> CUSTOMER NAME AND ADDRESS REPORT   Click this entry. The border appears.
>
> [↓]   Click the down arrow of the Font Size selection box on the toolbar. It currently has the value of 14.
>
> [↑]   Click to view the 12.

■■■■■■■■■■■■■■■■■■■■■■

Figure 3.35

The new NAME column heading entered in the Page Header band.

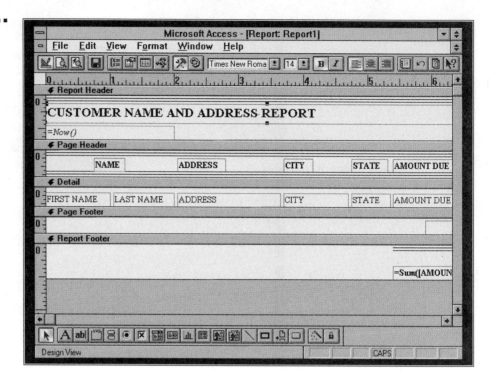

| 12 | Click to change the font size to 12 point. |

13. Shrink the header box.

| CUSTOMER NAME AND ADDRESS REPORT | If the border with handles is not present, click this entry. |
| **Click and drag** | Position the pointer to the top-middle handle of the field border. The pointer should turn into ⇕. Drag the top border downward to equalize the space above and below the text and the borderlines. |

14. Increase the size of the Report Header band.

| **Click and drag** | Position to the top of the page header borderline. The pointer should change into ⇕. Drag to the bottom of the Page Header band. |

15. Select and drag the existing fields to the bottom of the Report Header band, using a click-and-drag procedure. You know that you are ready for a drag operation, because the pointer turns into an open hand. (Look at Figure 3.36 for guidance.)

16. Enter the company name as part of the header.

| | Click the Label button in the toolbox. A label icon now appears as the pointer. Position the pointer to the leftmost area of the Report Header band above the report name and click. |
| Type **ABC COMPANY** | Enter the company name. |

Handle for extending box to the right

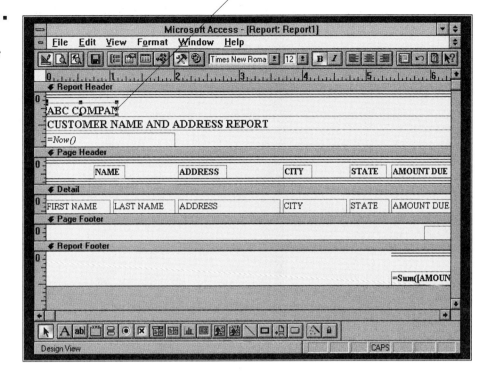

Figure 3.36

The company name included in the Report Header band.

17. Change the font size of the company name to 12. First, click the company name.

  Click the down arrow of the Font Size selection box on the toolbar. It currently has the value of 10.

12 Click to change the font size to 12 point. Your screen should now look like Figure 3.36.

18. Center the titles in the Report Header band.

Click and drag Position the pointer to the center handle on the right-hand side of the field border (see Figure 3.36). The pointer should turn into ⟷. Drag the right border to the edge of the report.

  Click the Center-Align Text button to center the text in the selected box. You will have to use the arrows of the horizontal scroll bar to move the screen display.

CUSTOMER NAME AND ADDRESS REPORT Click this title to select it.

Click the Center-Align Text button to center the text in the selected box. Your screen should look like Figure 3.37.

19. Change the field size of the amount due field and the grand total field. (You can also drag the field to the left to shrink it instead of using the Properties sheet.)

Click Double-click the amount due field in the Detail band. The Properties sheet for this field should now appear.

■ ■
Figure 3.37

The centered data in the Report
Header band.

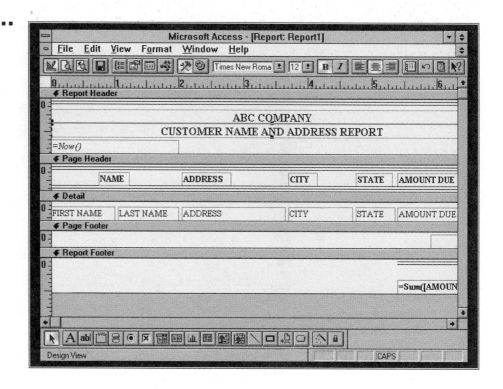

	Click the down arrow of the vertical scroll bar until the Width entry appears.
Click	Position the cursor to the right of the "1" of the "1.5 in" entry.
Backspace	Erase the 1. The entry should now be "0.5 in" (Figure 3.38).
	Double-click the control-menu button of the Properties sheet.
=SUM([AMOUNT DUE]]	Double-click the grand total field for the amount due in the Report Footer band. The Properties sheet for this field should now appear.
	Click the down arrow of the vertical scroll bar until the Width entry appears.
Click	Position the cursor to the right of the "1" of the "1.5 in" entry.
Backspace	Erase the 1. The entry should now be "0.5 in".
	Double-click the control-menu button of the Properties sheet.

20. Preview the report.

	Click to invoke Print Preview. Your screen should look like Figure 3.39.

Figure 3.38

The Properties sheet for the amount due field.

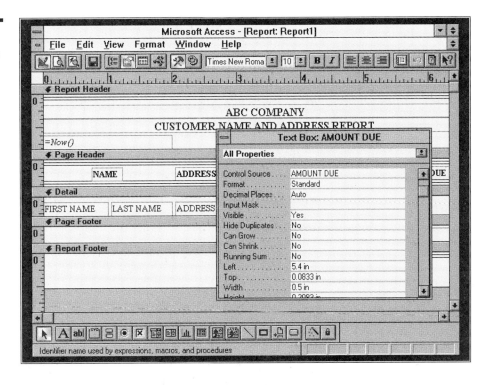

Figure 3.39

The report shown in the Print Preview window.

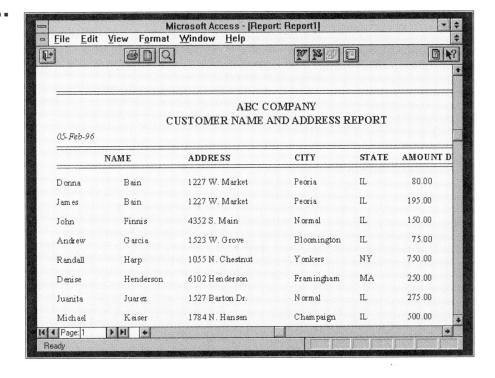

21. Print the report.

[printer icon]   Click to invoke the Print dialog box.

[**OK**]   Print the document.

22. Save the report.

[icon]   Return to the Report Design window.

[disk icon]   Click to invoke the Save As dialog box.

Type **CUSTOMER NAME AND ADDRESS**   Enter the name of the report.

[Enter]   Save the report.

[icon]   Restore the Report Design window.

[icon]   Double-click the control-menu button to return to the database window.

HINTS/HAZARDS   If you inadvertently "misplace" a field or text box, reposition it by dragging it to the desired location in the report layout.

CHAPTER REVIEW   Access allows you to make changes to the structure of a database table. You can add, delete, and rearrange fields in the table structure. You can also control how data are to be entered in a table via the Properties sheet of a field. The Properties sheet allows you to enter default values in a field, control how data in a field are to be displayed, create an input mask for making data entry easier, validate data as it is being entered and display an error message if it is incorrect, and force any data entered to uppercase.

The Replace command changes records for a field at one time, in accordance with selection criteria.

The Access 2.0 package allows you to delete a record or a group of records from a table by selecting the desired record(s) and then pressing the Del key. Access then verifies that you want the record(s) deleted. Once confirmed, the record(s) are physically removed from the table.

The Reports feature of Access lets you format a report via a report template for information contained in a table. The Report Design window provides a number of bands for you to use in describing the report, including bands for specifying report and column headings and any fields you want to print. A band also generates totals for any numeric fields.

KEY TERMS AND CONCEPTS

AutoReport
Default Value cell
Design view
Detail band
expression builder
field list
Format cell
Group Footer band
Group Header band
Groups/Totals report
Input Mask cell
input mask characters
Input Mask Wizard
Insert Row command
Is Null operator
Mailing Label report
Page Footer band
Page Header band
palette

Print Preview
Properties sheet
Replace command
Replace dialog box
Report Design window
Report Footer band
Report Header band
report template
Report Wizards
Reports sheet
ruler ribbon
Single-Column report
Summary report
Tabular report
toolbox
Validation Rule cell
Validation Text cell
wizard button

CHAPTER QUIZ

Multiple Choice

1. Which of the following Access commands changes records in a table?
   a. Zoom
   b. Mask
   c. Report
   d. Replace
   e. Change

2. The _____ sheet for a field is used to control how data are to be entered/displayed for a table.
   a. Control
   b. Properties
   c. Display
   d. none of the above

3. The Report Wizard feature lets you do which of the following?
   a. establish a report title
   b. print column headings
   c. number each page
   d. print totals
   e. all of the above
   f. Only a, b, and c

4. Which of the following report bands is automatically used to hold page numbers?
   a. Page Header band
   b. Detail band
   c. Page Footer band
   d. none of the above

5. Which of the following statements is true about the input mask for a field?
   a. It can be used to allow only uppercase characters.
   b. It can be used to allow only numeric digits.
   c. It can be used to allow only alphabetic characters.
   d. It can be used to allow optional or required characters.
   e. All of the above statements are true.

True/False

6. The Input Mask Wizard creates an input mask for frequently used data type fields.

7. The Del key can physically remove a record from a table.

8. The Report Wizards allow you to create only two types of reports.

9. The Validation Rule cell is typically used in conjunction with the Validation Text cell of the Field Properties box.

10. The toolbox makes controlling data entry much easier.

Answers

1. d   2. b   3. e   4. c   5. e   6. t   7. t   8. f   9. t   10. f

Exercises

1. The _____ sheet allows you to effect more control over how data are entered in a table.

2. To quickly change the structure of a table, click the _____ _____ icon of the datasheet toolbar.

3. Insert a row in the table structure by clicking the _____ _____ icon of the Design view toolbar.

4. A(n) _____ _____ allows you to control what characters can be entered in a field.

5. Commonly used data type fields can be controlled via the Input Mask _____.

6. The _____ cell of the Table Field Properties box allows you to use predefined formats.

7. Before a record can be deleted it must be _____ using the mouse.

8. The _____ character of an input mask causes all characters that follow to be converted to lowercase.

9. The _____ character of an input mask requires only the letters A through Z.

10. The Validation Rule entry of the Field Properties box can use the _____ _____ to create the validation rule.

11. The _____ tab of the database window Reports sheet allows you to create report.

12. The _____ band contains the data fields in the report layout area.

13. The Report Wizards allow you to create _____ different kinds of reports.

14. The _____ _____ band in the Report Design Window generates totals of numeric columns.

15. The _____ allows you to enter field names or labels as well as other types of controls in a report.

16. Access lets you use a _____ and drop procedure for moving fields or labels within a report

17. To preview a report to see how it will print, you invoke the _____ _____ feature.

18. To delete a field or heading, you must first select the item with the mouse and then press the _____ key.

19. When you are placing labels in a report, Access allows you to change the font style as well as the font _____.

20. The Properties sheet for a field/control can be activated by _____ - _____ the mouse.

COMPUTER EXERCISES

1. Perform the following tasks using the PAYMAST table, created previously.
   a. Look at the structure of the database records.
   b. Make certain that only an uppercase letter is entered for the middle-initial field.
   c. Make certain that only the department values of 10, 15, or 20 are used. Generate an error message if some other value is entered.
   d. Delete record 5.
   e. Create the report shown in Figure 3.40 and print it. You will have to resize and reposition fields in the Detail band to make your report look like the figure.
   f. When you create the report using the Report Wizard, specify that it is to be sorted by department number. Save the report as PAYROLL REGISTER REPORT.
   g. Use the technique covered in this chapter for adding fields to a record. Add the following fields to the PAYMAST table. Give each field an appropriate length.

   ADDRESS
   CITY
   STATE
   ZIP

   h. Use the Datasheet window to fill in data for each record.

Figure 3.40

The report for the PAYMAST table.

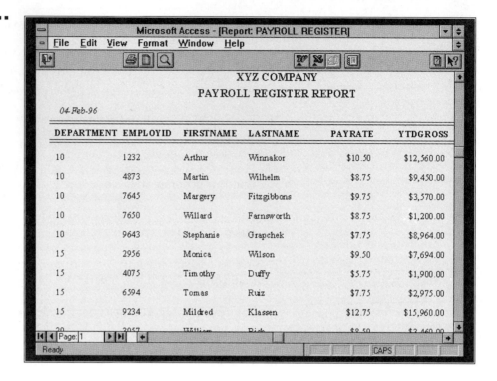

2. This exercise requires the INVENTORY PURCHASES table. For information about the structure of this table, use the Design Structure command.

Create a report template, INVLIST1, that corresponds to Figure 3.41. *Hint:* Be sure to resize the fields so that they are the same as in the figure. Resize the fields like you did when you centered the headings: drag the handles of a border box to the desired location.

Figure 3.41

The required report for the INVENTORY PURCHASES table.

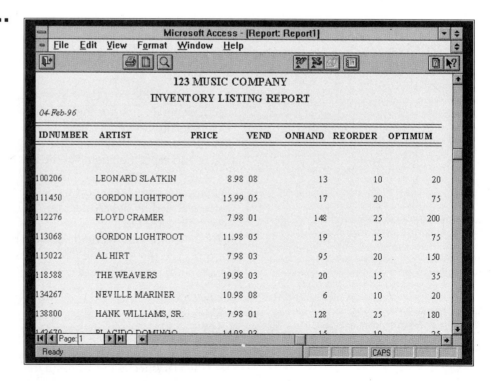

4

ACCESS
PRINT
FEATURES

CHAPTER OBJECTIVES

After completing this chapter, you should be able to

- **Use advanced Access Report features**
- **Use the label generator**
- **Use the Mailmerge capability**
- **Create graphs**

This chapter covers advanced uses of the Report feature: the ability to have multiple lines print per record, to include calculations in a report, to create labels using the Label command, the Mailmerge capability of Access, and its ability to generate graphs depicting data contained in a database table.

ADVANCED REPORT FEATURES

The Access reports you have printed thus far with the Report feature have been relatively simple. The advanced commands in this section let you print reports with subtotals and other calculations as well as reports that format information from each record into multiple lines within a column of print.

SUBTOTALS

Subtotals can be generated in reports when a table has been ordered into record groups. Generating subtotals for groups of records is referred to as **control-break**, or **level-break**, **processing**. To generate such a report, you use the Access **Groups/Totals Report Wizard**.

Suppose you want to create a report that shows the total number of records for each zip code in the CUSTOMER DATA table. The new report will have the same format as CUSTOMER NAME AND ADDRESS REPORT, except it will include the subtotal specifications (see Figure 4.6).

 Hands-On Exercise: Creating a Report with Subtotals

In generating this report, you will create the bulk of the report specification using the Report Wizards. Activate the SALES database, then issue the following commands.

1. Specify the table and type of report to be generated.

    Click to invoke the Reports sheet of the database window.

    Click to invoke the New Report dialog box.

    Click the down arrow of the text box. A listing of available tables appears.

CUSTOMER DATA   Click this table.

 Report Wizards   Click to invoke the Report Wizards dialog box, which prompts you for the type of report you want.

2. Select the report type.

Groups/Totals   Click this report type.

    Click to invoke the Groups/Totals Report Wizard dialog box.

3. Specify the fields to be included in the report.

FIRST NAME   Click this field name in the Available fields selection box.

Figure 4.1

The Groups/Totals Report Wizard dialog box for including the desired fields in the report.

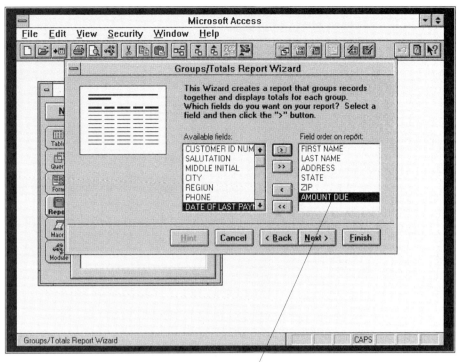

List of fields selected for the report

>	Click to include the FIRST NAME field.
LAST NAME	Click this field name.
> (twice)	Click to include the LAST NAME and ADDRESS FIELDS.
STATE	Click this field name.
> (twice)	Include the STATE and ZIP fields.
AMOUNT DUE	Click this field name.
>	Click to include the AMOUNT DUE field. Your dialog box should now look like Figure 4.1.
Next >	Click to move to the next dialog box. Access now prompts you to determine how the records in the report are to be grouped.

4. Specify how the records are to be grouped.

ZIP	Click the ZIP field in the Available fields selection box.
>	Click to include the ZIP field in the Group records by list box. Your screen should now look like Figure 4.2.
Next >	Access now prompts you about how the records are supposed to be arranged in the report by zip code (Figure 4.3). The "Normal" value tells Access to group together those records with the same value in the ZIP field.

Figure 4.2

The specification that the records are to be grouped in order by zip code.

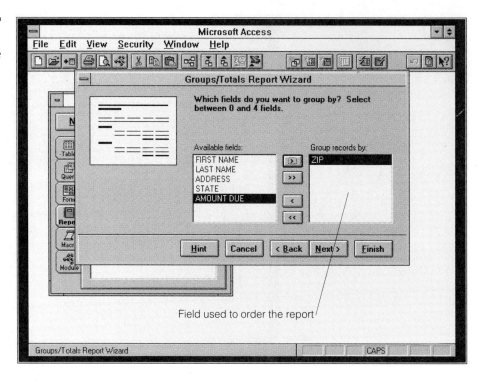

Field used to order the report

Figure 4.3

The specification that the records with the same zip-code value are to be grouped together.

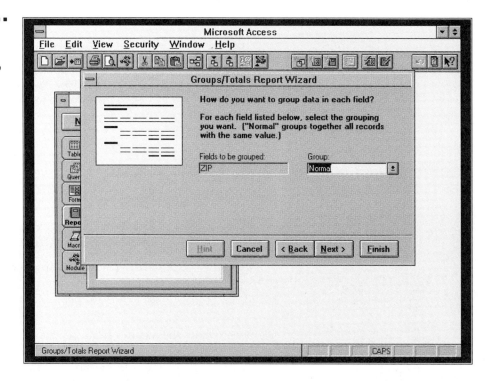

> **Next >**

Access now prompts you about how the records are to be arranged within zip codes.

5. Specify the order of the report as alphabetical order by name.

LAST NAME   Click this field name in the Available fields selection box.

Figure 4.4

The specification for the order of the records within each zip-code grouping in the report.

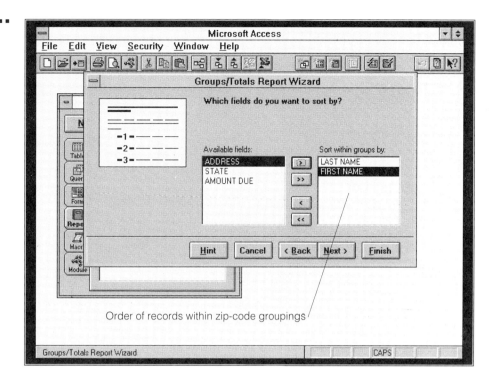

Order of records within zip-code groupings

>	Click to include the LAST NAME field.
FIRST NAME	Click this field name.
>	Click to include the FIRST NAME field. Your dialog box should now look like Figure 4.4.
Next >	Access now prompts you for the report style.

6. Determine the characteristics of the report.

Portrait	Change the report so that it appears on standard 8.5-by-11-inch paper.
Next >	Access now provides you with the option to use a report title that is different from the name of the table.
Type CUSTOMERS BY ZIP CODE REPORT	Enter the new report title.
Calculate Percentages	Click the check box that starts out with this label to deactivate this feature. If this feature is active, meaningless percentages will print on each subtotal. Your screen should look like Figure 4.5.

7. View the report.

Finish	Access now prepares the report based on these specifications. When finished, it displays the Print Preview window for the generated report.

Figure 4.5

The specification for the new report title.

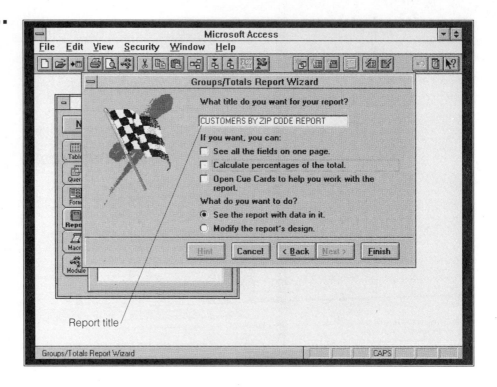

Figure 4.6

The Print Preview window for the generated report.

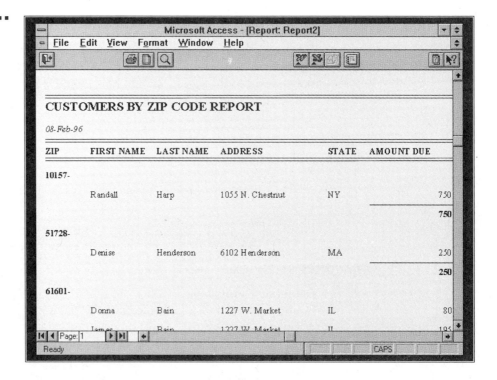

8. Maximize the Print Preview window.

    Maximize Print Preview to see the generated report. Your screen should now look like Figure 4.6. (Use the scroll bars to position in this manner.)

Figure 4.7

The Design view with the toolbox at the bottom.

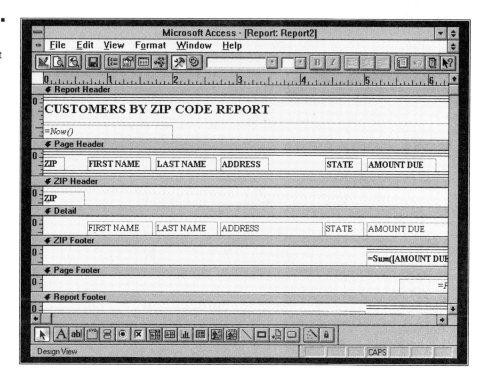

9. View the report template.

 Click the Close Window button on the toolbar. The Report Design window now shows the specifications that Access used for creating the report. If your toolbox is in the way, do step 10; otherwise, go to step 11 (if your screen looks like Figure 4.7).

10. Move the toolbox to the bottom of the window.

Drag   Click and drag the toolbox to the bottom of the window. Your screen should look like Figure 4.7.

11. Change the report header.

CUSTOMERS BY ZIP CODE REPORT   Click this entry. The border appears.

Click the down arrow of the Font Size selection box on the toolbar. It currently has the value of 14.

Click to view the 12.

12   Click to change the font size to 12 point.

12. Shrink the header box.

CUSTOMERS BY ZIP CODE REPORT   If the border with handles is not present, click this entry.

Click and drag   Position the pointer to the top-middle handle of the field border. The pointer should turn into ⇕. Drag the top border downward to equalize the space above and below the text and the borderlines.

13. Increase the size of the Report Header band.

Click and drag   Position to the top of the page header borderline. The pointer should change into ↕. Drag to the bottom of the Page Header band.

14. Drag the existing fields to the bottom of the Report Header band, using a click-and-drag procedure. You know that you are ready for a drag operation, because the pointer turns into an open hand. (Look at Figure 4.8 for guidance.)

15. Enter the company name as part of the header.

   Click the Label button in the toolbox. A label icon now appears as the pointer. Position the pointer to the leftmost area of the Report Header band above the report name and click.

Type **ABC COMPANY**   Enter the company name.

16. Change the font size of the company name to 12.

Click   Click the mouse in another area of the Design view window and then click the text box with the text that you just entered. It should now be surrounded by a box with handles.

   Click the down arrow of the Font Size selection box on the toolbar. It currently has the value of 10.

12   Click to change the font size to 12 point. Your screen should now look like Figure 4.8.

Figure 4.8

The company name included in the report header.

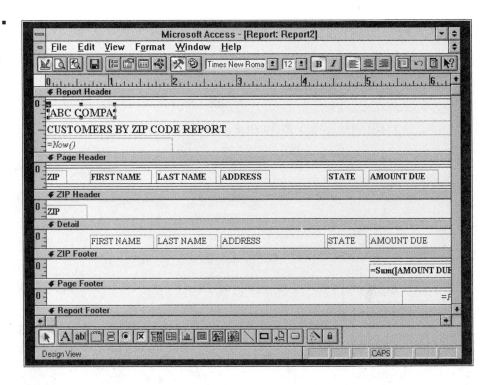

Figure 4.9

The centered data in the Report Header band.

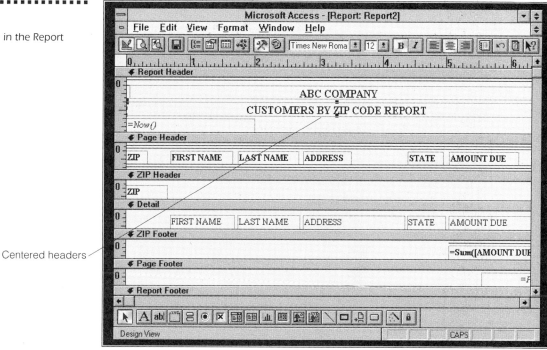

Centered headers

17. Center the titles in the Report Header band.

Click and drag   Position the pointer to the center handle on the right-hand side of the field border. The pointer should turn into ⟷. Drag the right border to the edge of the report.

    Click the Center-Align Text button to center the text in the selected box. You will have to use the arrows of the horizontal scroll bar to move the screen display.

CUSTOMERS BY ZIP CODE REPORT   Click this title to select it.

    Click the Center-Align Text button to center the text in the selected box. Your screen should look like Figure 4.9.

18. Enter identifying text for the subtotals.

    Click the Label button in the toolbox. Position the pointer to the left of the "=Sum([AMOUNT DUE])" formula in the ZIP Footer band and click.

Type **SUBTOTAL**   Enter the text of the label.

Click and drag   Click outside the label box and then click the box and drag it to the location shown in Figure 4.10.

19. Preview the report.

    Click to invoke Print Preview.

    Your screen should look like Figure 4.11. (You may have to use the scroll bars to position your report to this view.)

Figure 4.10

The label for the zip-code subtotal.

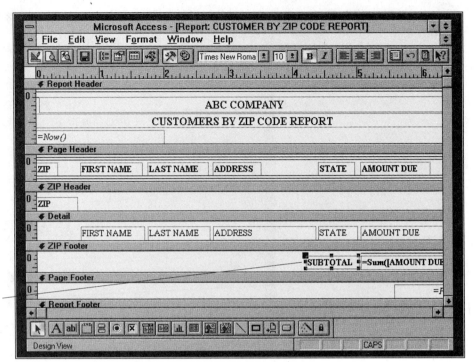

Label box for the subtotal

Figure 4.11

The report shown in the Print Preview window.

Print button

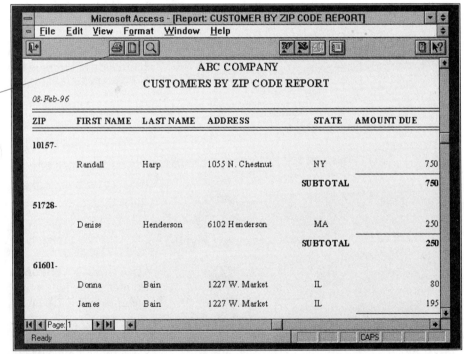

HINTS/HAZARDS

If you inadvertently dragged the right margin of the report to the right, you may get an error message like that shown in Figure 4.12. In this example, the right margin of the report should not be to the right of the 6.5-inch mark on the ruler. If it happens to be larger than that figure, you have to drag the right margin of the print area to the left so that it is around that 6.5-inch position.

Figure 4.12

The alert dialog box indicating that the right margin of the printable area of the report extends beyond the acceptable calculated location.

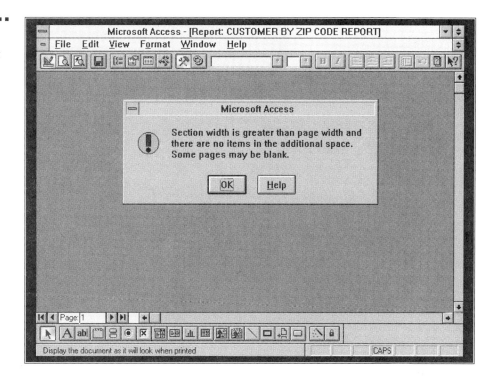

20. Print the report.

Click to invoke the Print dialog box.

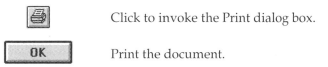   Print the document.

21. Save the report.

Return to the Report Design window.

Click to invoke the Save As dialog box.

Type **CUSTOMERS BY ZIP CODE REPORT**   Enter the name of the report.

Enter   Save the report.

Restore the Report Design window.

Double-click the control-menu button to return to the database window.

MULTIPLE-LINE REPORTS

In this portion of the chapter, we will create multiple-line reports like the one shown in Figure 4.24. Notice that this report appears to have the first- and last-name data fields joined. It also has the information about the city, state, and zip-code data joined.

When we generated previous reports, the first-name and last-name fields were separated by spaces and appeared as separate fields/columns in the

Figure 4.13

The empty unbound box for entering a formula along with the label control automatically included by Access.

Field number (usually deleted)

Unbound text box holds the formula/expression

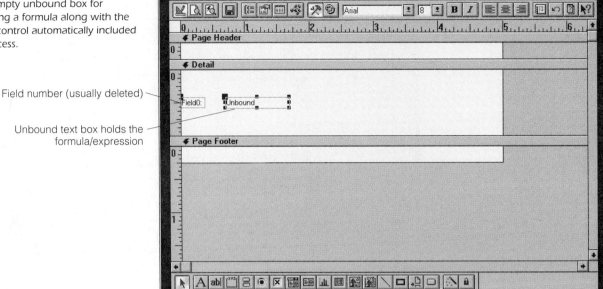

report. This is because the Report feature of Access has been treating them as two discrete pieces of data. But often we want the first name and last name to appear joined together, with only a space separating them (the common way of representing these two fields).

We achieve this joining of text fields through a process known as **concatenation**, which is accomplished via a three-step process.

1. Create an unbound text box in the Detail band. This may create both a data cell and a label cell (Figure 4.13) or just a label cell.

2. Use the Properties sheet to enter the concatenation expression/formula in the Control Source cell (Figure 4.14).

3. Change and move the label cell to reflect the contents of the formula entered in the text box. You can also just delete the label. Figure 4.15 shows the label control deleted and replaced with the name label in the Page Header band. It also shows the unbound text control containing the concatenation expression.

This concatenation is accomplished via an **expression**. This expression can be defined via the **Expression Builder dialog box** (Figure 4.16) or simply entered from the keyboard. The Expression Builder requires an extensive use of mouse commands for generating the various portions of the Access formula. In our applications, we will be entering the formulas from the keyboard.

Concatenation Formula   Fields are concatenated in a report layout by joining the fields together with the Access **cocatenation character**—an ampersand (&). When you concatenate text fields, most of them have lower-order spaces (spaces in the right-hand portion of the field). These spaces must be removed before the fields can be joined. The ampersand is Access's way of forcing string concatenation of two operands (fields). When a field is being joined to another

■ ■

Figure 4.14

The Properties sheet for the unbound box with the concatenation expression/formula in the Control Source cell.

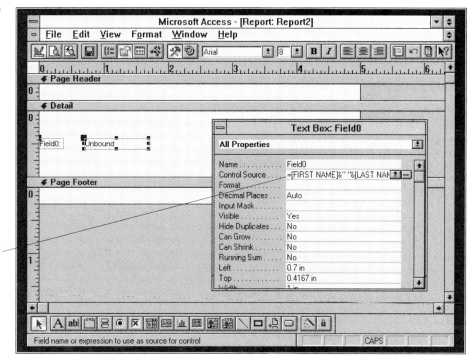

Expression/formula for the text box

■ ■

Figure 4.15

The concatenation expression moved to a different location after the label control was deleted and a label box created in the Page Header band for holding the column heading.

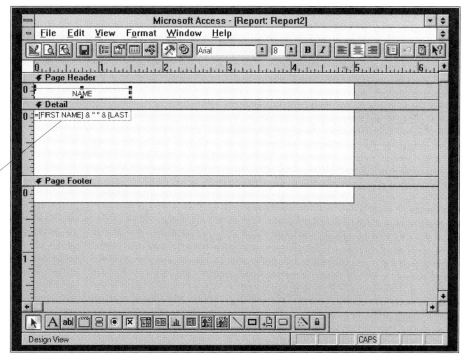

Completed text box

field via the & command, a space usually has to be included between the fields to make the data readable. For example, you would not want to see JimBain entered as a name. It is not only more readable but also more correct to display such data as Jim Bain. To concatenate the first-name and last-name fields requires the statement:

```
=[FIRST NAME]&" "&[LAST NAME]
```

Figure 4.16

The Expression Builder dialog box for concatenating the name fields.

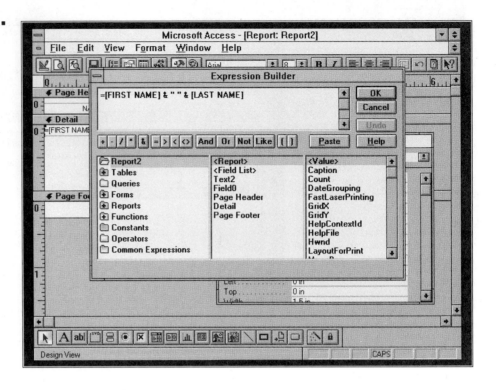

The space is embedded between the first-name and last-name fields by including a space between double quotation marks ("). Notice that the ampersands (&) surround this alphanumeric constant.

Suppose you want to report data from the CUSTOMER DATA table in the format shown in Figure 4.24. We will call this report NEW LISTING REPORT. The report will have a page header as shown. The first-name and last-name fields will be concatenated so no extra blanks appear between them. Addresses will appear as two lines in one column (the city, state, and zip fields will be concatenated), and the phone number and amount due will appear next to the address. The report will contain only one final total. Place commas in any numeric fields.

In building this report, we will be using the Report Wizards to enter some fields; then, once the report has been assembled, we will be entering other fields and headings manually. The last-name field will simply serve as a placeholder to avoid a lot of field movement once the report is built by the wizard. The report will also be in name order within zip-code order.

 Building the NEW LISTING REPORT Specification

Activate the SALES database, then issue the following commands.

1. Specify the table and type of report to be generated.

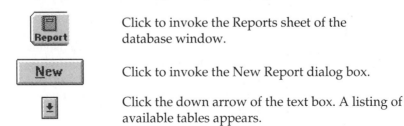

Click to invoke the Reports sheet of the database window.

Click to invoke the New Report dialog box.

Click the down arrow of the text box. A listing of available tables appears.

CUSTOMER DATA   Click this table.

Report <u>W</u>izards   Click to invoke the Report Wizards dialog box, which prompts you for the type of report you want.

2. Select the report type.

Tabular   Click this report type.

| OK | Click to invoke the Tabular Report Wizard dialog box.

3. Specify the fields to be included in the report.

LAST NAME   Click this field name in the Available fields selection box.

| > | (twice)   Click to include the LAST NAME and ADDRESS fields.

PHONE   Click this field name.

| > | (twice)   Include the PHONE and AMOUNT DUE fields. Your dialog box should now look like Figure 4.17.

| Next > | Click to move to the next dialog box. Access now prompts you to determine how the records in the report are to be grouped.

4. Specify the order of the report as alphabetical order by name.

LAST NAME   Click this field name in the Available fields selection box.

| > | Click to include the LAST NAME field. Your dialog box should now look like Figure 4.18.

Figure 4.17

The Tabular Report Wizard dialog box for including the desired fields in the report.

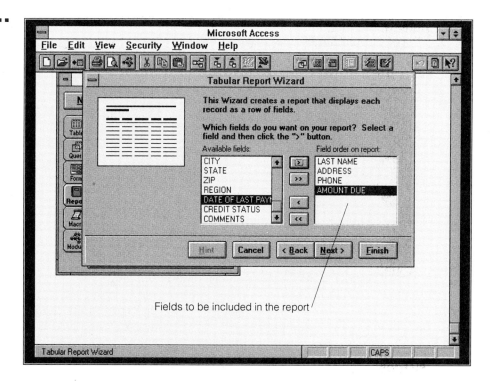

■ ■ ■ ■ ■ ■ ■ ■ ■ ■ ■ ■ ■ ■ ■ ■ ■ ■ ■ ■

Figure 4.18

The specification for the order of the records within last name in the report.

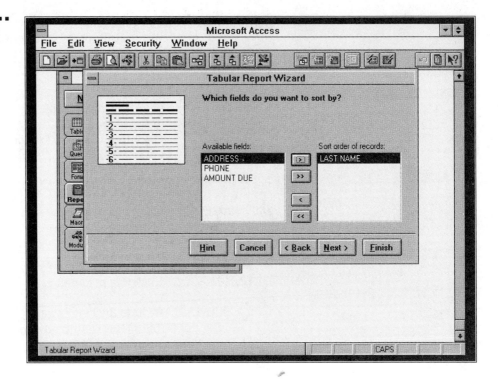

      Access now prompts you for the report style.

5. Determine the characteristics of the report.

Portrait   Change the report so that it appears on standard 8.5-by-11-inch paper.

      Access now provides you with the option to use a report title that is different from the name of the table.

Type **CUSTOMER NAME AND ADDRESS REPORT**   Enter the new report title.

6. View the report.

Finish   Access now prepares the report based on these specifications. When finished, it displays the Print Preview window for the generated report.

7. Maximize the Print Preview window.

      Maximize Print Preview to see the generated report. Your screen should look like Figure 4.19. (Use the scroll bars to position in this manner.)

8. View the report template.

     Click the Close Window button on the toolbar. The Report Design window now shows the specifications that Access used for creating the report. If your toolbox is in the way, do step 9; otherwise, go to step 10.

Figure 4.19

The Print Preview window for the generated report.

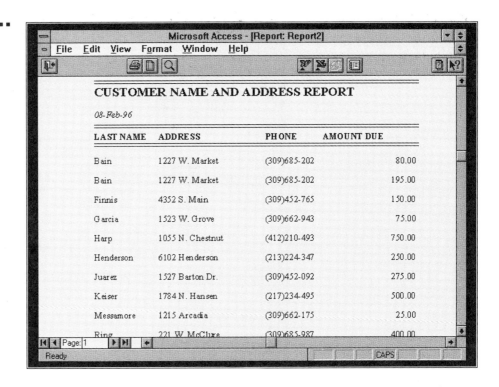

9. Move the toolbox to the bottom of the window.

Drag   Click and drag the toolbox to the bottom of the window.

10. Increase the size of the Detail band.

Click and drag   Position to the top of the page footer borderline. The pointer should change into ⭥. Drag to below the report footer border to increase the size of the Detail band. Your Detail band should now look like Figure 4.20.

11. Change the report header.

CUSTOMER NAME AND ADDRESS REPORT   Click this entry. The border appears.

▼   Click the down arrow of the Font Size selection box on the toolbar. It currently has the value of 14.

▲   Click to view the 12.

12   Click to change the font size to 12 point.

12. Shrink the header box.

CUSTOMERS BY ZIP CODE REPORT   If the border with handles is not present, click this entry.

Click and drag   Position the pointer to the top-middle handle of the field border. The pointer should turn into ⭥. Drag the top border downward to equalize the space above and below the text and the borderlines.

Figure 4.20

The Design view with the Detail band enlarged.

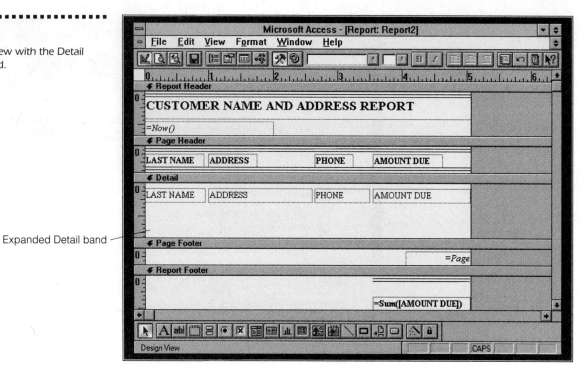

Expanded Detail band ——

13. Increase the size of the Report Header band.

Click and drag   Position to the top of the Page Header borderline. The pointer should change into ↕. Click and drag to the middle of the Page Header band (until the border is at the 1¼-inch mark on the vertical ruler). Look at Figure 4.21 for guidance.

14. Drag the date field to the bottom of the Report Header band using a click-and-drag procedure. You know that you are ready for a drag operation, because the pointer turns into a hand. (Look at Figure 4.21 for guidance.)

15. Enter the third line of the report header.

   Click the Label button in the toolbox. A label icon now appears as the pointer. Position the pointer to the leftmost area of the Report Header band above the date and click.

Type **IN ORDER BY ZIP CODE**   Enter the third line of header text.

16. Enter the company name as part of the header.

   Click the Label button in the toolbox. Position the pointer to the leftmost area of the Report Header band above the report name and click.

Type **ABC COMPANY**   Enter the company name.

Figure 4.21

The additional two lines included in
the report header.

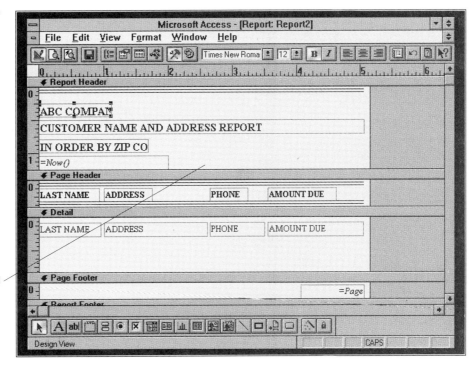

Completed Report Header band

17. Change the font size of the new header line to 12.

Click	Click the third line of the header. It should now be surrounded by a box with handles.
⬦	Click the down arrow of the Font Size selection box on the toolbar. It currently has the value of 10.
12	Click to change the font size to 12 point.

18. Perform the commands from step 17 on the first header line. Your screen should now look like Figure 4.21.

19. After selecting a header field, use the following commands to center the three header lines in the Report Header band.

Click and drag	Position the pointer to the center handle on the right-hand side of the field border. The pointer should turn into ⬌. Drag the right border to the edge of the report.
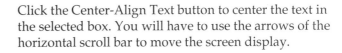	Click the Center-Align Text button to center the text in the selected box. You will have to use the arrows of the horizontal scroll bar to move the screen display.

After you have finished, your screen should look like Figure 4.22.

20. Create the concatenation expression for the first-name and last-name fields.

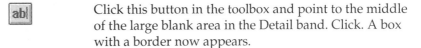	Click this button in the toolbox and point to the middle of the large blank area in the Detail band. Click. A box with a border now appears.

Figure 4.22

The rearranged fields in the Detail and Page Header bands of the Report Design window.

Centered headers

New heading

Unbound text field for the name fields

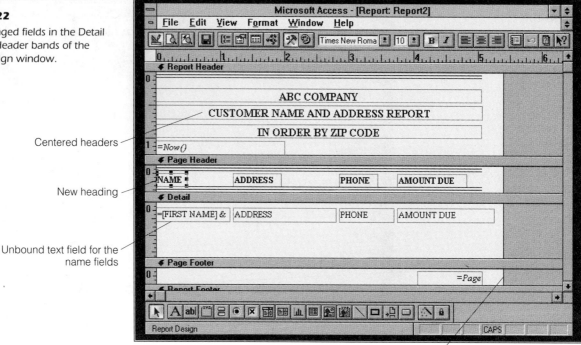

Resized right margin

	Open the Properties sheet for the unbound text field.
Control Source	Click this cell.
Type =[FIRST NAME]&" "&[LAST NAME]	Enter the concatenation formula.
	Double-click the control-menu button of the Properties sheet.
LAST NAME	Click the LAST NAME field in the Detail band.
Del	Erase the field.
Click and drag	Move the concatenation control/field to the location formerly occupied by the LAST NAME field.

21. Erase the column heading and enter a new one.

LAST NAME	Click this heading.
Del	Erase the heading.
A	Click this button in the toolbox. Position to the area originally occupied by the LAST NAME column heading and click to position the label box.
Type NAME	Enter the heading.

22. Resize the report right margin and move fields to the right. Use Figure 4.22 as a guide for moving the fields. Drag the right margin to the $5\frac{3}{8}$-inch mark. After you have moved the other fields, make the formula field slightly larger. Don't forget to move the heading controls too. Your screen should now look like Figure 4.22.

Figure 4.23

The completed Detail band.

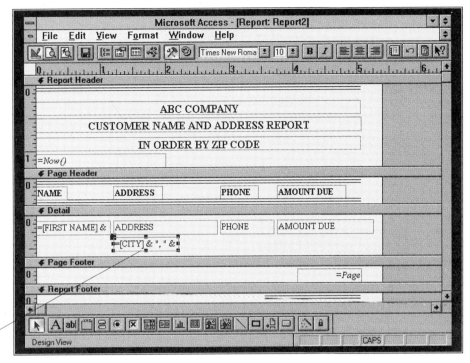

Unbound text box containing the
concatenation expression
repositioned for printing

23. Create the concatenation expression for the city, state, and zip fields.

abl	Click this button in the toolbox and point to the middle of the large blank area below the left border of the address field. Click. A box with a border now appears.
	Open the Properties sheet for the unbound text field.
Control Source	Click this cell.
Type =[CITY]&", "&[STATE]&" "[ZIP]	Enter the concatenation formula.
	Double-click the control-menu button of the Properties sheet.

24. Reposition the control box, if necessary, as shown in Figure 4.23.

25. Shrink the Detail band to look like Figure 4.23.

26. Drag the right margin of the concatenation field beneath the ADDRESS box so that it extends beyond the right margin of the ADDRESS box. This will allow the CITY, STATE, and ZIP fields to print properly. Also, shrink the AMOUNT DUE field so that it does not extend beyond the lines of the report.

27. Change the specification for the order of the data in the report. (Remember, we want it in name order within zip code.)

	Click on the toolbar to invoke the Sorting and Grouping dialog box.
	Click in the LAST NAME cell.

ZIP	Click this field.
Field/Expression	Click this cell beneath the ZIP entry.
⬇	Click to display the list of fields.
LAST NAME	Click this field.
⊟	Double-click the control-menu button of the Sorting and Grouping dialog box.

28. Preview the report.

🔍	Click to invoke Print Preview. Your screen should look like Figure 4.24. (You may have to use the scroll bars to position your report to this view.)

29. Print the report.

🖨	Click to invoke the Print dialog box.
OK	Print the document.

30. Save the report.

📲	Return to the Report Design window.
💾	Click to invoke the Save As dialog box.
Type **NEW LISTING REPORT**	Enter the name of the report.

• •

Figure 4.24

The report shown in the Print Preview window.

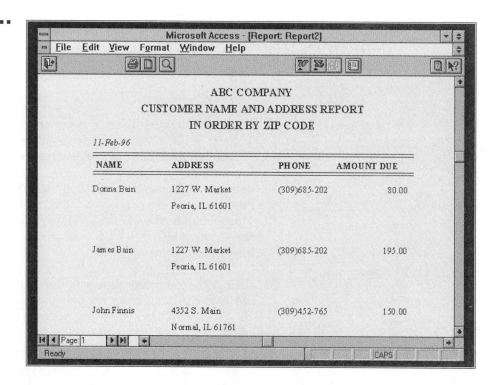

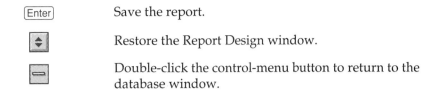

Enter   Save the report.

   Restore the Report Design window.

   Double-click the control-menu button to return to the database window.

HINTS/HAZARDS   If you inadvertently enter extra blank lines in the Detail band, you can get rid of them by decreasing the size of the Detail band via a drag operation.

EMBEDDING CALCULATIONS WITHIN A REPORT TEMPLATE

Besides providing subtotals of numbers falling within certain subgroups, the Report feature also lets you specify **report calculations** to be performed as a report is printed. For instance, Access can multiply a number of inventory units in one numeric field by an item price in another numeric field to generate an extension value in a new field in the report. Calculations can also involve numeric constants or combinations of fields and constants.

To explore this feature, activate the INVENTORY DATA table from the SALES database. You will use this inventory table to generate a report that multiplies the number in the on-hand field (the number of items) by the number in the price field (the price per item) and shows the extension in a new field. Figure 4.25 shows the structure of the INVENTORY DATA table. With the

Figure 4.25

The structure of the INVENTORY DATA table.

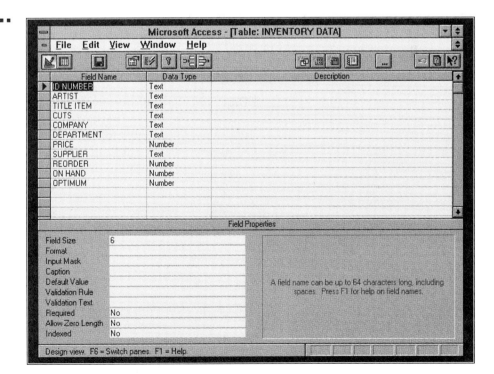

exception of the price field, all numeric fields are integer to allow only whole (no fractional) unit values. The report you will generate, called INVENTORY CALCULATION, will look like Figure 4.30. You will, of course, use an expression to create the formula for the **extension field**. The expression that you will use is:

```
=[PRICE]*[ON HAND]
```

 Hands-On Exercise: Creating the INVENTORY CALCULATION Report Template

1. Specify the table and type of report to be generated.

        Click to invoke the Reports sheet of the database window.

        Click to invoke the New Report dialog box.

        Click the down arrow of the text box. A listing of available tables appears.

INVENTORY DATA   Click this table.

 **Report Wizards**   Click to invoke the Report Wizards dialog box, which prompts you for the type of report you want.

2. Select the report type.

Tabular   Click this report type.

[**OK**]   Click to invoke the Tabular Report Wizard dialog box.

3. Specify the fields to be included in the report.

ID NUMBER   Click this field name in the Available fields selection box.

[>] (twice)   Click to include the ID NUMBER and ARTIST fields.

PRICE   Click this field name.

[>]   Include the PRICE field.

ON HAND   Click this field name.

[>]   Include the ON HAND field.

[**Next >**]   Click to move to the next dialog box. Access now prompts you to determine how the records in the report are to be sorted.

4. Specify the order of the report as ID number order.

ID NUMBER   Click this field name in the Available fields selection box.

[>]   Click to include the ID NUMBER field.

 [**Next >**]   Access now prompts you for the report style.

5. Determine the characteristics of the report.

Portrait Change the report so that it appears on standard 8.5-by-11-inch paper.

 Access now provides you with the option to use a report title that is different from the name of the table.

Type **INVENTORY VALUATION REPORT** Enter the new report title.

6. View the report.

 Access now prepares the report based on these specifications. When finished, it displays the Print Preview window for the generated report.

7. Maximize the Print Preview window.

Maximize Print Preview to see the generated report. Your screen should look like Figure 4.26. (Use the scroll bars to position in this manner.)

8. View the Report Design window.

Click the Close Window button on the toolbar. The Report Design window now shows the specifications that Access used for creating the report. If your toolbox is in the way, do step 9; otherwise, go to step 10.

Figure 4.26

The Print Preview window for the generated report.

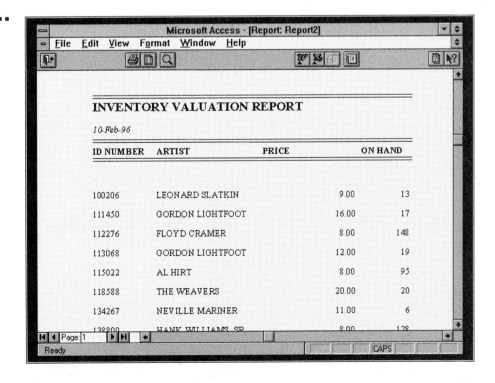

Figure 4.27

The Design view with the right margin enlarged.

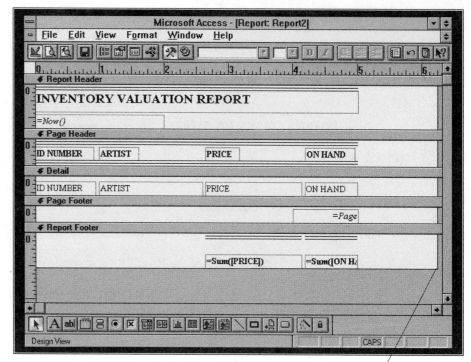

Repositioned margin

9. Move the toolbox to the bottom of the window.

Drag   Click and drag the toolbox to the bottom of the window.

10. Increase the size of the right-hand margin.

Click and drag   Position to the right side of the white area representing the right-hand margin of the report. The pointer should change into ⟷. Drag this border to the right to the 6¼-inch mark on the top ruler. (Use the area below the title box to accomplish this.) Your screen should now look like Figure 4.27.

11. Change the report header, right margin of report, data fields, and lines all at once.

Point   Position to the 5-inch mark on the ruler (this position should be above the right-hand portion of the field and line control boxes). The pointer should now change into ↓.

Click   Click the mouse, and the rightmost field boxes, line boxes, and heading boxes are selected.

Click and drag   Click and drag any handle (the best might be the middle-right handle of the heading) to the 6-inch mark on the ruler. Your screen should now look like Figure 4.28.

Click   Click anywhere outside the current box to turn off all selections.

INVENTORY VALUATION REPORT   Click this title to select it.

Figure 4.28

The Report Design window with the far-right controls (fields) enlarged.

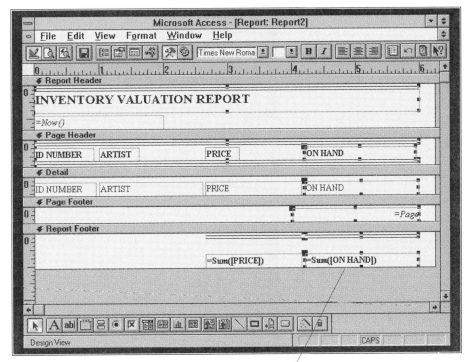

Resized fields and lines

 Click the Center-Align Text button to center the text in the selected box.

12. Use the commands above to decrease the on-hand (data and label) and =SUM([ON HAND]) fields so that the right margin of these boxes is to the left of the 5-inch mark on the ruler. Use Figure 4.29 as a guide.

13. Create the expression for the extension field.

    `abl`   Click this button in the toolbox and point to the right of the on-hand field in the Detail band. Click. A box with a border now appears.

     Open the Properties sheet for the unbound text field.

Control Source   Click this cell.

Type `=[ON HAND]*[PRICE]`   Enter the formula for calculating the extension.

Format   Click this cell.

     Click the down arrow.

Standard   Select this format for displaying the calculated data.

      Double-click the control-menu button of the Properties sheet. Refer to Figure 4.29.

14. Create a column heading.

    `A`   Click this button in the toobox. Position to the area in the Page Header band above the extension field and click to position the label box.

Figure 4.29

The rearranged fields in the Report Design window along with the extension fields added.

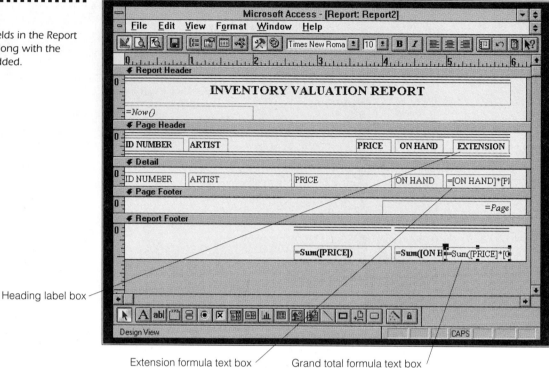

Heading label box

Extension formula text box   Grand total formula text box

| Type **EXTENSION** | Enter the heading. Depending on how you positioned the text box, you may now have to drag the box to position it properly over the new column. See Figure 4.29. |

15. Create the grand total formula for the extension column.

abl	Click this button in the toolbox and point to the right of the =SUM([ON HAND]) field in the Report Footer band. Click. A box with a border now appears.
	Open the Properties sheet for the unbound text field.
Control Source	Click this cell.
Type **=SUM([PRICE]*[ON HAND])**	Enter the formula for calculating the grand total of the extension. (Be sure to include the parentheses.)
Format	Click this cell.
↓	Click the down arrow.
Standard	Select this format for displaying the calculated data.
—	Double-click the control-menu button of the Properties sheet.

16. Drag column headings so that they are right-justified above the data columns (Figure 4.29).

Figure 4.30

The report shown in the Print Preview window.

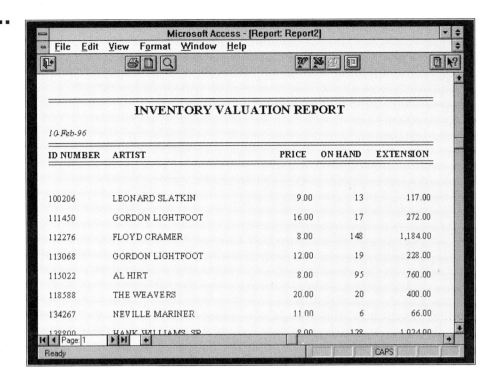

17. Preview the report.

    Click to invoke Print Preview. Your screen should look like Figure 4.30. (You may have to use the scroll bars to position your report to this view.)

18. Print the report.

    Click to invoke the Print dialog box.

    Print the document.

19. Save the report.

    Return to the Report Design window.

    Click to invoke the Save As dialog box.

Type **INVENTORY CALCULATION**   Enter the name of the report.

Enter   Save the report.

    Restore the Report Design window.

⊟   Double-click the control-menu button to return to the database window.

PRINTING LABELS

Printing labels is an application frequently used in business. Most businesses have to communicate with clients or customers. To generate labels, the **Mailing Label command** of the Report Wizards makes generating mailing labels a straightforward task.

Before you use the Access wizards to generate labels, however, you must have some understanding of the characteristics of the typical label application. For example, are you using a dot matrix or laser printer? How many labels are on each row? What is the size of the label you will be using? Do you want to use envelopes instead? You must address all these issues before you generate any labels.

The labels that are used for dot matrix printers are less costly than those for laser printers. Thus, many people who use laser printers first test their label specifications by printing on regular paper. Laser labels cannot easily be used with dot matrix printers. Because of print requirements by certain manufacturers, some labels have a row of half labels at the top and bottom of the page that cannot be used for label generation.

Dot matrix labels have pin-feed holes along the side to control how the forms are fed past the print head. Besides their size, labels vary as to how many appear in a row. If a label form has only one label per row, it is called a one-up label; a label form that has five labels across is referred to as a five-up form.

The **Mailing Label Wizard** lets you define the physical attributes of your labels based on predefined specifications supplied by Avery, a computer forms manufacturer. In the following example you will generate three-up labels (Figure 4.35).

When you are creating labels, you have the option of including variable as well as constant data. The constant data—data that don't change—could be the return address information, whereas the variable data is the information about the addressee. You can also include graphical images or logos, if desired.

The Mailing Label Wizard for designing a label is shown in Figure 4.31. The available fields are in the left list box. Below that is a text box for entering constant data to be included in the label. The buttons below the text box are for adding punctuation and spacing to the label as well as indicating when a new line is to be entered in the label. When Access places a second field on the same line, it automatically deletes any spaces to the right of the last text character (it creates its own concatenation expression).

 HANDS-ON EXERCISE: CREATING MAILING LABELS

Activate the SALES database, then issue the following commands.

1. Specify the table and type of report to be generated.

     Click to invoke the Reports sheet of the database window.

     Click to invoke the New Report dialog box.

     Click the down arrow of the text box. A listing of available tables appears.

CUSTOMER DATA   Click this table.

   Click to invoke the Report Wizards dialog box, which prompts you for the type of report you want.

Figure 4.31

The Mailing Label Wizard dialog box for designing a label.

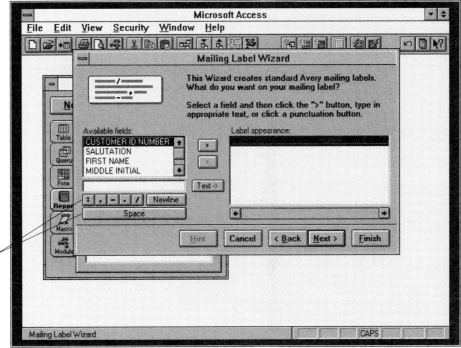

Command buttons for controlling
punctuation and line breaks

2. Select the report type.

Mailing Label   Double-click this report type to invoke the Mailing Label
Wizard dialog box (Figure 4.31).

3. Specify the fields to be included in the first label line.

FIRST NAME   Click this field name in the Available fields selection
box.

> Click to include the FIRST NAME field.

Space   Click to add a blank space. A dot now appears on the
label line.

LAST NAME   Click this field name.

> Click to include the LAST NAME field.

Newline   Click to position to the next label line.

ADDRESS   Click this field name.

> Include the ADDRESS field.

Newline   Click to position to the next label line.

CITY   Click this field name.

> Include the CITY field.

,   Click to insert a comma.

....

Figure 4.32

The completed Mailing Label Wizard dialog box for generating the mailing labels for the CUSTOMER DATA table.

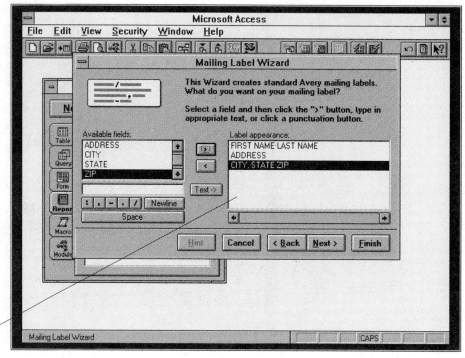

Completed label specification

Space	Click to add a space.
STATE	Click this field name.
>	Include the STATE field.
Space	Click to add a space.
ZIP	Click this field name.
>	Include the ZIP field. Your label specification should now look like Figure 4.32.

4. Specify the order of the labels.

Next >	Click to move to the next dialog box. Access now prompts you to determine how the records in the label report are to be sorted.
ZIP	Click this field name.
>	Include the field in the Sort order text box.

HINTS/HAZARDS   If you inadvertently insert the wrong field, remember to use the [<] button to remove the last field entered. This button can be used for more than one field.

Figure 4.33

The available Avery label types displayed in a dialog box.

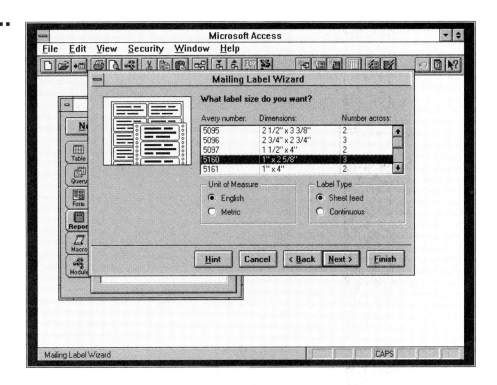

5. Specify the type of Avery label to use.

Next >	Move to the next dialog box. You are now prompted to pick the type of label (Figure 4.33).
5160	Select the Avery label that is 1 inch by 2⅝ inches and three-up.

6. Specify the font to use.

Next >	Move to the next dialog box. You are now prompted to pick the font for the label (Figure 4.34). We will accept the defaults.
Next >	Move to the next dialog box, accepting the defaults.
Finish	The Print Preview window for the labels appears.
▲	Maximize Print Preview (Figure 4.35).

7. Print the report.

🖨	Click to invoke the Print dialog box.
OK	Print the report.

Figure 4.34

The dialog box for determining the font to use in generating the labels.

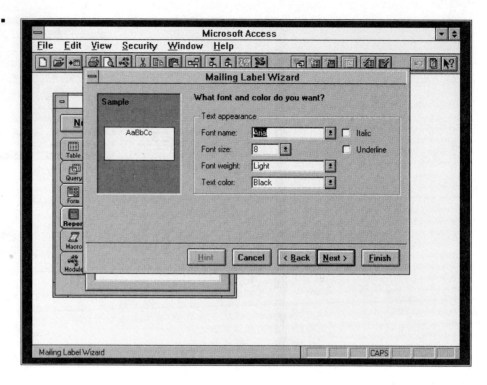

Figure 4.35

The Print Preview window for the three-up labels.

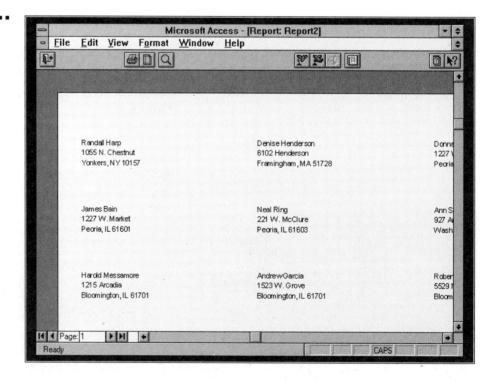

8. View the Report Design window for the label generation.

 Return to the Report Design window. Your screen should look like Figure 4.36. Notice that Access has created all of the concatenation expressions for you via the description of the label that you entered in a prior Report Wizard dialog box.

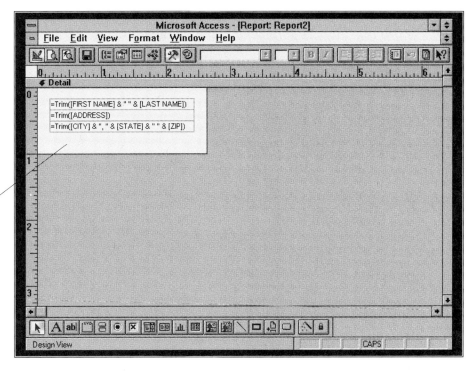

Figure 4.36
The report specification Design view generated by Access for printing the mailing labels.

Concatenation expressions

9. Save the report.

⊞	Click to invoke the Save As dialog box.
Type **GENERATE CUSTOMER LABELS**	Enter the name of the report.
Enter	Save the report.
⬍	Restore the Report Design window.
—	Double-click the control-menu button to return to the database window.

USING ACCESS FOR A MERGE OPERATION

Despite technological advances, most communication is still conducted via the written word, and writing letters is still extremely important in business. Writing the same letter to 100 different people, however, poses some real problems for the typical business. In many situations, it is important to modify each letter so it appears to have been typed individually for the recipient. People do not like "Dear Customer" letters.

With Access's **merge capability** and a letter-quality printer, each letter in a bulk lot can look as though it was individually typed. Figure 4.37 shows an example of such a letter.

This individualized look is accomplished by creating a merge report design like the one in Figure 4.38. This report template consists of two types of text. The **constant text** is the text that does not change from one letter to the next. It resides in label boxes.

The **variable text** is text that is obtained from an Access database table. The variable-text fields appear as text boxes in the report layout. Each text box holds the formula for the field(s) contained in that box (starts with an equal sign [=]).

• •

Figure 3.37

A sample letter generated by a merge operation.

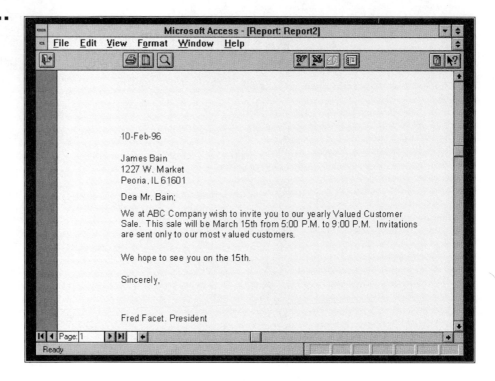

• •

Figure 3.38

The merge template shown in the Report Design window.

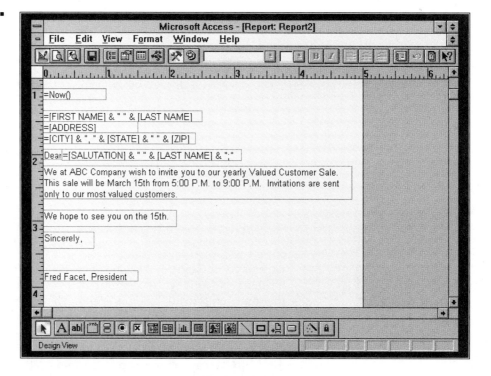

When the report template is printed, the merge operation is performed and each data record in the specified database table is used to generate a separate letter. The date field is also an Access field, and will automatically include the current system date when the letters are printed.

In this example, each letter is assumed to appear on preprinted letterhead for the company. This is why it starts at the 1-inch mark.

HANDS-ON EXERCISE: EXECUTING A MERGE OPERATION

Activate the SALES database, then issue the following commands.

1. Specify the table and type of report to be generated.

Reports	Click to invoke the Reports sheet of the database window.
New	Click to invoke the New Report dialog box.
⬇	Click the down arrow of the text box. A listing of available tables appears.
CUSTOMER DATA	Click this table.
Blank Report	Click to invoke a blank Report Design window.
▲	Maximize the Report Design window.

2. Get rid of the Page Header/Footer bands.

Format	Open the Format Menu.
Page Header/Footer	Click this entry, and the bands disappear from the report specification. The Detail band is all that remains.

3. Increase the size of the Detail band.

Point	Position to the bottom margin of the Detail band. The pointer changes into ⬍.
Click and drag	Drag the bottom margin to the 4-inch mark on the vertical ruler.
⬆	Click the scroll arrow of the vertical scroll bar to get to the top of the Detail band. Your screen should now look like Figure 4.39.

4. Indicate to Access that it is to go to the top of the next page after it prints a letter.

Right click	With the pointer anywhere in the Detail band, click the right mouse button to invoke the SpeedMenu.
Properties...	Select this option to invoke the Properties sheet for the Detail band (Figure 4.40).
Force New Page	Select this cell.
⬇	Click to display the list of options.
After Section	Select this option to go to the top of a new page after printing the record (letter).
▬	Double-click the control-menu button of the Properties sheet.

Figure 4.39

The blank, resized Detail band for the merge letter.

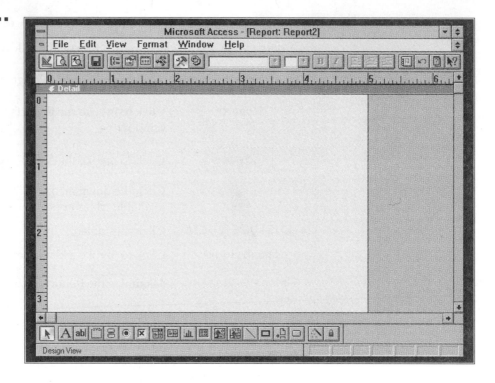

Figure 4.40

The Properties sheet for the Detail band.

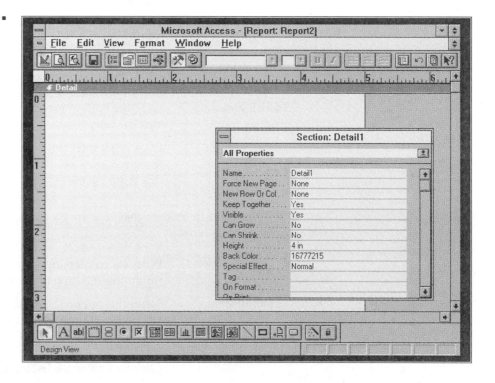

5. Use the Expression Builder to include today's date in the letter.

 Click this button in the toolbox and then position to the middle of the Detail band and click to display the text box. Notice that it has a box with a field number in it. In the next step we will get rid of that box.

Figure 4.41

The concatenation expression built using the Expression Builder.

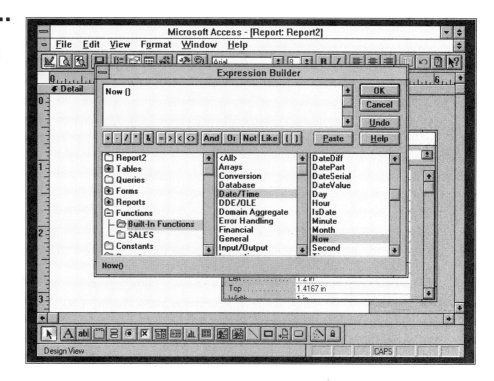

Click	Click the mouse anywhere in the Detail band to deselect the text box.
Click	Click the box with the field number in it.
Del	Delete the box.
Click	Click the unbound box to select it.
	Open the Properties sheet for this object.
Control Source	Click this cell.
...	Click to invoke the Expression Builder dialog box.
Functions	Double-click this entry in the first column.
Built-In Functions	Click this entry.
Date/Time	Click this entry in the second column.
	Click the down arrow of the vertical scroll bar of the third column to view the Now function.
Now	Double-click this entry. Your screen should now look like Figure 4.41.
OK	Place the function in the Control Source cell of the Properties sheet.
Format	Select this cell.
	Click the down arrow to get a list of display options.
Medium Date	Select this entry.
	Double-click the control-menu button of the Properties sheet. The formula is now placed in the text box.

Drag	Drag the box so that the top is at the vertical 1-inch mark (see Figure 4.38).
▤	Left-justify the date along the left margin.

6. Change the font size to 10.

▾	Display the options for the font size.
10	Select 10 point.

7. Create text boxes and manually enter the concatenation formulas using the Properties sheet for each text box of the addressee part of the letter. Change the font size of each box to 10 point. Use the formulas and box placements as shown in Figure 4.38. Delete any field number boxes.

8. Use text and label boxes as indicated for the rest of the letter. Be sure to reset the font size to 10 for each box. Use Figure 4.38 as a guide. Delete any field number boxes.

9. Preview the report.

▣	You should now see the Bain letter onscreen.

10. Print the first three letters.

🖨	Click to invoke the Print dialog box.
From	Click the From text box.
Type **1**	Enter the first page number.
To	Click the To text box.
Type **3**	Enter the last page number.
OK	Print the document.

11. Save the report.

▯←	Return to the Report Design window.
💾	Click to invoke the Save As dialog box.
Type **CUSTOMER MERGE**	Enter the name of the report.
[Enter]	Save the report.
▴▾	Restore the Report Design window.
▭	Double-click the control-menu button to return to the database window.

GRAPHING DATA IN A REPORT

Depicting large amounts of numeric data as a graph makes it easier to get an idea of overall trends as well as makes the data easier to understand. Access makes the process of graphing numeric data relatively easy by including graphing capabilities via the **Graph Wizard**, which is invoked with the **Graph button** in the toolbox. In the following example, we are going to use an existing report (CUSTOMERS BY ZIP CODE REPORT) and summarize the amount due by zip code as a graph on the first page of the report. This graph will thereby provide an overall summary of the information contained in the report.

HANDS-ON EXERCISE: GRAPHING THE AMOUNT DUE BY ZIP CODE

Activate the SALES database, then issue the following commands.

1. Specify the table and type of report to be generated.

 Click to invoke the Reports sheet of the database window.

CUSTOMERS BY ZIP CODE REPORT   Select this report name.

 Click this button to get the Form Design window.

 Click the Graph button in the toolbox.

Point and click   Place the + of the pointer under the "Z" of the word "ZIP" in the Report Header band and click. Your computer now displays the Graph Wizard dialog box shown in Figure 4.42 and spends considerable time processing data.

Figure 4.42

The Graph Wizard dialog box.

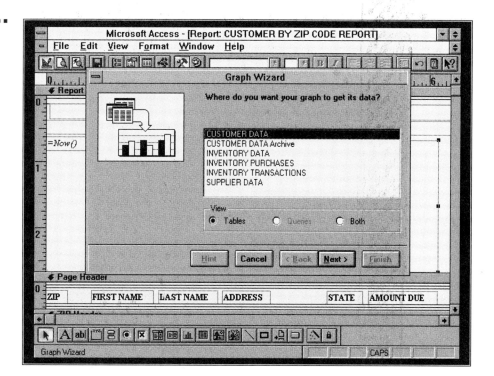

■ ■

Figure 4.43

The fields to include in the graph.

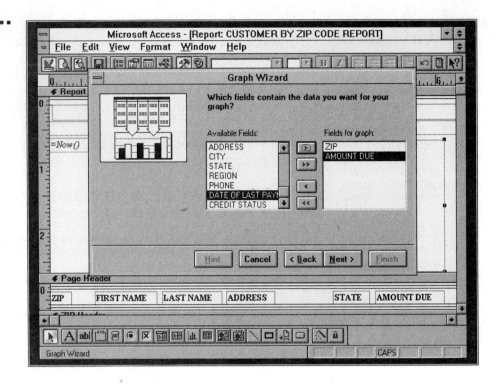

2. Use the CUSTOMER DATA table in creating the graph.

CUSTOMER DATA	Select this table.
Next >	Access now prompts you to select the fields to include.
ZIP	Click this field name in the Available fields selection box.
>	Copy to the Fields for graph box.
AMOUNT DUE	Click this field name.
>	Copy to the Fields for graph box. Your dialog box should now look like Figure 4.43.
Next >	Access now prompts you to specify how to present the data. We want to sum the amount due data (the default).
Next >	Access now asks if you want to link the data from your table. You do not want to do this. The No button should be the default.
No	Access now requests that you to choose the graph type (Figure 4.44).
(pie chart)	Click the pie chart, and you should see a graph like that shown in Figure 4.44.
Next >	Access now wants you to enter a title for the graph.
Type **AMOUNT DUE BY ZIP CODE**	Enter the graph title.
Finish	Generate the graph in the Report Header band (Figure 4.45).

Figure 4.44

The dialog box for selecting the graph type.

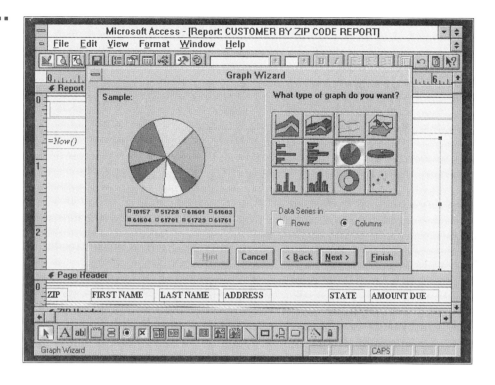

Figure 4.45

The graph generated in the Report Header band of the Report Design window.

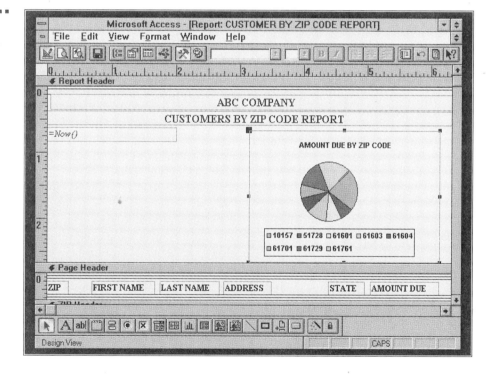

3. Preview and print the report.

You should now see the report with the pie chart onscreen.

Click to invoke the Print dialog box.

   OK   Print the document.

4. Save the report under another name.

Return to the Report Design window.

File Open the File menu.

Save As... Select this option.

Type **CUSTOMER BY ZIP CODE REPORT - GRAPHED** Enter the new name.

[Enter] Save the report.

Restore the Report Design window.

Double-click the control-menu button to return to the database window.

CHAPTER REVIEW

Based on how the Report Wizards build reports, it appears to a beginning Access user that multiple lines cannot be generated per record. Wizards also do not provide the ability to create fields that are the result of calculations performed using data from record fields. Once a basic report has been generated using a Report Wizard, these features can be added to the report. This saves you a lot of time because you can start with an existing report design and add enhancements in the Report Design window of Access.

The Properties sheet is an important Access tool for controlling what happens. Access maintains a Properties sheet on any object created. An object can be a band in a report, a label box, a text box, and so forth. Concatenation expressions and formulas are placed in reports via these Properties sheets.

The Access package has a number of advanced report features. One is the ability to create subtotals via the Groups/Totals Report Wizard feature, which can be used only on ordered tables (Access must be told the order of the table). A report in which subtotals are generated for groups of records is often referred to as a control-break or level-break report.

Although it might appear that Access allows you to print only one line per record, lines can be added to the Detail band to generate multiple lines per record. Joining fields requires using the concatenation character (and placing a space or any needed punctuation) between fields. This is accomplished by setting up a relationship in the Expression Builder dialog box or by entering a concatenation expression in a Properties sheet.

Access also has a Mailing Label Wizard that can quickly design a report for generating labels. Access allows you to access a number of predesigned label formats for Avery-style labels.

You can also use Access to generate merged documents. Constant text is contained in label cells, and variable data for the letter is contained in text cells. Only the Detail band is needed for a merge operation.

Finally, data contained in a table can be used to generate a graph, which can be included in a report form. For instance, if you want a visual summary of a report, a graph can be placed in the Report Header band, as shown in this chapter.

KEY TERMS AND CONCEPTS

concatenation	Graph button
concatenation character	Graph Wizard
constant text	Groups/Totals Report Wizard
control-break (level-break)	Mailing Label command
processing	Mailing Label Wizard
expression	merge capability
Expression Builder dialog box	report calculations
extension field	variable text

CHAPTER QUIZ

Multiple Choice

1. Which of the following statements is true for forcing multiple lines to appear within a data column?
   a. The semicolon (;) must be placed where each line is to end within a column.
   b. Both the + and the ; may be required.
   c. Only the colon is needed to indicate the end of a line.
   d. Full-screen editing places each heading on a separate line.
   e. None of the above statements is true.

2. Which of the following characters concatenates fields?
   a. &
   b. :
   c. ;
   d. +
   e. none of the above

3. Calculation formulas can be built using the:
   a. Properties sheet
   b. Expression Builder
   c. both of the above
   d. none of the above

4. The Control Source cell of the Properties sheet, when used to control concatenation, can be changed by:
   a. the Expression Builder
   b. entering the formula directly in a formula cell in the Detail band
   c. first deleting and then entering a new expression.
   d. none of the above

5. A formula is placed in a _____ box.
   a. label
   b. formula
   c. text
   d. field
   e. none of the above

True/False

6. The $ deletes blanks on the left-hand side of a field.

7. Up to a maximum of two lines can be printed per specified field using the Reports feature of Access.

8. Subtotals almost always result in a page break.

9. The Mailing Label Wizard lets you print up to three labels across.

10. Arithmetic statements in a report template can contain only field names.

Answers

1. e   2. a   3. c   4. a   5. c   6. f   7. f   8. f   9. f   10. f

Exercises

1. Define or describe each of the following:

   a. level break

   b. concatenation

   c. Graph Wizard

   d. Mailing Label Wizard

2. A _____ is generated when the contents of a field change from one record to the next.

3. The _____ character is used to join fields.

4. Subtotals can be generated only on _____ data fields.

5. The _____ button of the initial Report Wizard dialog box enables you to include all fields from a table in a report.

6. To include additional lines in a report band requires that you enlarge that band via a _____ operation.

7. The _____ option tells Access to generate a report using standard 8.5-by-11-inch paper.

8. The _____ button of a Report Wizard dialog box aborts the report generation and returns you to the database window.

9. Placing the pointer in the _____ ribbon of the Report Design window and clicking allows you to select and make changes to multiple objects at one time.

10. A _____ box is used to hold the concatenation expressions in a report.

11. The Properties sheet is invoked for an unbound box to enter any type of _____.

12. An entity used to control how a formula will operate, when to begin printing at the top of a page, is the _____ _____ of an object.

13. A _____ must be embedded between fields when a concatenation expression is used.

14. When you are entering a formula or expression, field names must be included within _____.

15. The _____ _____ Wizard allows you to quickly generate mailing labels.

16. The label selection for a two-up label is the _____ by Avery, whereas the three-up label is _____.

17. The _____ capability of Access allows you to create individualized letters.

18. When you are developing a merge operation, only the _____ band is needed for the report specification.

19. The ability to summarize large amounts of numeric data visually is made possible using the _____ feature of Access.

20. _____ data does not change from one letter to the next in a merge operation.

COMPUTER EXERCISES

1. Perform the following tasks using the PAYMAST table, created previously.
   a. Create a multiple-line report like that shown in this chapter. Design the report layout yourself.
   b. Generate mailing labels for all employees via the Mailing Label Wizard.
   c. Generate a Groups/Totals report on total pay by department.
   d. Using the report generated in step c, place a summary graph in the Report Header band.

2. This record-keeping project deals with tracking donations that have been made to your college's or university's foundation. A foundation office is extremely important for providing needed funds to a school. The efforts put forth by the foundation office generate the funds for construction, faculty travel, research, and equipment.

When people donate money to an institution, it is critical that the organization receiving the money record that donation and generate a timely thank-you letter. Recording the donation properly is important because it allows the institution to keep track of individual donors and retrieve information about those donors when needed. For example, you may be interested in all individuals who have made donations of more than $1,000 during the past five years. Another point that may interest you is the geographic location of donors. An efficiently built record-keeping system lets you quickly and easily answer these types of questions.

However, properly acknowledging the contribution quickly is even more important. When people make contributions to any type of institution, their gift has some element of sacrifice to it.

This project requires use of the ALUMNI table provided on your student disk. Figure 4.46 shows the structure of the ALUMNI table.

Let's examine some of the fields. The SALUT field contains room for just about any salutation you wish to use in a letter, depending on the individual(s) giving the gift. The salutation might be "Dear Mr. and Mrs.," "Dr. and Ms.," "Ms.," or any variation. This field is especially useful when generating letters for a donor.

The FIRST NAME, MIDDLE, and LAST NAME fields are used to record the name of the principal donor. The SPOUSE FIRST and SPOUSE MIDDLE fields are used to record the name of the spouse, if any, who should be included in recording the donation.

The GIFT TYPE field is used to classify the gift. The three classifications are determined by the size of the gift:

- $1–499 = Regular (R)
- $500–999 = Dean's Circle (D)
- $1,000 and up = President's Club (P)

The DATE field contains the date the gift was received, and the AMOUNT field records the size of the gift.

Create and print a report called GIFT EDIT, which contains the information about each gift. Figure 4.47 shows the report to be generated. This report is produced to allow manual comparison of each printed record about each gift with the original document to ensure that all gifts and the information about each were recorded properly. If any errors are detected, they are corrected immediately.

When building the report, make the changes indicated below.

a.   Concatenate these fields:

        FIRST and SPOUSE FIRST
        CITY, STATE, and ZIP,
        GIFT TYPE—leave as is

b.   Use the Mailing Label Wizard to generate labels for each contributor. Place these label settings in the ALUM LABEL report. Print the labels on regular paper.

c.   Design your own thank-you letter and send each contributor a personalized letter using the merge capability of Access covered in this chapter.

Figure 4.46

The structure of the ALUMNI table.

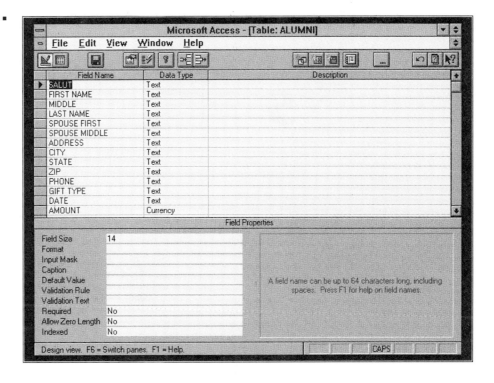

Figure 4.47

The report to be generated by the GIFT EDIT report specification.

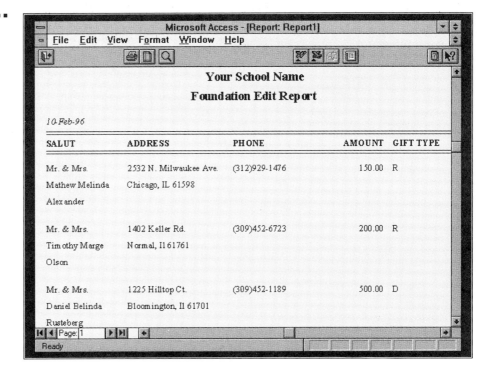

5

THE QUERY
FEATURE OF
ACCESS

CHAPTER OBJECTIVES

After completing this chapter, you should be able to

- **Create selection queries of a database**

- **Use queries for copying tables and creating new tables**

- **Use calculations in queries**

- **Use the Query feature to link tables**

- **Use the Update command with multiple tables**

This chapter introduces the following Access topics: Query Design window, dynaset, query (QBE) techniques, techniques for linking tables, the Update command, and elementary Access command files.

QUERIES

Chapter 3 introduced entering elementary queries using the Access Find command. This section introduces you to using the **Query By Example (QBE) grid** of the Query Design window to construct selection queries that ask questions about your data. A **query** is a set of instructions that specifies how Access should organize or change your data. You use the Query Design window to build a model of the information you want, specifying the tables and desired fields.

Access allows you to build two types of queries: select queries and action queries. A **select query** gets data from a table but does not do anything with the data except display it. An **action query** does something with the data after it is obtained. In this chapter we will be making extensive use of the select query.

Access **Query Wizards** allow you to build four different types of queries. The query type appears as part of the title bar of the Query Design window. The four query types are as follows:

- **Crosstab Query** displays data in a compact, spreadsheet-like format.
- **Find Duplicates Query** creates a query that finds duplicate records in a single table or query.
- **Find Unmatched Query** finds records in one table that have now-related records in another table.
- **Archive Query** creates a query that copies records from an existing table into a new table.

These four action queries are usually created using Query Wizards whereas the select query is created by the user from the Query Design window. Access does not provide wizards for select queries because, as you will see shortly, creating a select query is a fairly straightforward process.

When you execute the query, a **result set** or **dynaset table** is generated that provides a view, or partial picture, of the data contained in one or more database tables. Access allows you to use a **dynaset** just as you would a database table to display, enter, and edit data. The difference is that instead of dealing with only one table in the Datasheet window, you may be dealing with a number of fields from several different tables that appear in the dynaset. The fields displayed are specified in the query. Any changes that you make to the fields are automatically included in records of the underlying specified tables.

ACCESS DYNASETS

As noted previously, a dynaset provides a picture of one or more database tables. Queries can use fields from one or more database tables to create a temporary dynaset table. Queries can be used to display data, enter data in a database table, generate a report, rearrange fields in a table, update a database table, or limit the fields that are accessible to a user.

Dynasets allow you to make changes to the data, even though that data is a copy of data actually contained in one or more tables. If you make a change to a field of the dynaset, the underlying table is also changed. This differs dramatically from some database packages, which let you look only at read-only copies of data when a query is executed. When you have finished using a dynaset, it no longer exists in memory.

Access allows you to save instructions governing the query that defined the dynaset and then reuse those query statements later via the **Queries sheet** of the database window. You can also save the dynaset to a table; however, the data in that table is not updated when you make changes to the tables that were used as input to the original query dynaset table.

In the following example, only those records containing the value Normal in the city field will be displayed. The **relational operator** in the example is assumed by Access to be the equal sign (=). If no relational operator is specified, Access always assumes it is the equal sign. Other relational operators that can appear in a query are shown in Table 5.1.

When a query requires examining several fields, the selection criteria for the fields must be linked with the **logical operators** found in Table 5.2.

In addition to using relational and logical operators, Access also supports some additional operators (see Table 5.3) that afford you tremendous flexibility in querying tables of data.

Table 5.1   Relational Operators

Operator	Description
<	Less than
<=	Less than or equal to
=	Equal to
>=	Greater than or equal to
>	Greater than
<>	Not equal to

Table 5.2   Logical Operators

Operator	Description
Not	The opposite of this expression must occur for this action to take place.
And	This condition requires that both conditions be true before any action will be taken.
Or	This condition requires that only one of the conditions be true for the action to be taken.
()	Parentheses group relations together. If nested parentheses are used, Access evaluates an expression by starting with the innermost set and working outward.

Table 5.3   *Other Operators*

Operator	Description
Is	Used with Null to determine whether a value is Null or Not Null (whether a field is empty or not empty).
Like	Determines whether a string value begins with one or more specified characters. You must use the wildcards * and ? for this to work properly, for example, Blo*.
In	Determines whether or not a string value is in a list of values, for example, In("IL", "IA", "MN", "IN").
Between	Determines whether a numeric value lies within a range of values, for example, Between 1 and 6.

THE TABLE USED BY QUERY

When you use the Queries sheet of the database window to create a query, Access places the conditions that you specify in a **Select Query window**. Unless you tell Access otherwise, it assumes that you want to create a select query. Once the query has been defined and saved, you can recall it using the Queries sheet of the database window to locate records that meet the specified conditions. The Query Design window does not contain data, only specifications in the QBE grid on how to sort and select the data stored in one or more tables. The query QBE grid can be used to specify the following items about the environment:

- One or more tables for use
- Fields and calculated fields
- Sets or characteristics of records to include
- Order of the records

CREATING A QUERY SPECIFICATION

When selected, the Queries sheet of the database window displays a list of queries that have been created. (This sheet should be empty right now; see Figure 5.1.)

The New button lets you create a query using the Query Design window. Once the New button is selected, Access displays a New Query dialog box that lets you decide whether to build the query yourself or use an Access Query Wizard (Figure 5.2). If, as in the examples used in this chapter, you select the New Query button, Access displays the Query Design window and an Add Table dialog box (Figure 5.3) that lets you indicate which tables to use in designing the query via the Add button.

Once you have selected the table to be included, you click the Close button, and the Query Design window and QBE grid remain onscreen (Figure 5.4). The upper portion of the window contains the selection box(es) for the selected table(s). Notice that the title bar indicates that you are building a select query. The bottom portion of the window contains the QBE grid and shows columns that are used to control which fields are to be included in the dynaset as well as

Figure 5.1

The database window with the
Queries sheet invoked.

Name of sheet

Query tab

Names of queries will appear here

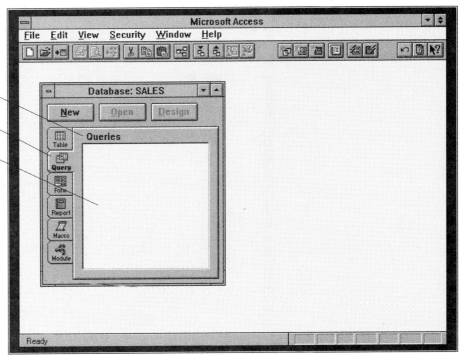

Figure 5.2

The New Query dialog box for
determining how the new query
is to be built.

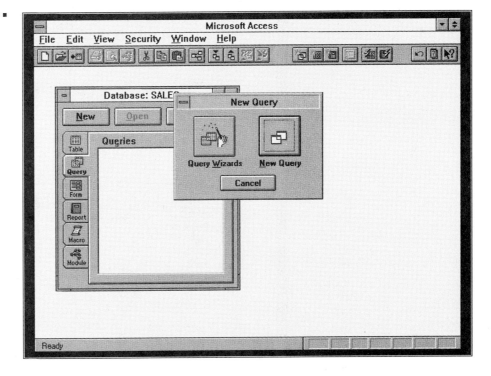

Figure 5.3

The Add Table dialog box for determining which tables are to be accessed in the query.

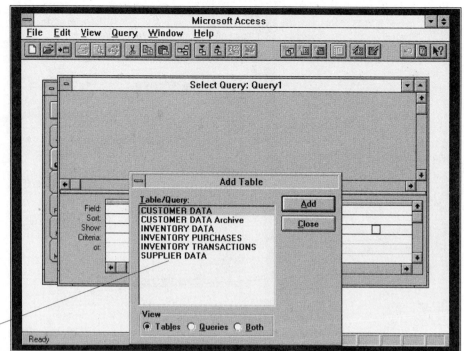

Tables in database that can be
added to the query

Figure 5.4

The Query Design window.

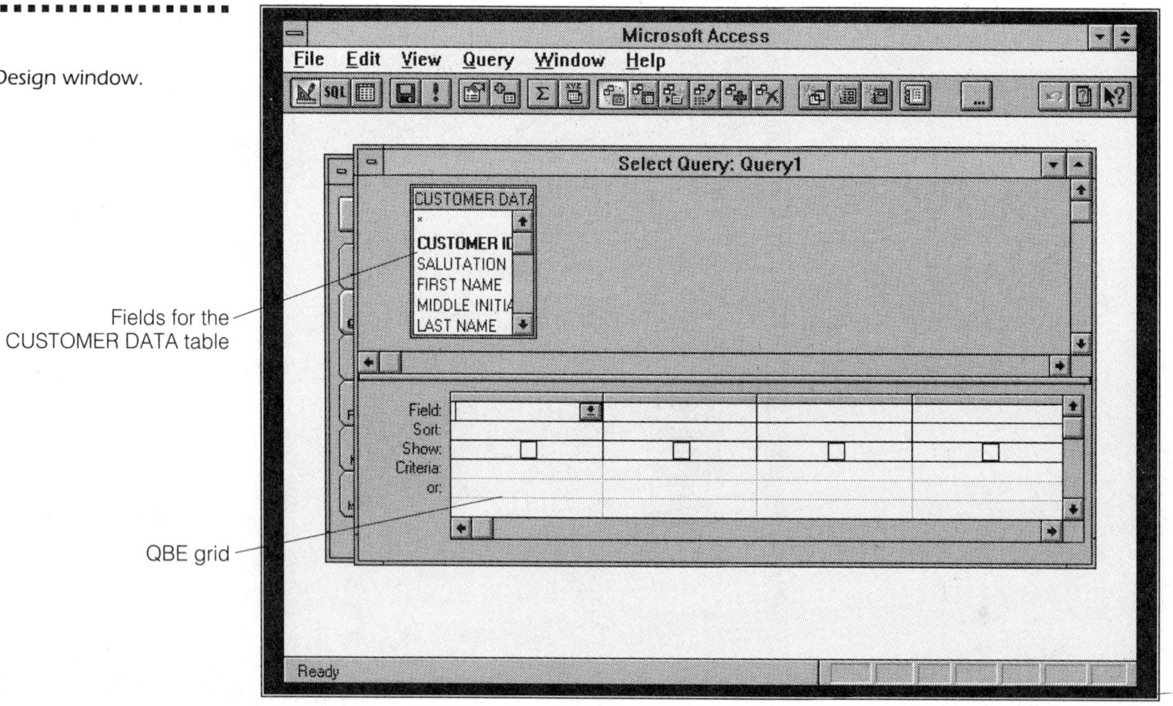

Fields for the
CUSTOMER DATA table

QBE grid

how the field is to be sorted, whether or not it is to be displayed, and any criteria to use in including records in the dynaset.

Field   The names of the fields to include in a query are specified via the **Field cell**. Fields can be included in one of four ways.

Figure 5.5

The list box of the Field cell used for including a field in a query dynaset.

List of fields from the CUSTOMER DATA table

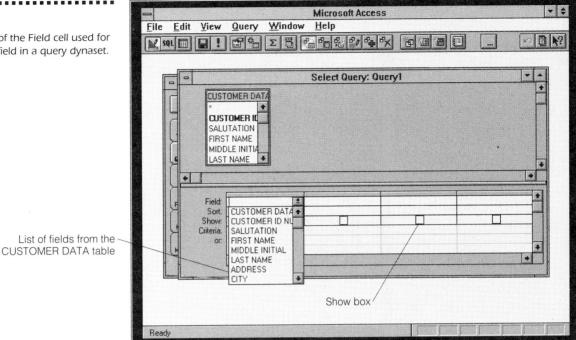

- An individual field can be dragged from the list box at the top to a column in the lower portion of the table.
- An individual field can be automatically included in the next QBE box by double-clicking the field name.
- The down arrow can be clicked to invoke a list box of fields from the table (Figure 5.5).
- All fields from the table can be included by double-clicking the title bar of the list box in the upper portion of the window and then dragging all of the fields in one drag operation to the lower portion.

Sort   The **Sort cell** displays a list box with the options Ascending, Descending, or (not sorted). This cell allows you to determine the order for records to appear in the dynaset. The order of fields in the QBE grid is important when you want to sort on multiple fields. Access moves from the left as field 1 to the right for the next field order.

Show   The **Show cell** is used to determine whether or not a field/column is to be displayed in the dynaset. Fields with an × in the show box appear in the dynaset generated by the query whereas fields with a blank box do not appear. Both types of fields can be used to control the records that appear in the dynaset.

Criteria   The **Criteria cell** is where you enter any selection criteria for including records in the dynaset for a specified field. After you finish entering the expression and press the Enter key, Access examines it and displays the expression using standard Access syntax. For example, if you type **Normal**, Access adds quotation marks and displays it as **"Normal"**.

If you don't include an operator, Access assumes the equal sign (=). For example, if you enter Normal in the city field, Access interprets that as the expression CITY = "Normal".

■■■■■■■■■■■■■■■■■■■■■■

Figure 5.6

The Zoom dialog box used for
examining a long criteria
specification.

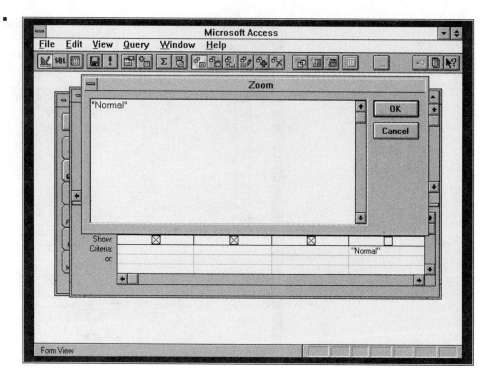

■■■■■■■■■■■■■■■■■■■■■■

Figure 5.7

The completed QBE grid for
displaying the first-name, last-name,
and amount due fields of all records
with a city value of Normal.

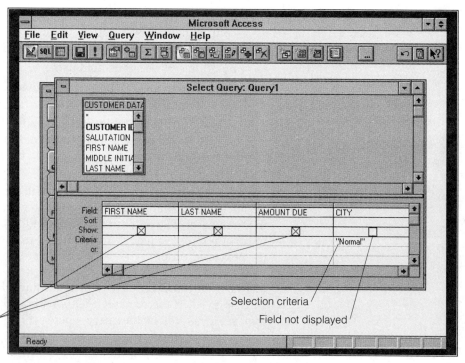

If you have a long series of criteria specifications and you want to review
them, the Criteria cell is rather small for that purpose. In such a situation, you
should use the **Zoom command** (Shift + F2) to invoke the Zoom dialog box to
examine the criteria formula (Figure 5.6).

Once the characteristics of the query have been entered (Figure 5.7), the
query is executed by clicking the **Run button** on the toolbar (Figure 5.8). Access
then displays the dynaset for the query using the Datasheet window (Figure 5.9).

When you access the Query Design window, the toolbar of the design window changes to include a number of query buttons. These buttons are summarized in Table 5.4.

Table 5.4   Query Toolbar Buttons

Button	Name	Function
	Design View	Switches to Design View of a query.
	SQL View	Opens the Query window in SQL view and displays the SQL statement for the current query.
	Datasheet View	Switches to the Datasheet view of the query.
	Save	Saves the design of the query to disk.
	Run	Runs the query displayed and shows the results in the Datasheet window.
	Properties	Shows or hides the Properties sheet for the selected item.
	Add Table	Chooses tables or queries whose field lists you want to add to the active query.
	Totals	Shows or hides the Total row in the QBE grid of the Query Design window.
	Table Names	Displays or hides the table names in the QBE grid.
	Select Query	Makes the active query a select query.
	Crosstab Query	Makes the active query a crosstab query.
	Make-Table Query	Makes the active query a make-table query.
	Update Query	Makes the active query an update query.
	Append Query	Makes the active query an append query.
	Delete Query	Makes the active query a delete query.
	New Query	Creates a query based on the active table or query.
	New Form	Creates a form based on the active query.
	New Report	Creates a report based on the active query.
	Database Window	Displays the database window.
	Build	Performs a task or creates an expression using the Expression Builder.
	Undo	Undoes the most recent action.
	Cue Cards	Displays the Cue Cards main menu.
	Help	Invokes Help when you click this button and then the feature about which you wish to obtain help.

Figure 5.8

The dynaset generated by the query shown in the Datasheet window.

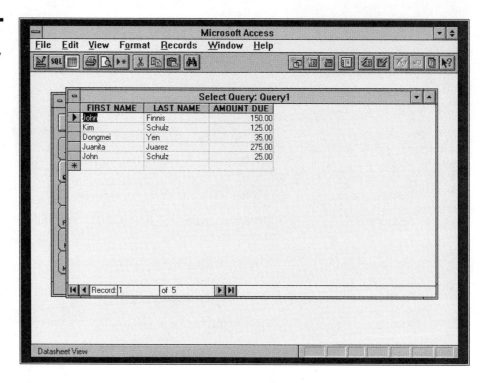

Figure 5.9

The dynaset including selected fields of all records.

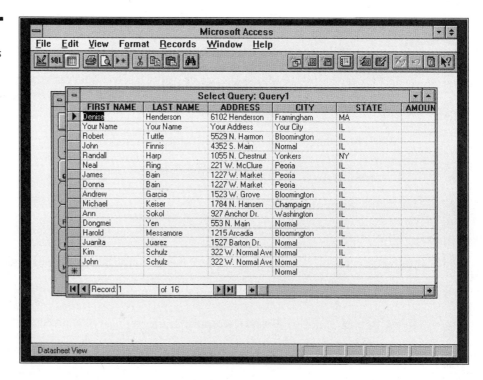

Hands-On Exercise: Creating the City Query

In preparation for this hands-on exercise, have the SALES database window open.

1. Activate the Queries sheet and start the build process.

Query	Click to invoke the Queries sheet of the database window (Figure 5.1).
New	Click to activate the New Query dialog box (Figure 5.2).
New Query	Select to activate the Add Table dialog box (Figure 5.3).
CUSTOMER DATA	Select this file.
Add	Add this filename to the top of the Query Design window.
Close	Close the Add Table dialog box. Your screen should look like Figure 5.4.

2. Use a drag operation to include the first-name field in the QBE grid.

FIRST NAME	Click this field and drag it to the Field cell in the first column of the QBE grid. FIRST NAME should now appear in the Field cell.

3. Use the list-box method of including field names for the last-name, amount due, and city fields.

Field	Click the rightmost corner of the Field cell of the next column. A list box of field names appears (Figure 5.5).
LAST NAME	Click this field name to include it in the Field cell.

4. Use the instructions of step 3 to include the amount due and city fields in the next two Field cells.

5. Exclude the city field from the dynaset.

⊠	Click the show box of the CITY field to exclude this column from the dynaset. The box should now have no ×.

6. Enter the query criteria.

Criteria	Click the Criteria cell of the CITY column.
Type Normal	The screen may jump to the left. When you click any other cell, Access includes the double quotation marks around Normal. If you move your QBE grid to the right, it should look like Figure 5.7.

7. Run the query.

  Click to run the query. The dynaset shown in Figure 5.8 should appear. Notice that even though the CITY field is not present, it is being used to control the appearance of the records in the dynaset.

8. Print the results of the query.

  Click to invoke the Print dialog box.

  Print the query dynaset.

9. Sort by last name and print.

  Click this button on the toolbar to return to the Query Design window.

Sort Click the Sort cell of the LAST NAME column.

  Click the down arrow to display the sort options.

Ascending Select from the list box.

  Click to run the query. The dynaset should appear, sorted in order by name.

  Click to invoke the Print dialog box.

  Print the query dynaset.

10. Save the query and exit.

  Click to return to Design view.

  Click to invoke the Save As dialog box.

Type **Name, Amount for City** Enter the name of the query.

[Enter] Save the query.

[—] Double-click the control-menu button to return to the database window.

Hands-On Exercise: Performing More-Complex Queries

The next query that you will create will have more fields (most of them will be resized). You will also enter additional selection criteria. The query specification that we will create will be a general-purpose specification that will be used for other queries.

You should have the SALES database invoked and the database window displayed.

1. Activate the Queries sheet and start the build process.

Query	Click to invoke the Queries sheet of the database window.
New	Click to activate the New Query dialog box.
New Query	Select to activate the Add Table dialog box.
CUSTOMER DATA	Select this file.
Add	Add this filename to the top of the Query Design window.
Close	Close the Add Table dialog box.

2. Use the list-box method of including field names for the first-name, last-name, address, city, state, and amount due field names.

Field	Click the rightmost corner of the Field cell of the first column. A list box of field names appears.
FIRST NAME	Click this field name to include it in the Field cell.

3. Use the instructions of step 2 to include the last-name, address, city, state, and amount due fields in the next five Field cells.

4. Run the query.

[!]	Click to run the query. The dynaset shown in Figure 5.9 should appear. Since no criteria data were entered, all records appear.

5. Use the drag operation on the field names to resize the columns as shown in Figure 5.10.

6. Save the query.

[icon]	Click to return to Design view.
[icon]	Click to invoke the Save As dialog box.
Type General Purpose Query	Enter the name of the query.

· ·
Figure 5.10
The dynaset containing resized fields for the display of records.

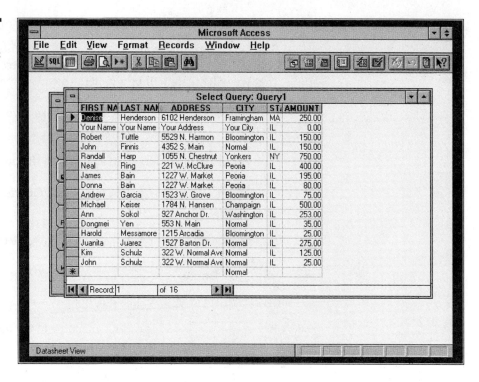

FIRST NA	LAST NAI	ADDRESS	CITY	ST/	AMOUNT
Denise	Henderson	6102 Henderson	Framingham	MA	250.00
Your Name	Your Name	Your Address	Your City	IL	0.00
Robert	Tuttle	5529 N. Harmon	Bloomington	IL	150.00
John	Finnis	4352 S. Main	Normal	IL	150.00
Randall	Harp	1055 N. Chestnut	Yonkers	NY	750.00
Neal	Ring	221 W. McClure	Peoria	IL	400.00
James	Bain	1227 W. Market	Peoria	IL	195.00
Donna	Bain	1227 W. Market	Peoria	IL	80.00
Andrew	Garcia	1523 W. Grove	Bloomington	IL	75.00
Michael	Keiser	1784 N. Hansen	Champaign	IL	500.00
Ann	Sokol	927 Anchor Dr.	Washington	IL	253.00
Dongmei	Yen	553 N. Main	Normal	IL	35.00
Harold	Messamore	1215 Arcadia	Bloomington	IL	25.00
Juanita	Juarez	1527 Barton Dr.	Normal	IL	275.00
Kim	Schulz	322 W. Normal Ave	Normal	IL	125.00
John	Schulz	322 W. Normal Ave	Normal	IL	25.00
			Normal		

Enter	Save the query. Now, when you want to use this QBE query specification, just click that entry in the Queries sheet and then click the Design button.
▭	Double-click the control-menu button to return to the database window.

7. Use this query specification for locating any record with an amount field of greater than $100. You should be at the Queries sheet of the Sales database.

General Purpose Query	Select this query from the Queries sheet.
Design	Click to display the Query Design window with the QBE grid.
→	Click the scroll arrow of the horizontal scroll bar of the QBE grid to view the AMOUNT DUE column.
Criteria	Click this cell of the AMOUNT DUE column.
Type **>100**	Enter the criteria.
!	Click to run the query. The dynaset shown in Figure 5.11 should appear.

8. Now add Peoria as the city field criteria so that only those records from Peoria with an amount due greater than 100 are included.

	Click to display the Query Design window with the QBE grid.

Figure 5.11

The dynaset of records with an amount due field greater than 100.

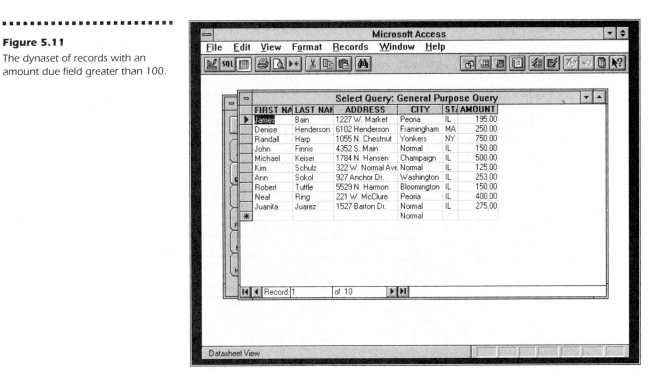

Click the scroll arrow of the horizontal scroll bar of the QBE grid to view the CITY column.

Criteria   Click this cell of the CITY column.

Type **Peoria**   Enter the criteria.

Click to run the query. The dynaset shown in Figure 5.12 should appear.

9. List any records from Peoria or Normal with an amount due field greater than 100.

Click to display the Query Design window with the QBE grid.

or   Click this cell of the CITY column.

Type **Normal**   Enter the criteria.

Click to run the query. The dynaset shown in Figure 5.13 should appear.

Click to display the Query Design window with the QBE grid.

10. Delete the three criteria entries of the QBE grid.

Drag   Click and drag over a Criteria cell entry. All of the text should be in reverse video.

Del   Delete the entry. Perform these commands on the remaining two fields.

Figure 5.12

The dynaset of records with the city of Peoria and an amount due field greater than 100.

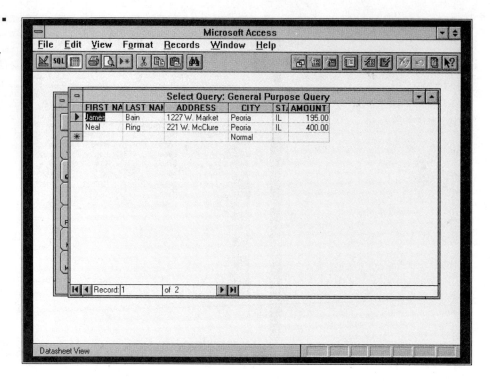

Figure 5.13

The dynaset of records with the city of Peoria or Normal and an amount due field greater than 100.

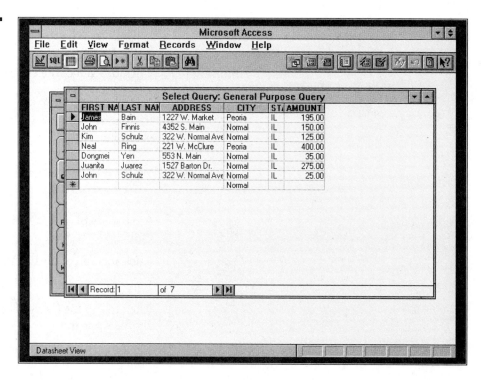

11. Use the date field to display only those records prior to December 10, 1995. First you must add the date of last payment field to the QBE grid.

DATE OF LAST PAYMENT   Double-click this field from the list box in the upper window to include it in the QBE grid.

Criteria   Click this cell of the DATE column.

Figure 5.14

The dynaset of records with the date value prior to December 10, 1995.

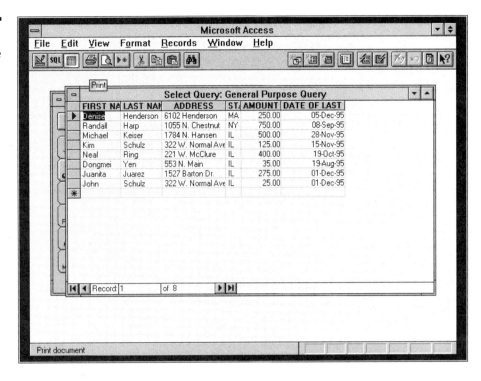

Figure 5.15

The Query Design window showing how Access has changed the date field of December 10, 1995 prior to performing the query.

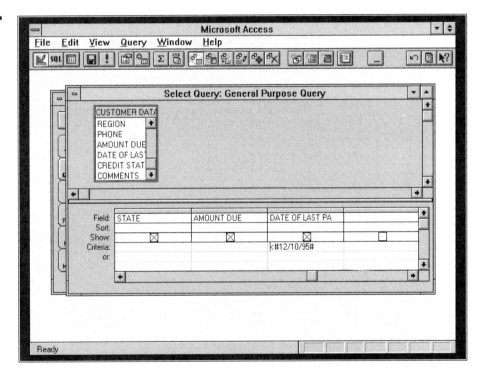

Type **<12/10/95**   Enter the criteria. Access converts this date to a number. Other types of string searches can be seen in Table 5.5.

   Click to run the query. The dynaset shown in Figure 5.14 should appear.

   Click to display the Query Design window with the QBE grid. Figure 5.15 shows how Access has changed the entry so that it can be properly evaluated and the dynaset created.

Table 5.5   *Examples of String Searches*

Expression	Task Performed
<=02/03/95	Matches dates on or before February 2, 1995.
<=G	In a character field, finds all records that start with "A" through "G" in a case-sensitive field.
*john	Matches records that include "john" somewhere in the field.
<>IL	Matches records that do not have the contents "IL".
Like "University*"	Matches records that include text beginning with "University". The * is the wildcard.

12. Exit without saving the changes to the query specification.

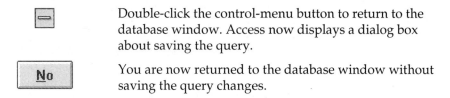

	Double-click the control-menu button to return to the database window. Access now displays a dialog box about saving the query.
No	You are now returned to the database window without saving the query changes.

13. Now, use a **wildcard** to find any records that start with "Jo" in the first-name field. Access uses the ? and * wildcards in the same fashion as DOS and Windows. You should be at the Queries sheet of the database window.

General Purpose Query	Select this entry in the Queries sheet of the database window.
Design	Click to display the Query Design window with the QBE grid.
Criteria	Click this cell of the FIRST NAME column.
Type **jo***	Enter the criteria.
!	Click to run the query. The dynaset shown in Figure 5.16 should appear.

14. Now, use a wildcard to find any records that contain "main" in the address field.

	Click to display the Query Design window with the QBE grid.
Click and drag	Select the entry of the FIRST NAME Criteria cell.
Del	Delete the criteria.
Criteria	Click the Criteria cell of the ADDRESS column.
Type ***main**	Enter the criteria.
!	Click to run the query. The dynaset shown in Figure 5.17 should appear.

Figure 5.16

The dynaset for any record in which the first-name field starts with "jo".

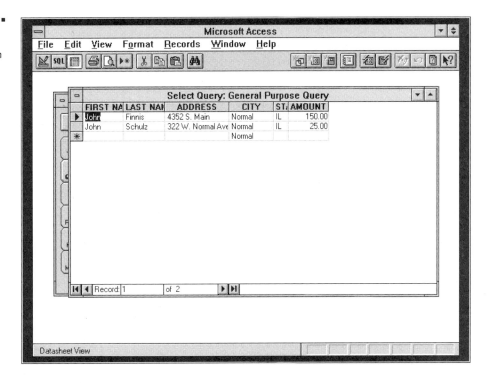

Figure 5.17

The dynaset for any record that contains "main" in the address field.

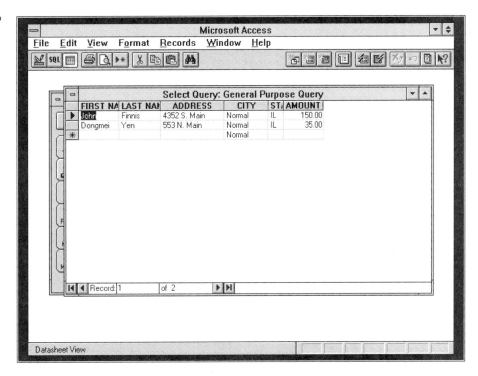

Click to display the Query Design window.

15. Save the changes made to the query specification in this session.

File   Open the File Menu.

Save As...   Select this option.

Figure 5.18

The Print Preview window for the
AutoReport generated by Access.

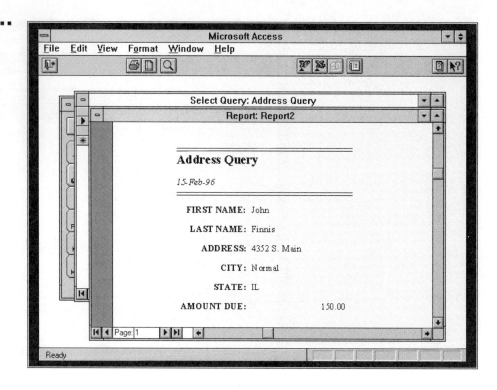

Type **Address Query**   Enter the name of the query.

⌈Enter⌉   Save the query.

    Double-click the control-menu button to return to the
    database window.

16. Activate Address Query and generate an AutoReport.

Address Query   Double-click this entry. The dynaset now appears.

    Click the New Report button on the toolbar. A Print
    Preview window like Figure 5.18 appears.

17. Print the report.

    Click to invoke the Print dialog box.

OK   Print the report.

    Double-click the control-menu button of the Print
    Preview window. Access now asks if you want to save
    the report.

No   Do not save the report.

    Double-click the control-menu button to return to the
    database window.

QUERY CALCULATIONS ON GROUPS OF RECORDS

When you are using the Query feature of Access, you may want to generate summary totals for groups of records within a table or totals for all of the records. Decisions are often made on this type of summarized data. Making calculations based on table values requires creating a query that employs Access's **SQL aggregate functions** to perform these calculations. Table 5.6 summarizes these functions. Since these functions are used against groups of records, they are called "aggregate."

Invoking an aggregate function is a two-step process:

1. Access must be told to add a Total line to the QBE grid by clicking the Totals button on the toolbar.

2. Once the Total line is present, press the F4 key or click the down-arrow icon to get a listing of the functions as shown in Figure 5.19.

 Hands-On Exercise: Generating Subtotals

Assume that you want to generate summary totals as well as counts of records for each zip code in the CUSTOMER DATA table. You should have the SALES database window active.

1. Activate the Queries sheet and start the build process.

    Click to invoke the Queries sheet of the database window.

    Click to activate the New Query dialog box.

Figure 5.19

The list box for the SQL aggregate functions for summarizing numeric fields of a table.

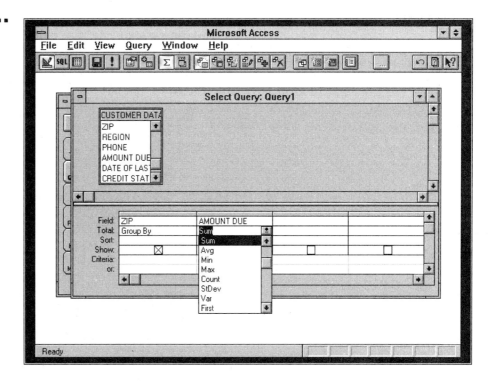

Table 5.6   SQL Aggregate Functions

Function	Description
Group By	Specifies the field on which to sort and develop the level break.
Sum	Totals the values in a field.
Avg	Averages the values of a field.
Min	Determines the smallest value in a field.
Max	Determines the greatest value in a field.
Count	Determines the number of values in a field (no null values included).
StDev	Determines the statistical standard deviation of the values in a field.
Var	Determines the statistical variation of the values in a field.
First	Determines the value of the field of the first record.
Last	Determines the value of the field of the last record.

New Query	Select to activate the Add Table dialog box.
CUSTOMER DATA	Select this file.
Add	Add this filename to the top of the Query Design window.
Close	Close the Add Table dialog box.

2. Use the double-click method of including field names for the zip, customer ID, and amount due fields.

ZIP	Double-click this field name to include it in the QBE grid. Now continue with the following fields: CUSTOMER ID AMOUNT DUE
Σ	Click to insert the Total line.
Total	Click the far-right corner of the Total cell of the CUSTOMER ID NUMBER column. A selection box of SQL aggregate functions appears (Figure 5.19).
Count	Click this option.
Total	Click the far-right corner of the Total cell of the AMOUNT DUE column. A selection box of SQL aggregate functions appears.
Sum	Click this option. Your QBE grid should now look like Figure 5.20.

Figure 5.20

The completed QBE grid for the SQL aggregate query.

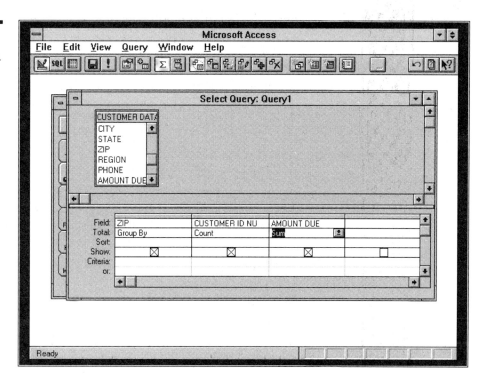

Figure 5.21

The dynaset for generating subtotals by zip code.

Number in each zip code

Total for each zip code

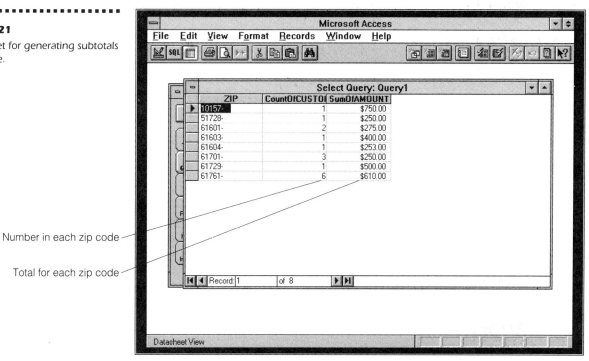

3. Run the query.

 Click to run the query. A dynaset like that shown in Figure 5.21 appears. This dynaset shows the zip-code number, the count of individuals in that zip code, and the subtotal of the AMOUNT DUE field for that zip code.

4. Save the query.

 Click to return to Design view.

 Click to invoke the Save As dialog box.

Type **Zip Code Total Query**   Enter the name of the query.

⌐Enter⌐   Save the query. Now, when you want to use this QBE query specification, just click that entry in the Queries sheet and then click the Design button.

 Double-click the control-menu button to return to the database window.

Hands-On Exercise: Generating Grand Totals

Assume that you want to generate a grand total as well as overall summary totals of records in the CUSTOMER DATA table. You should have the SALES database window active.

1. Activate the Queries sheet and start the build process.

 Click to invoke the Queries sheet of the Database window.

 Click to activate the New Query dialog box.

 Select to activate the Add Table dialog box.

CUSTOMER DATA   Select this file.

 Add this filename to the top of the Query Design window.

 Close the Add Table dialog box.

2. Use the double-click method of including field names for the customer ID and amount due fields. We will need one copy of the amount due field for each summary total to be generated. Since we want to generate a grand total value—an overall average—as well as find out the largest and smallest values, we will need four copies of the amount due field in the QBE grid.

CUSTOMER ID   Double-click this field name to include it in the QBE grid. Now double-click the AMOUNT DUE field four times so that there are four copies of this field in the QBE grid.

Σ   Click to insert the Total line.

Total   Click the far-right corner of the Total cell of the CUSTOMER ID NUMBER column. A selection box of SQL aggregate functions appears.

Count   Click this option.

Total	Click the far-right corner of the Total cell of the first AMOUNT DUE column. A selection box of SQL aggregate functions appears.
Sum	Click this option.
Total	Click the far-right corner of the Total cell of the second AMOUNT DUE column. A selection box of SQL aggregate functions appears.
Avg	Click this option.
Total	Click the far-right corner of the Total cell of the third AMOUNT DUE column. A selection box of SQL aggregate functions appears.
Min	Click this option.
➡	Click the scroll arrow of the horizontal scroll bar to view the fourth AMOUNT DUE column.
Total	Click the far-right corner of the Total cell of the fourth AMOUNT DUE column. A selection box of SQL aggregate functions appears.
Max	Click this option. Your SQL grid should now look like Figure 5.22.

3. Run the query.

!	Click to run the query. A dynaset like that shown in Figure 5.23 appears. This dynaset contains one row with each of the specified values in a field. The column name indicates which function is displayed.

Figure 5.22

The completed QBE grid for Grand Total Query.

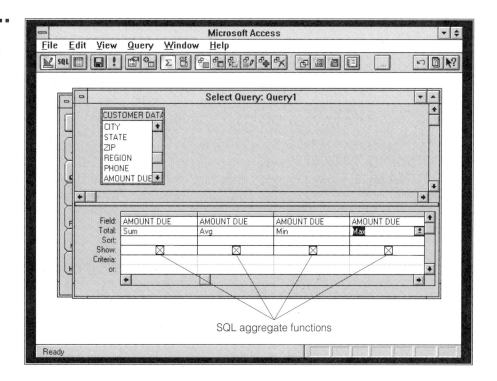

Figure 5.23

The dynaset for generating the summary totals.

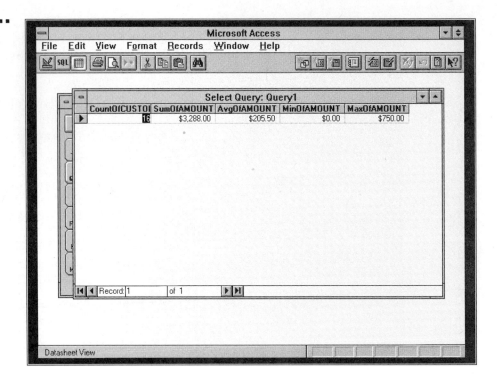

4. Save the query.

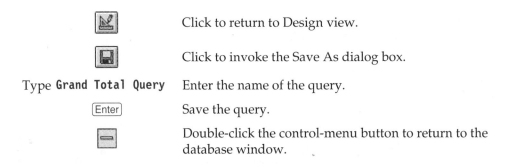

Click to return to Design view.

Click to invoke the Save As dialog box.

Type **Grand Total Query**   Enter the name of the query.

[Enter]   Save the query.

Double-click the control-menu button to return to the database window.

PERFORMING TABLE MAINTENANCE VIA QUERIES

Access makes use of queries to perform what is many times referred to as table or file maintenance. Table/file maintenance refers to making backup copies of a table, appending records to a table, deleting records from a table, and creating other tables from selected fields of a table. These tasks are accomplished via Query Wizards or by selecting a different query type from the Datasheet window.

CREATING BACKUPS AND OTHER TABLES

Access allows you to use the **Make-Table Query** dialog box to quickly create a complete or partial copy of a table. This new table can include all or selected fields of a table and, as such, provides an easy way of making a backup copy in the database of a table. This is easier than using DOS's BACKUP command to make a complete backup copy of the database and sending that to diskette. It is, however, somewhat dangerous because if anything happens to the database on disk, the original table along with its backup is also destroyed (remember, any table is simply a small part of an Access database).

If you want to make a table, you start out with the Select Query query type. At the Query Design window, click the Make-Table Query button on the toolbar. The Query Properties dialog box appears (Figure 5.24), prompting you to enter the name of the table to receive the fields and their data. Once the filename is specified, you indicate which fields are to be used in the new table (Figure 5.25). After you have indicated which fields are to be used, you can run the query.

Figure 5.24

The Query Properties dialog box for specifying the name of the table to receive the copy.

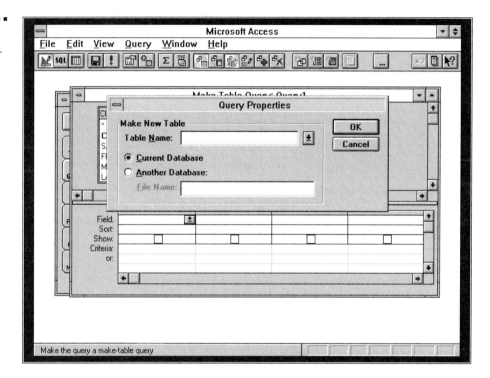

Figure 5.25

The Make-Table Query QBE grid.

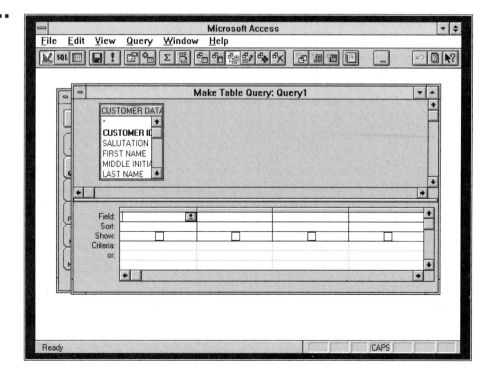

You now activate the database window, select the Table tab to activate the Tables sheet, and activate the CUSTOMER BACKUP table to bring up the Datasheet window displaying the table and its records. Once you have finished examining the table, close the Datasheet window and do not save the query to disk since it is no longer needed.

 Hands-On Exercise: Creating a Copy of the CUSTOMER DATA Table

You should have the SALES database window active.

1. Activate the Queries sheet and start the build process.

Query (icon)	Click to invoke the Queries sheet of the database window.
New	Click to activate the New Query dialog box.
New Query	Select to activate the Add Table dialog box.
CUSTOMER DATA	Select this file.
Add	Add this filename to the top of the Query Design window.
Close	Close the Add Table dialog box.

2. Change the default select query to a make-table query.

(icon)	Click to invoke the Query Properties dialog box (Figure 5.24).
Type **CUSTOMER BACKUP**	Enter the name of the file to receive the table copy.
(Enter)	Name the file. The Make Table Query label now appears in the Query Design window title bar (Figure 5.25).

3. Use the double-click method of including all field names at once in the QBE grid.

CUSTOMER DATA	Double-click the title bar of the selection box for the CUSTOMER DATA table and field names list box in the upper window of the Query Design window. All of the field names are now selected.
Drag and drop	Click the CUSTOMER ID NUMBER field and then use a drag-and-drop operation to drag the icon to the first Field cell of the QBE grid. Once the drag icon appears in the Field cell, release the mouse button. Your QBE grid should now look like Figure 5.26.

4. Create the table.

!	Click to run the query. A message box appears, indicating how many records (rows) will be copied to the new table (Figure 5.27).
OK	Create the table.

Figure 5.26

The completed QBE grid.

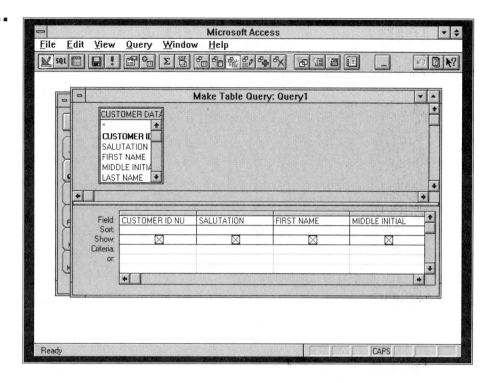

Figure 5.27

The message box indicating how many records will be added to the new table.

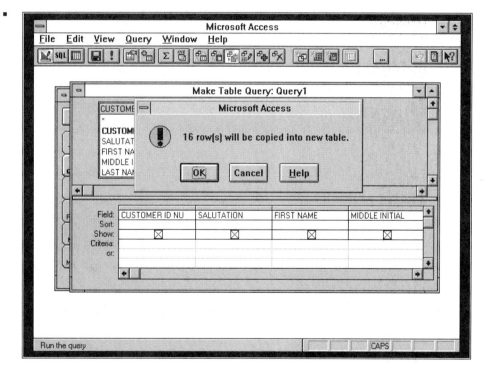

Figure 5.28

The CUSTOMER BACKUP table just created.

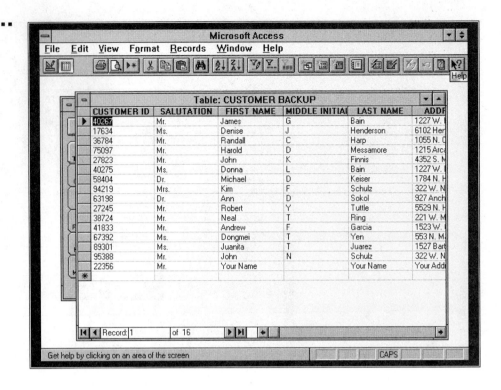

5. Close the query without saving it.

`—`	Double-click the control-menu button.
No	Do not save the query. You are returned to the database window.

6. Activate the newly created table.

Table	Click the Table tab to activate the Tables sheet.
CUSTOMER BACKUP	Double-click the filename to activate the Datasheet window. The table shown in Figure 5.28 should appear.
`—`	Close the table and return to the database window.

INCLUDING ONLY SELECTED FIELDS

Suppose that you want to allow another user access to selected data without having to worry about that individual accessing fields that contain sensitive information. You can accomplish this by creating a new table that has only those fields that you want another user to see. For example, in a merge operation, another user would need only such data as the salutation, first- and last-name, address, city, state, and zip fields.

Hands-On Exercise: Including Selected Fields

You should have the SALES database window active.

　1. Activate the Queries sheet and start the build process.

　Click to invoke the Queries sheet of the database window.

　Click to activate the New Query dialog box.

　Select to activate the Add Table dialog box.

CUSTOMER DATA　Select this file.

　Add this filename to the top of the Query Design window.

　Close the Add Table dialog box.

　2. Change the default select query to a make-table query.

　Click to invoke the Query Properties dialog box.

Type NAME AND ADDRESS DATA　Enter the name of the file to receive the table copy.

　Name the file. The Make Table Query label now appears in the Query Design window title bar.

　3. Use the double-click method of including all individual field names at once in the QBE grid.

SALUTATION　Double-click this field name from the CUSTOMER DATA list box to include the field name in the QBE grid. Continue with the following fields:

　　　FIRST NAME
　　　LAST NAME
　　　ADDRESS
　　　CITY
　　　STATE
　　　ZIP

Your QBE grid should now look like Figure 5.29.

　4. Create the table.

　Click to run the query. A message box appears, indicating how many records will be copied to the new table (Figure 5.27).

　Create the table.

Figure 5.29

The completed QBE grid for creating the NAME AND ADDRESS DATA table.

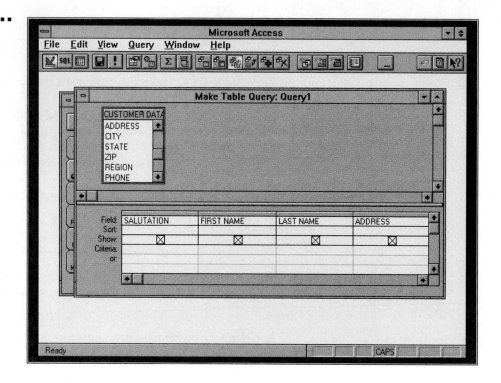

5. Close the query without saving it.

 Double-click the control-menu button.

 Do not save the query. You are now returned to the database window.

6. Activate the newly created table.

 Click the Table tab to activate the Tables sheet.

NAME AND ADDRESS DATA Double-click the filename to activate the Datasheet window. The table shown in Figure 5.30 should appear. The column widths in the datasheet have been adjusted to display all fields of each record.

 Close the table and return to the Database window.

VIEWING DATA BY LINKING TABLES

Assume that you have an inventory application that has a master table containing every inventory item as its inventory stock information. You also have an inventory transaction table that keeps track of the number of items and the dates of transactions. In addition, you have a customer table and supplier table. Your objective is to link these four tables so reports or queries for information from all tables can be contained, for example, in one report. The Query feature of Access easily does this. You can create a query to display or print records from more than one table.

Figure 5.30

The NAME AND ADDRESS DATA table displayed with the column widths adjusted.

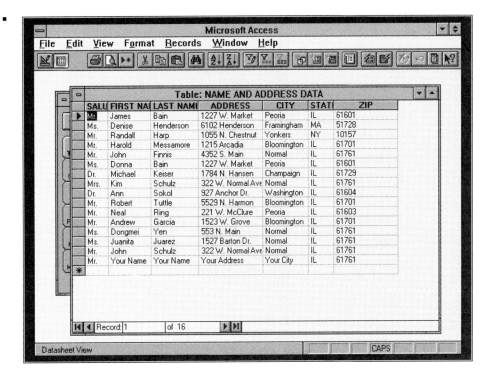

Figure 5.31

The structure of the INVENTORY DATA table.

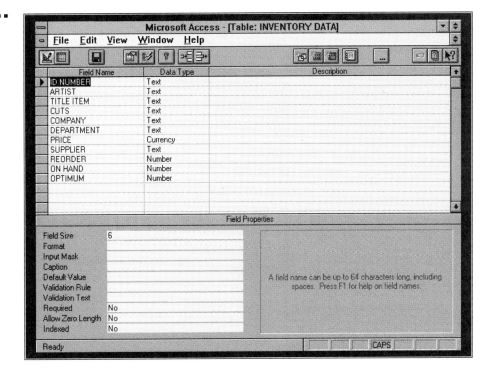

• • • • • • • • • • • • • • • • • • • •

Figure 5.32

The structure of the INVENTORY TRANSACTIONS table.

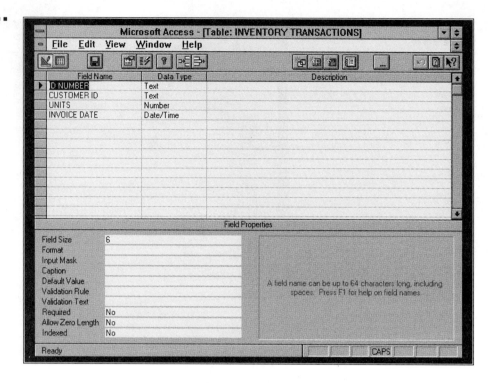

• • • • • • • • • • • • • • • • • • • •

Figure 5.33

The structure of the CUSTOMER DATA table.

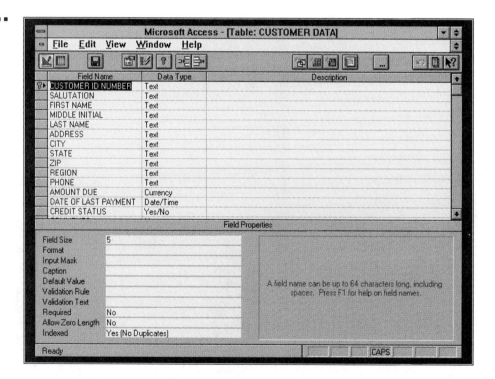

The first database table used in this application is the INVENTORY DATA master table. Figure 5.31 shows the structure of this table. The second database table in this application is the INVENTORY TRANSACTIONS transaction table. Figure 5.32 shows the structure of the INVENTORY TRANSACTIONS table. The CUSTOMER DATA and SUPPLIER DATA table structures are shown in Figures 5.33 and 5.34, respectively.

Figure 5.34

The structure of the SUPPLIER DATA table.

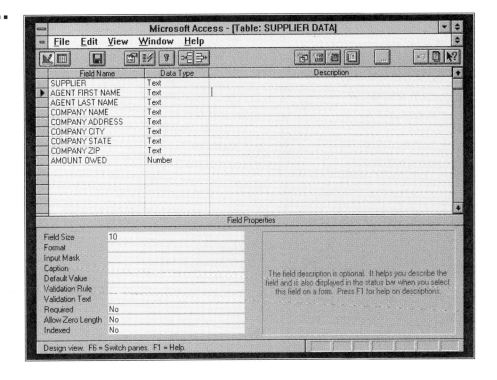

Figure 5.35

Multiple tables specified in a select query operation.

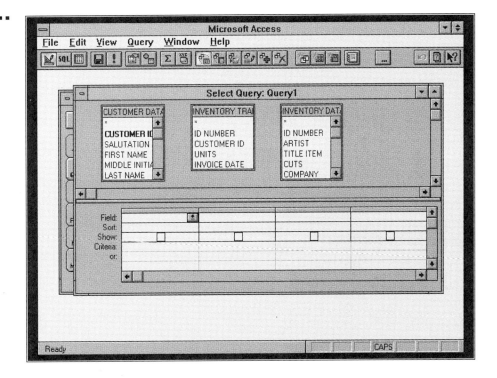

Tables to be linked must appear in the window above the QBE grid (Figure 5.35).

One limitation imposed by Access is that any two tables to be related or joined must share a **common field**. In this case, the ID number field is the common field between the INVENTORY TRANSACTIONS and INVENTORY DATA tables. It is this field that lets Access link the two tables and display

■■■■■■■■■■■■■■■■■■■■

Figure 5.36

The CUSTOMER DATA and INVENTORY TRANSACTIONS table linked via the customer ID field.

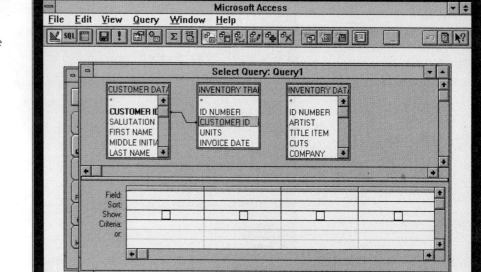

information from both tables in one line of a display or report. The supplier field is used to link the INVENTORY DATA and SUPPLIER DATA tables. These two examples show the same named field linking tables. Using the same name in two tables allows you to make a linking application easier to understand but is not required by Access. For example, we will also be using the field named customer ID number of the CUSTOMER DATA table to link with the INVENTORY TRANSACTIONS table via the customer ID field.

Linking tables together using Access is accomplished using a graphical approach. The field being used in one table to link to another table is clicked and then dragged to the corresponding field in another table in the upper window of the Query Design window (Figure 5.36). Once the tables have been linked, you can include any fields from any table in the query QBE grid.

 Hands-On Exercise: Linking the Four Tables

You should have the SALES database window active.

1. Build a new query and add the four tables.

▲	Maximize the database window. (Do this now so there'll be room for all of the tables above the QBE grid.)
Query	Click to invoke the Queries sheet of the database window.
New	Click to activate the New Query dialog box.
New Query	Select to activate the Add Table dialog box.
CUSTOMER DATA	Select this file.

Figure 5.37

The four tables to be linked together.

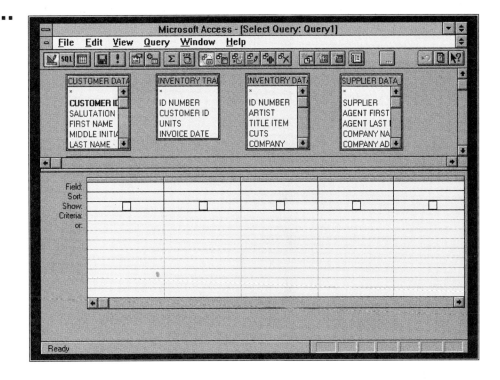

		Add this filename to the top of the Query Design window.
INVENTORY TRANSACTIONS		Select this file.
	Add	Add this filename to the top of the Query Design window.
INVENTORY DATA		Select this file.
	Add	Add this filename to the top of the Query Design window.
SUPPLIER DATA		Select this file.
	Add	Add this filename to the top of the Query Design window.
	Close	Close the Add Table dialog box. Your screen should look like Figure 5.37.

HINTS/HAZARDS

If you inadvertently leave out a table, you can add it to the query by issuing the command sequence Query, Add Table. The Add Table dialog box appears, and the desired table can be added to the query specification.

Figure 5.38

The tables linked via the customer ID number and customer ID fields.

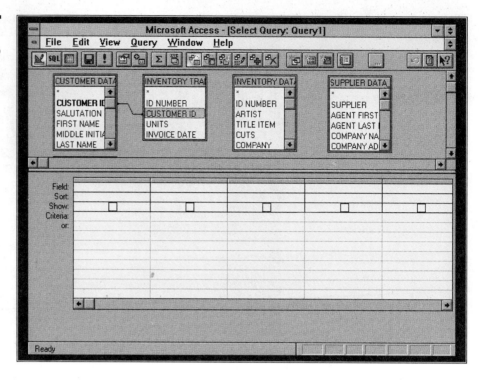

2. Link the tables based on the common fields.

Drag   Drag the CUSTOMER ID NUMBER field of the CUSTOMER DATA table to the CUSTOMER ID field of the INVENTORY TRANSACTIONS table. A line should now link the fields of the two tables (Figure 5.38).

Drag   Drag the ID NUMBER field of the INVENTORY TRANSACTIONS table to the ID NUMBER field of the INVENTORY DATA table. A line should now link the fields of the two tables.

Drag   Drag the SUPPLIER field of the INVENTORY DATA table to the SUPPLIER field of the SUPPLIER DATA table. A line should now link the fields of the two tables. Your screen should now look like the top of Figure 5.39.

3. Include fields from the CUSTOMER DATA table.

FIRST NAME	Double-click this field.
LAST NAME	Double-click this field.

4. Include fields from the INVENTORY DATA table.

ARTIST	Double-click this field.
TITLE ITEM	Double-click this field.
PRICE	Double-click this field.

5. Include fields from the INVENTORY TRANSACTIONS table.

UNITS	Double-click this field.

Figure 5.39

The completed QBE grid for the multitable link.

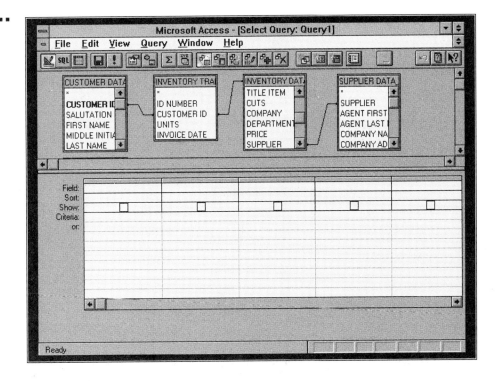

6. Include fields from the SUPPLIER DATA table.

COMPANY NAME   Double-click this field. Your Query Design window should now look like Figure 5.39.

HINTS/HAZARDS   If you forget to include a field in the QBE grid, drag it until your cursor is on the field that's just to the right of where you want the new field to go. When the mouse button is released, Access inserts the field to the left of the field in which the pointer resided.

7. Display the dynaset for the query.

[!]   The dynaset of the linked tables appears in the Datasheet window (Figure 5.40).

8. Save the query.

[icon]   Click to return to Design view.

[≑]   Restore the Query Design window.

File   Open the File menu.

Save   Invoke the Save As dialog box.

Figure 5.40

The dynaset generated via the
linked tables.

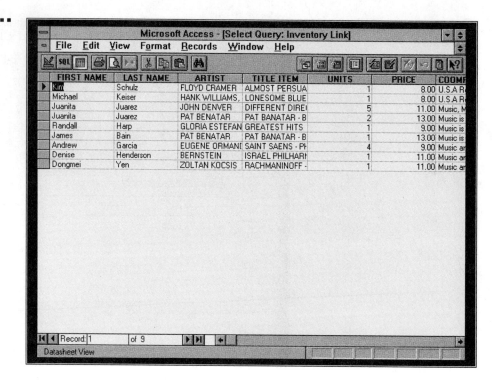

FIRST NAME	LAST NAME	ARTIST	TITLE ITEM	UNITS	PRICE	COOMF
Kim	Schulz	FLOYD CRAMER	ALMOST PERSUA	1	8.00	U.S.A R
Michael	Keiser	HANK WILLIAMS,	LONESOME BLUE	1	8.00	U.S.A R
Juanita	Juarez	JOHN DENVER	DIFFERENT DIRE	5	11.00	Music, M
Juanita	Juarez	PAT BENATAR	PAT BANATAR - B	2	13.00	Music is
Randall	Harp	GLORIA ESTEFAN	GREATEST HITS	1	9.00	Music is
James	Bain	PAT BENATAR	PAT BANATAR - B	1	13.00	Music is
Andrew	Garcia	EUGENE ORMANI	SAINT SAENS - PI	4	9.00	Music an
Denise	Henderson	BERNSTEIN	ISRAEL PHILHARI	1	11.00	Music an
Dongmei	Yen	ZOLTAN KOCSIS	RACHMANINOFF -	1	11.00	Music an

Type **Inventory Link**   Enter the name of the query.

 [Enter]   Save the query.

   Double-click the control-menu button to return to the database window.

INCLUDING CALCULATIONS

You are now going to add an **extension field** that Access automatically calculates for each record, multiplying the price field contents by the units field contents.

Hands-On Exercise: Creating the Extension Field

1. Begin the process of adding the field.

Inventory Link   Click the Inventory Link query in the Queries sheet of the database window.

 Design   Click the Design button. The design for this query is now displayed.

   Maximize the Query Design window.

2. Delete the company name column.

Point and click   Position the pointer in the thin gray line above the COMPANY NAME entry of the QBE grid. The pointer should turn into ↓. Click the pointer to select the entire column.

[Del]   Delete the field.

Figure 5.41

The QBE grid with the inserted extension field.

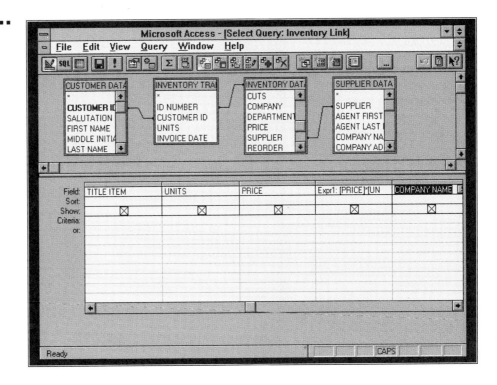

3. Enter the formula in the Field cell.

Type **[PRICE]*[UNITS]**   Enter the formula.

4. Rebuild the company name from the SUPPLIER DATA list box.

COMPANY NAME   Double-click this entry. Your QBE grid should now look like Figure 5.41.

5. Run the query.

    After resizing fields, you should now see a screen like Figure 5.42. Notice that the extension field has the column heading of "Expr1" and that there are no decimal positions in the calculated result. In the following steps we are going to change this.

6. Return to the Query Design window.

    Click to return to Design view.

Expr1:   Click the cell with the formula.

Shift + F2   Issue the Zoom command to display the formula (Figure 5.43).

7. Change the formula to display the label EXTENSION and display the numbers in dollars-and-cents format.

Home   Position to the beginning of the formula.

Figure 5.42

The dynaset with the resized fields showing the extension field.

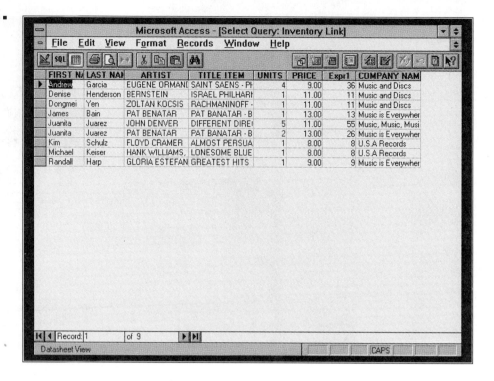

Figure 5.43

The Zoom dialog box for the query calculation.

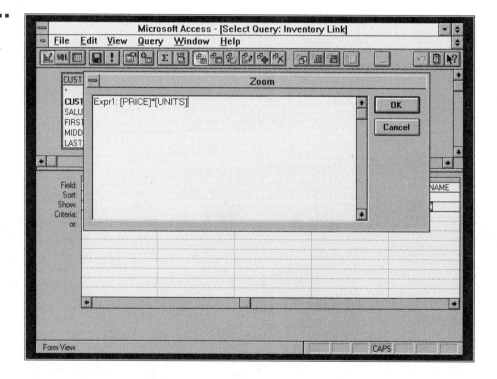

Del (5 times)	Delete the Expr1 portion of the formula. Be certain to leave the colon.
Type **EXTENSION**	Enter the new label.
→	Press the right arrow to move past the colon.

Figure 5.44

The dynasheet with the new label and numeric display format.

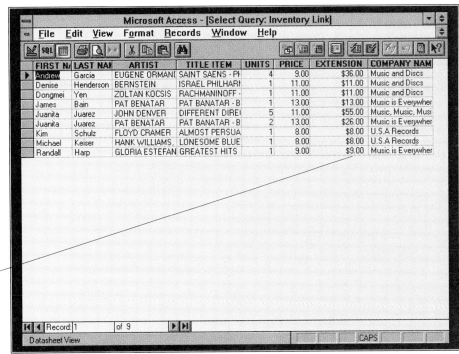

Changed column with currency display

8. Enter the currency function around the rest of the formula to display the extension as dollars and cents.

Type **CCUR(**	Enter the first part of the function.
[End]	Go to the end of the formula.
Type **)**	Finish the formula.
[Enter]	Close the Zoom dialog box.

9. Run the query.

| | If you resize the EXTENSION column, you should see a dynasheet like that shown in Figure 5.44. |

10. Save the table using a new name.

	Click to return to Design view.
	Restore the Query Design window.
File	Open the File menu.
Save As...	Invoke the Save As dialog box.
Type **Inventory Link Calc**	Enter the new query name.
[Enter]	Save the query.
	Double-click the control-menu button to return to the database window.

PERFORMING A TABLE UPDATE USING A QUERY

You can use a query involving linked tables to update the data in the master or **parent table**. For example, you can use the units data from the INVENTORY TRANSACTIONS table to update the on-hand field of the INVENTORY DATA table. In order to accomplish this, however, the on-hand field must be in the QBE grid. Once this is accomplished, use the Query, Update, Run command to specify the table update. Access displays a dialog box indicating the number of records that will be updated. Once the update is accomplished, the information in the INVENTORY TRANSACTIONS table must be placed in a history table or erased from that table (you don't want to perform an update using the same data twice).

Before you issue the **Update command**, you should verify that the INVENTORY DATA table has the same values as those shown in Figure 5.45. To get your table to look like the figure, select the columns between the artist and on-hand fields and use the Format, Hide Columns command to suppress their display.

Hands-On Exercise: Performing an Update Using a Query

1. Build a new select query and add the inventory tables.

Query	Click to invoke the Queries sheet of the database window.
New	Click to activate the New Query dialog box.
New Query	Select to activate the Add Table dialog box.
INVENTORY DATA	Select this file.
Add	Add this filename to the top of the Query Design window.
INVENTORY TRANSACTIONS	Select this file.

Figure 5.45

The INVENTORY DATA table before the update is performed.

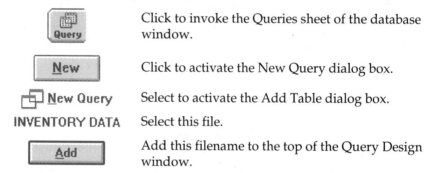

Figure 5.46

The completed Query Design
window for the select query.

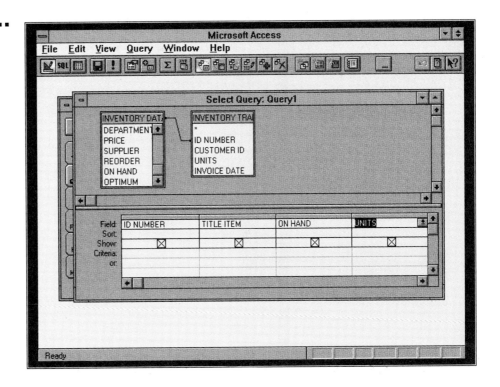

Add	Add this filename to the top of the Query Design window.	
Close	Close the Add Table dialog box.	

2. Link the tables based on the common fields.

Drag — Drag the ID NUMBER field of the INVENTORY TRANSACTIONS table to the ID NUMBER field of the INVENTORY DATA table. A line should now link the fields of the two tables (Figure 5.46).

3. Include fields from the INVENTORY DATA table.

ID NUMBER — Double-click this field.

ARTIST — Double-click this field.

ON HAND — Double-click this field.

4. Include the field from the INVENTORY TRANSACTIONS table.

UNITS — Double-click this field. Your Query Design window should now look like Figure 5.46.

5. Run the select query.

! — Display the records in the dynaset (Figure 5.47).

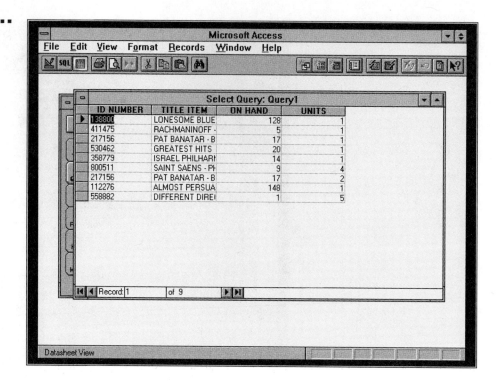

Figure 5.47

The records of the select query
displayed in the dynaset.

6. Create the update query.

          Return to Design view.

Query   Open the Query menu.

Update   Select this option. The Update To row has now been
                   added to the QBE grid (Figure 5.48).

7. Add the query expression.

Type [ON HAND]-[UNITS]   In the Update To cell of the ON HAND column of the
                          QBE grid, enter the update formula. This formula will
                          result in the current contents of the ON HAND field
                          being reduced by the amount in the UNITS field. Be sure
                          to include the brackets and a space in the ON HAND
                          field name. Your QBE grid should now look like
                          Figure 5.48.

8. Perform the update.

          Click to invoke the dialog box shown in Figure 5.49,
                   indicating how many records will be changed in the
                   update.

Figure 5.48

The QBE grid with the inserted Update To row and the update formula entered.

Row added

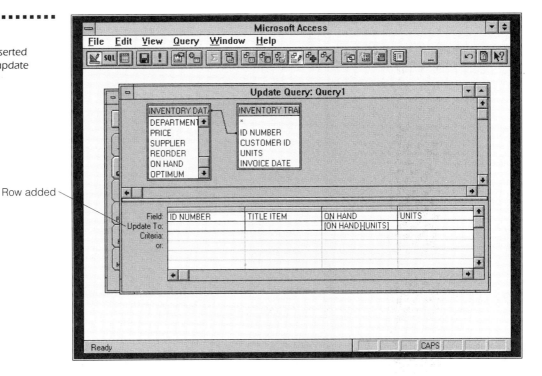

Figure 5.49

The dialog box indicating how many rows (records) will be changed in the update.

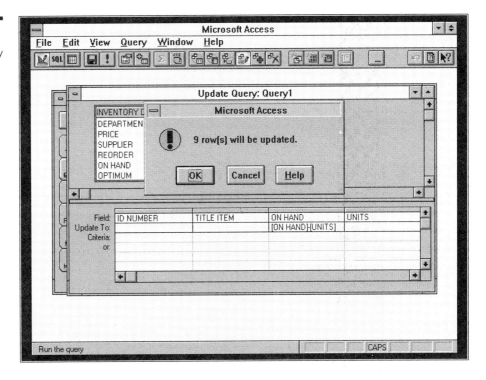

Figure 5.50

The dialog box indicating an
incorrectly named field.

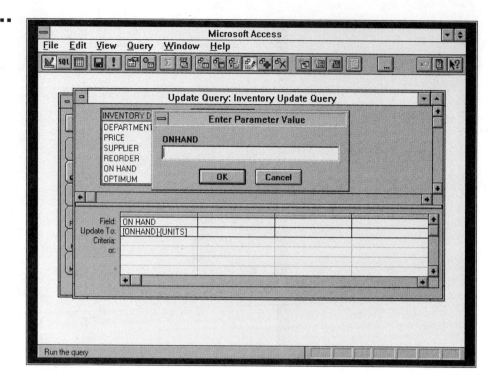

HINTS/HAZARDS

If you inadvertently enter the field name incorrectly, Access displays a dialog box like that shown in Figure 5.50. This means that Access does not know what to do with the ONHAND field and wants you to give it some direction. Of course, in such a situation, you would select the Cancel button and make the correction. If you select OK, Access will zero out any fields in the specified column of the QBE grid (the ON HAND field).

    Perform the update. The records in the INVENTORY DATA table have now been changed.

9. Save the update query and view the INVENTORY DATA table to verify the changes.

    Click to invoke the Save As dialog box.

Type **Inventory Update Query**   Enter the name of the query.

[Enter]   Save the query.

    Double-click the control-menu button of the Query Design window. Notice that your update query has a different icon than the other queries listed.

10. View the updated INVENTORY DATA table.

Table   Click the Table tab of the database window to activate the Tables sheet.

Figure 5.51

The updated INVENTORY DATA table.

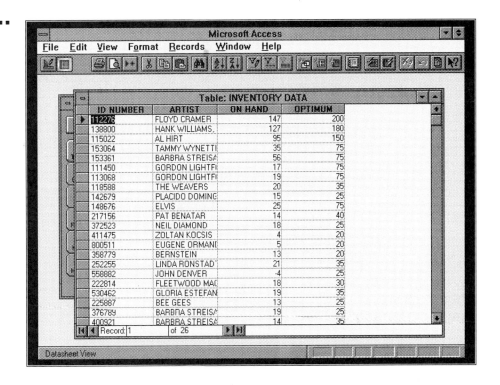

INVENTORY DATA   Double-click to activate the table in the Datasheet window. Compare this listing (Figure 5.51) with that shown in Figure 5.45. Notice that the on-hand entries have been changed for the records shown in Figure 5.47.

HINTS/HAZARDS

In a real-life situation, you would now append the records in the INVENTORY TRANSACTIONS table to a year-to-date history table. Such a table details all of the purchases for a business for the current year. This data can then be used to evaluate purchase trends as well as provide an audit trail.

CHAPTER REVIEW

The Access 2.0 package lets you create simple and complex queries via Query Wizards or at the Query Design window. Because many keystrokes are required, frequently used queries should be saved to a query specification which can then be accessed via the Queries sheet of the database window.

When Access executes a query, the result is displayed in a dynaset. This dynaset looks like the Datasheet window but has the title bar "Select Query: Query1". Only those records that match the selection criteria are displayed in the dynasheet.

Access also lets you link or relate tables via common fields. Once the table link has been established, you can display or print fields from different tables. When Access displays the fields/records of a query, you can edit any fields that are displayed or used to set up the relation. The underlying table data is automatically updated by Access.

You can also include calculations in a query. The calculation can comprise fields from related tables. It can also contain numeric constants. If you want summary totals, Access can generate them using SQL aggregate functions, which are made available to the QBE grid by clicking the Totals button on the toolbar.

The make-table action query can be used to create a temporary backup of a table or to include selected fields from one table in another table. Use the make-table query to make a copy of a table if you want to test the effects of a command on a table and you want to be able to quickly restore the original values to the table after it has been changed.

The Update command can also be used at the Query Design window to use information from a field of one table to update the contents of the same field in another table. The tables must be linked by a common field.

KEY TERMS AND CONCEPTS

action query
Archive Query
common field
Criteria cell
Crosstab Query
dynaset
dynaset table
extension field
Field cell
Find Duplicates Query
Find Unmatched Query
logical operator
make-table query
parent table
Queries sheet

query
Query By Example (QBE) grid
Query Wizards
relational operator
result set
Run button
select query
Select Query window
Show cell
Sort cell
SQL aggregate functions
Update command
wildcard
Zoom command

CHAPTER QUIZ

Multiple Choice

1. Which of the following statements about an Access dynaset table is true:
   a. A dynaset is shown as read-only.
   b. A dynaset is actually a datasheet showing all records of a table.
   c. A dynaset contains fields that meet the specified criteria which can be assembled from several linked tables.
   d. None of the above statements is true.

2. Which of the following definitely cannot be used against a linked dynaset table?
   a. SQL aggregate functions
   b. report
   c. make-table
   d. calculation
   e. All of the above can all be used.

3. Which of the following database window sheets lets you link tables?
   a. Queries
   b. Tables
   c. Forms
   d. Macros

4. Which of the following commands lets you update a field of linked tables?
   a. Update
   b. Modify Command
   c. Set Query
   d. Replace Records

5. An extension field can be viewed by using which of the following commands?
   a. Build Expression
   b. Zoom command
   c. Edit command
   d. none of the above

True/False

6. A make-table query is automatically erased by Access after it executes.

7. The entries that actually control how a query executes appear in the QBE grid of the Query Design window.

8. Access requires that you include only one copy of a numeric field in the QBE grid to generate the SUM, AVG, and MAX values for a dynaset.

9. Linking tables requires that both tables share one common field.

10. Only two tables can be linked using the linking capability of Access.

Answers

1. c   2. e   3. a   4. a   5. b   6. t   7. t   8. f   9. t   10. f

Exercises

1. A complex query typically uses one or more relational operators as well as one or more _____ operators.

2. A _____ is a set of instructions that specifies how Access should organize or change your data.

3. The _____ sheet of the database window allows you to access or build a query.

4. The logical operators are _____ , _____ , and _____ .

5. The output of a query is referred to as a _____ table.

6. Before data in tables can be linked, both tables must have a _____ field.

7. The cell of the QBE grid that determines which records are to be included in a query is the _____ cell.

8. An extension field has the title of _____ placed as the heading of the dynaset.

9. The _____ cell of the QBE grid allows you to indicate to Access which fields are to be included in a dynaset.

10. The query wildcards are _____ and _____.

11. The _____ button of the Query Design window toolbar is clicked to create an Access table.

12. The _____ operator is used to find any occurrences of regions 2 through 5 in a query.

13. The _____ cell of the QBE grid allows you to determine the order of the records in the dynaset.

14. Clicking the Totals button inserts a _____ row in the QBE grid.

15. The Show cell must contain a(n) _____ to display a field in the dynaset.

16. Clicking the _____ button causes the query to be executed and the dynaset generated.

17. Access automatically places _____ _____ around text used in a Criteria cell.

18. Use SQL aggregate _____ for generating statistics about numeric fields of an Access dynaset.

19. The _____ query automatically erases the query from the Queries sheet when it is run.

20. Access graphically shows which fields are used to link files by displaying a _____ between the table fields.

COMPUTER EXERCISES

The PAYTRANS and PAYMAST tables will be used for these exercises. The structure of the PAYTRANS table is shown in Figure 5.52, and the structure of the PAYMAST table is shown in Figure 5.53.

1. Create a query specification that displays a dynaset like that shown in Figure 5.54. Use this specification for finding out the answers to the queries below. Be sure to print each dynaset that you generate.
   a. Display those employees in Department 15.
   b. Display those employees with a PAY RATE > $9.00.
   c. Display those employees with a YTD GROSS > $5,000.
   d. Create a query that shows the count of all employees, the grand total YTD GROSS, and the average YTD GROSS.

Figure 5.52

The structure of the PAYTRANS table.

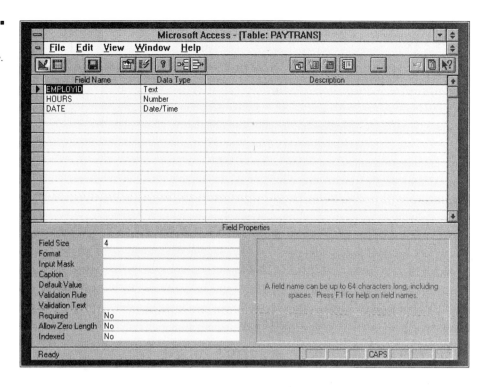

Figure 5.53

The structure of the PAYMAST table.

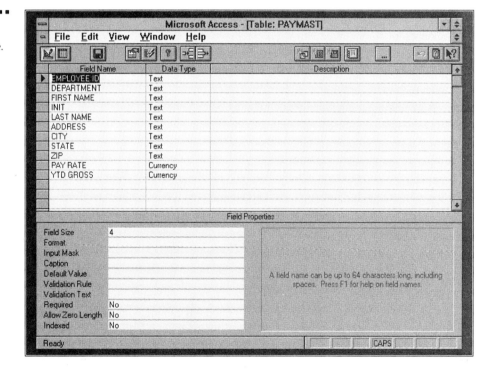

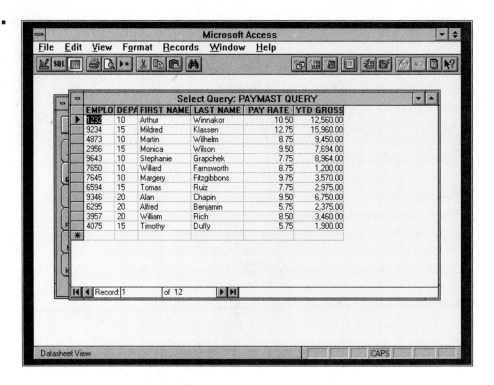

2. Create a make-table query that will incorporate the following fields in a PAYROLL NAME AND ADDRESS table.

   ```
   FIRST NAME
   LAST NAME
   ADDRESS
   CITY
   STATE
   ZIP
   ```

3. Create a query that links the PAYMAST and PAYTRANS tables so that the HOURS field from the PAYTRANS table and the calculated GROSS PAY field appears between the PAY RATE and YTD GROSS columns of the dynaset displayed in Figure 5.54. Print the dynaset.

4. In this exercise you will perform the update processing for a payroll application. You will use two tables from the PROJECTS database, PAYMAST and PAYTRANS. The PAYTRANS table is the transaction table containing time-card information.

   The EMPLOYID field contains the employee identification number. Use this number to locate the corresponding record in the PAYMAST table for the update. The HOURS field contains the number of hours this employee has worked this period. The DATE field contains the period end date. The PAYMAST table is the master table containing information about each employee.

   The EMPLOYID field is the field that matches with the PAYTRANS record. When the EMPLOYID field of the transaction table matches with the EMPLOYID field of the PAYMAST table, you can perform a payroll update. The FIRST NAME and LAST NAME fields contain the name for this employee. The PAY RATE field contains the hourly rate of pay. The rate of pay is multiplied by the HOURS field to obtain the gross pay.

Once the gross pay has been calculated, add it to the YTD GROSS field to get the new YTD GROSS figure.

Edit the record with the 4456 ID number. Place your name in this record and enter an appropriate hourly rate and year-to-date gross pay information.

Print the updated PAYMAST table.

5. Use a query table to set up the following query for the CUSTOMER DATA table: ZIP = 61761 and AMOUNT > 50 OR CITY = BLOOMINGTON. Include name and address data in the query. Print the dynaset.

6. This exercise requires the INVENTORY DATA and SUPPLIER DATA tables. Create a query that combines the two tables using the SUPPLIER field as the common field. Print the dynaset.

7. This exercise requires the ALUMNI table. Create a query that limits the records selected to those that are in the Dean's Circle. Print the dynaset. Save the query as ALUMNI DEAN.

6

CREATING
INPUT FORMS
AND MACROS

CHAPTER OBJECTIVES

After completing this chapter, you should be able to

- **Use Access to build special data-entry screens**

- **Use the Form Wizards to build a form**

- **Customize your own form**

- **Create an Access macro**

- **Add command buttons to a form**

FORMS

Database applications have one common problem: The paper form that is the source of the data does not resemble the screen used when entering the data. For example, the Access Datasheet window shows the records and fields in a tabular format. Field names are often cryptic notations that give a user little indication of what should be typed in each field. Another problem that Access has is if the record contains a significant number of fields, it is difficult to display more than a few onscreen at one time.

Access solves this problem by letting you create a customized data-entry form that is similar to that of the source document. Figure 6.1 shows one such form.

The Access **Form Wizards** make this task even easier by prompting you through five fairly simple steps and then quickly generating the form for you. The New Form dialog box (Figure 6.2) is activated when you click the New command button with the Forms sheet displayed in the database window. This dialog box requires that you select a table from a selection box like that used in generating reports. Once the table is selected, you indicate how the form is to be generated—manually or by using Form Wizards.

When the Form Wizards button is selected, Access prompts you on the style of form (Figure 6.3). This dialog box allows you to select a form type from those outlined in Table 6.1.

Once the form type is selected, Access displays a dialog box like that shown in Figure 6.4, prompting you on which fields to include in the form. To select all fields, press the [>>] button and then the Next button to progress to the next dialog box.

This field specification dialog box has two list boxes—Available fields and Field order on form—with which you indicate the fields to be included in the form. Use the buttons for selecting fields. The [>] button takes the selected field and includes it in the form. As you click this button, the field is moved to the Field order on form list box on the right.

The [>>] button selects and moves all the fields from the Available fields list box to the list box on the right.

Figure 6.1

Data-entry form created for the CUSTOMER DATA table.

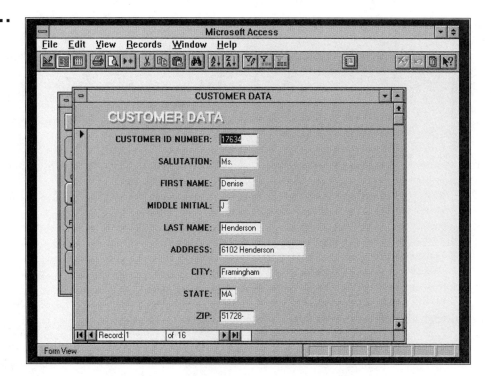

Figure 6.2

The New Form dialog box for specifying the table to be used and how the form is to be generated.

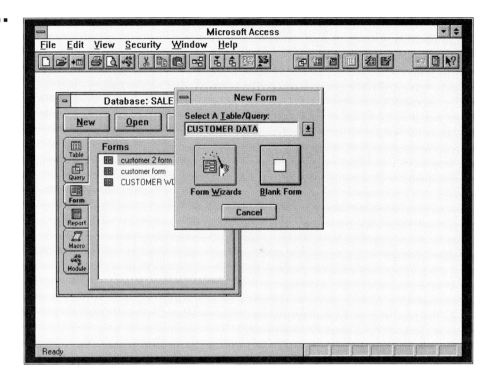

Figure 6.3

The Form Wizard dialog box for specifying which type of Form Wizard to use.

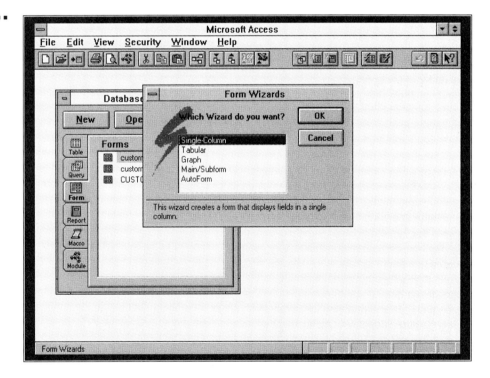

The [<] button deselects the highlighted field in the Field order on form list box and moves it back to the Available fields list box.

The [<<] button deselects all the fields in the list box on the right and moves them back to the Available fields list box.

The next Form Wizard dialog box prompts you for the type of field box display to be used in the form (Figure 6.5). As the style is selected, the sample portion of the dialog box shows how the form will appear.

Figure 6.4

The Form Wizard dialog box for specifying which table fields to use.

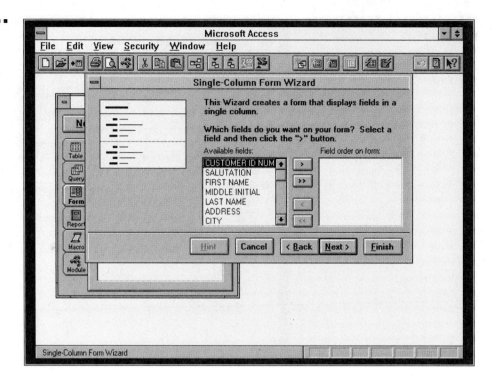

Figure 6.5

The Form Wizard dialog box for specifying which style to use.

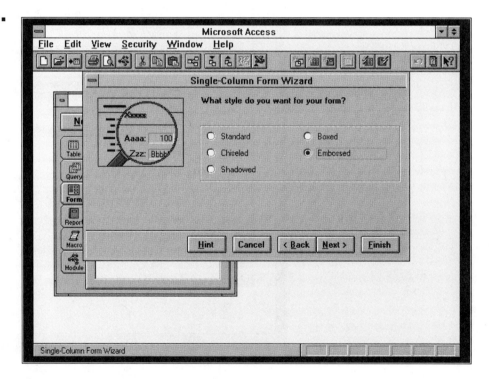

The last dialog box (Figure 6.6) is for indicating the title of the form. Unless you change it, the table name is used. Click the Finish button to assemble the form and display it to the screen with the table data present (Figure 6.1). The name of the table is in the header portion of the form. The detail portion of the form contains the field name and the contents of the field.

This ability to automate the forms generation process greatly eases the task of creating a form. The underlying form specifications are shown in Figure 6.7.

Figure 6.6

The Form Wizard dialog box for specifying the form title.

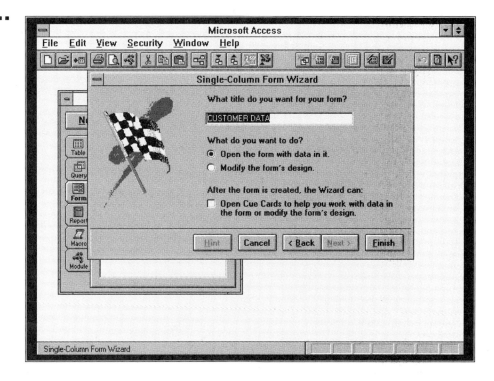

Figure 6.7

The Form Design window showing the underlying specifications used in creating the form.

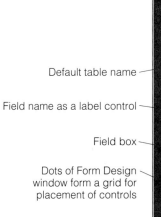

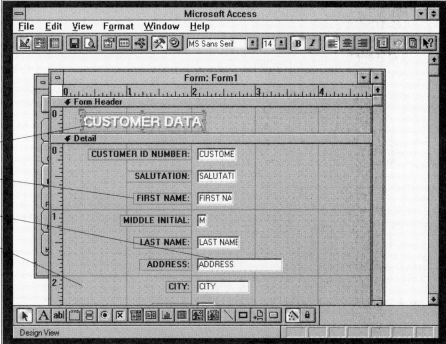

Default table name

Field name as a label control

Field box

Dots of Form Design window form a grid for placement of controls

Once you have generated a basic form, you can use it as a jumping off point to design your own form. You can choose which fields to include in the form and display additional descriptive data onscreen. You can also add additional **controls** that allow you to add many Windows-like features such as text, data fields, text boxes, list boxes, radio buttons, command buttons, or any other item that might appear on a form.

Table 6.1   *Form Types of the Form Wizards*

Form Type	Characteristics
Single-Column	Places all form fields in one column as text, and the contents of each field in a text box.
Tabular	Creates a form that has each record on one row, similar to the Datasheet window display.
Graph	Creates a form that incorporates a graph.
Main/Subform	Creates a form that contains another form.
AutoForm	Places all form fields in one column as text, and the contents of each field in a text box like the Single-Column form type. All subsequent dialog boxes are bypassed, and the form is created automatically.

Once you have created a form, you can use it to enter new records, delete records, or change existing records in a database. To enter new data or to display existing data, the forms are activated via the Forms sheet of the database window.

Figure 6.7 shows the two basic elements of the Form Design window: descriptive data (labels and titles) and **field boxes**.

CREATING A FORM USING THE FORM WIZARDS

This section introduces you to the use of the Form Wizards. As you will see, generating a form via the Form Wizards is a straightforward task that requires you to make some decisions, but Access does most of the work.

 Hands-On Exercise: Using the Form Wizards

1. Start the form design session. You should have the SALES database window active.

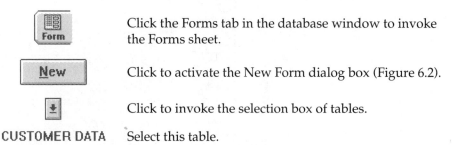

Click the Forms tab in the database window to invoke the Forms sheet.

Click to activate the New Form dialog box (Figure 6.2).

Click to invoke the selection box of tables.

CUSTOMER DATA   Select this table.

2. Select the type of form and build it.

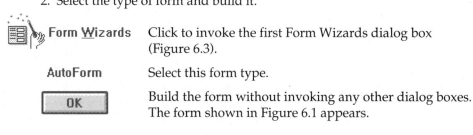

Click to invoke the first Form Wizards dialog box (Figure 6.3).

AutoForm   Select this form type.

Build the form without invoking any other dialog boxes. The form shown in Figure 6.1 appears.

3. View the form in the Form Design window to see the specifications used in displaying the form to the screen.

    Click to invoke the Form Design window (Figure 6.7).

4. Save the form.

    Click to invoke the Save As dialog box.

Type **CUSTOMER COLUMN**   Enter the name of the form.

Enter   Save the form.

—   Double-click the control-menu button of the Form Design window to return to the Forms sheet of the database window. The CUSTOMER COLUMN entry for this form should now be visible.

5. Invoke the form.

CUSTOMER COLUMN   Click the form name.

Open   The form appears onscreen (Figure 6.1).

▲   Maximize the Form Design window. Your screen should look like Figure 6.8.

Let's spend a moment examining exactly what Access has accomplished by creating the form design shown in Figure 6.7. The name of the table has

Figure 6.8
The CUSTOMER COLUMN form used to display the CUSTOMER DATA table.

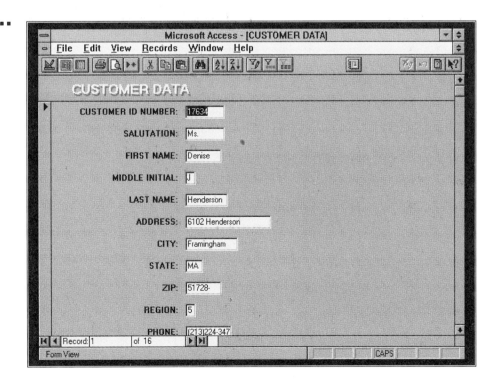

Figure 6.9

The controls added to the comments field.

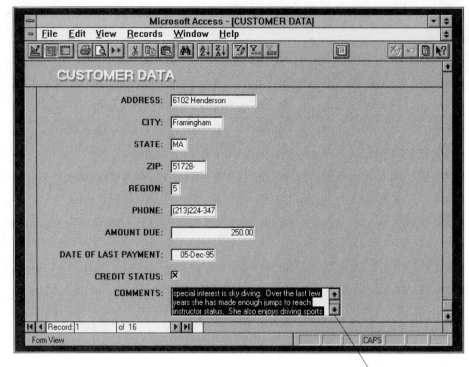

Access control

been placed in the form header. The field names have been positioned along the left side of the form specification. The field boxes are aligned in a column. Access has added a control to the comments field (Figure 6.9). The arrows allow you to scroll through text in the memo field. The credit status field has been entered so that an × represents a "Y" in the credit status field when it is clicked with a mouse.

Access has also made some changes to the toolbar. Clicking the Search button for a specific record in this table invokes the Find dialog box shown in Figure 6.10. The New Record button permits you to add records to the table using the form. The Print button allows you to send the information in the active window to the printer.

Like other windows in Access, the speedbar at the bottom of the Forms Design window contains the pointer location to allow you to track your location in the database table.

6. Use the speedbar to view records in the table and then enter a record.

▶❙	Click to position to the last record in the table. The John Schulz record should now be displayed.
◀	Click to position to the previous record in the table. The Kim Schultz record should now be displayed.
❙◀	Click to position to the first record in the table. The Denise Henderson record should now be displayed.
Click	Place the insertion point in the LAST NAME field.
🔍	Click to invoke the Find dialog box (Figure 6.10).

7. Find the Donna Bain record and increase the amount due by five dollars.

Figure 6.10

The Find dialog box invoked by clicking the Search button of the Form Design window.

Print button

New Record button

Search button

Speedbar

Pointer location in the table

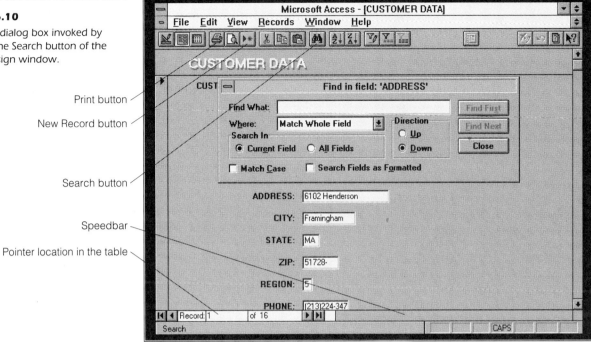

Type Bain	Enter the last name in the Find What box.
⦿ **D**own	Click to initiate the search from the present pointer location to the end of the table.
Find Fi**r**st	Click to find the first occurrence. You cannot see the record, however, because the Find dialog box is in the way.
Click and drag	Click the title bar of the Find dialog box and reposition as shown in Figure 6.11. You can now see the James Bain record.
Find Next	Click to find the next occurrence (the Donna Bain record).
Close	Close the Find dialog box.
⬇	Click the scroll arrow of the vertical scroll bar to view the AMOUNT DUE field on the form.
AMOUNT DUE	Double-click the AMOUNT DUE field to select the existing data.
Type 85	Enter the new amount in the AMOUNT DUE field.

8. Enter a new record.

▸⁎	Click to invoke a blank record like that shown in Figure 6.12. Enter the following data. Be sure to use the Enter or Tab key after you type the data for a field to position to the next field. There is no data for the COMMENTS field.

Figure 6.11

Repositioning the Find dialog box.

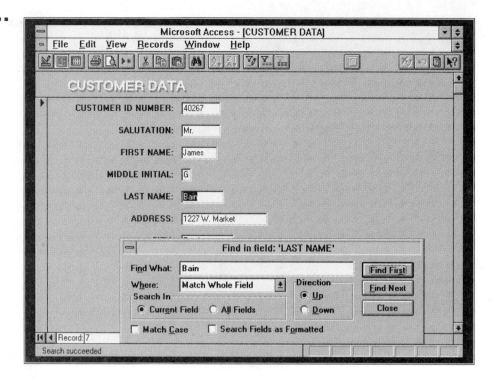

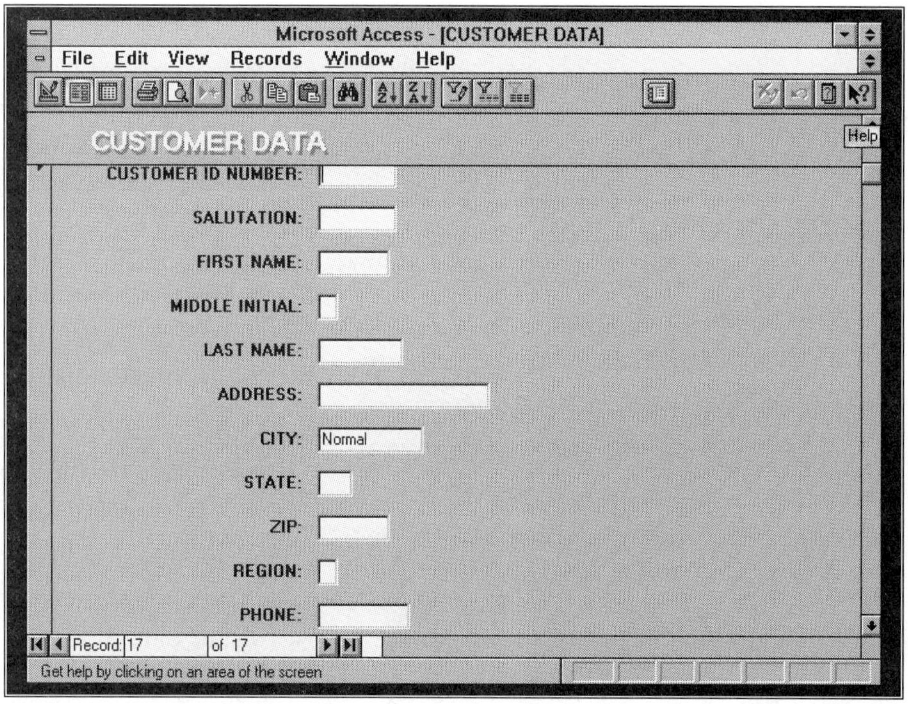

Figure 6.12

The blank record form for adding a new record to the CUSTOMER DATA table.

```
CUSTOMER ID NUMBER    33579
         SALUTATION    Mr.
         FIRST NAME    Samuel
     MIDDLE INITIAL    F
          LAST NAME    Linton
            ADDRESS    3462 W. Addison
               CITY    Bloomington
              STATE    IL
                ZIP    61704
             REGION    2
              PHONE    (309)663-2462
         AMOUNT DUE    125.00
DATE OF LAST PAYMENT    01/03/96
      CREDIT STATUS    -1
```

9. Return to the database window.

 Restore the Form Design window.

 Double-click the control-menu button to save the table, close the Form Design window, and return to the database window.

CREATING A CUSTOM DATA-ENTRY FORM

The form just created does not really correspond with paper forms that are typically used in the business world. One problem with this form is that the fields all appear along the left side. Another problem is that the descriptive text for the form comes from the table and field names. Such text is not necessarily indicative of the data to be entered by someone who is not knowledgeable about Access. Adding such things as more-descriptive headings, better field placement, and graphics make a form easier to use.

Later in this chapter we will modify the CUSTOMER COLUMN form to create a customized form, CUSTOMER TABULAR FORM, which will be loaded and modified. Each item on the form is called a control. A control, as indicated previously, can be a field, text, or any Windows entity. These controls on the existing form will have to be moved to new locations, and some of the field names will be changed. This is accomplished via a series of drag operations.

Selecting a Control   Each field entry on the current form is composed of two pieces: the field name and the field contents with the field name present. When you select a field box or its field name, the entry clicked is surrounded by a rectangle with handles. You can use a drag operation to increase or decrease the size of the box. The selected field (field box or field name) also has a large square in the upper-left corner. The unselected field of the pair has only a large square in its upper-left corner. This is depicted in Figure 6.13.

These handles give hints about how the fields can be moved. If you want to use a drag operation to position both parts of a field at one time, position the pointer to one of the small handles (the typical **hand icon** appears, indicating that a drag operation can occur) and click and drag to the desired location. Both boxes move together in this process.

If, however, you want to move only one box in the pair of fields, position the pointer to the large square in the upper-left corner of the selected control.

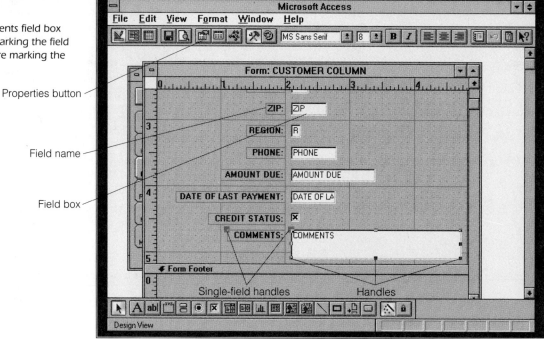

Figure 6.13

The selected comments field box with the handles marking the field and the large square marking the field name.

The pointer now turns into a hand with the index finger extended. This **index finger icon** indicates that you can drag only this box without the other box following automatically.

Selecting Multiple Controls   The discussion to this point has involved selecting a single control and making a change to it. Access also allows for **selecting multiple controls** and changing them all at once. This is accomplished by holding down the Shift key while using a click-and-drag operation to include other controls. As the drag operation is executed, a light-colored rectangle allows you to visually determine which controls have been included in the selection. Once the mouse button is released, the controls that were contained in the rectangle all have handles, indicating that they are selected. You can now perform any command, and that command will be executed against all of the selected controls.

Resizing a Control   You select a control in a form by clicking it. The control is then surrounded by a border of eight handles (see Figure 6.13). These handles allow you to resize the control. **Resizing a control** might be necessary if you have increased the size of the font for text contained in a control. In such a situation, you would grab the right-corner handle and drag it downward and to the right until the box is big enough to hold the text of the control. You can also use these handles to make a control smaller (for example, a field that is bigger than necessary to handle the majority of records).

As you add or delete text from a label control or want to increase or decrease the size of the field box, position the pointer to a handle and use the pointer's arrow configuration (not a hand) to change box size via a drag operation.

If you want to delete a control, select it (the border with handles appears), and press the Del key.

Properties   Every Access control (field, text, windows control) has properties. The properties for a control govern its appearance for such attributes as size,

Figure 6.14

An example of a Properties sheet for a control (the comments field).

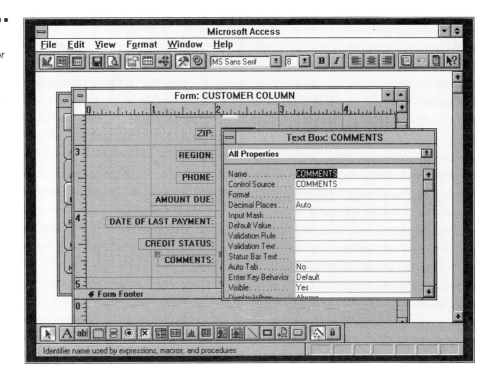

color, text alignment, and use of Windows-like entities as well as many other attributes. Changing the appearance or characteristics of a control many times requires accessing its properties via its Properties sheet. Activate the Properties sheet of a control by double-clicking the control or by selecting a control and then clicking the Properties button on the toolbar (Figure 6.13).

Once the properties for a control are activated, a screen like Figure 6.14 appears.

Properties sheets with a vertical scroll bar have a list of subproperties that are not showing. These Properties sheets work the same as others we have examined previously.

Toolbox The **toolbox** allows you to add standard and custom controls to a form. The toolbox functions in the same fashion as when building reports. The **A** text control, for example, allows you to insert text within a form. As discussed in the context of reports, to insert a control in a form, you click the desired control and then position the pointer to the form (the pointer has now changed to a crosshair and a graphic representing the control being built) and click where you want the control to be placed. You can now invoke the properties for that control and make any changes.

If the toolbox is not onscreen, select View from the menu bar and then click Toolbox in the list of active windows.

Hands-On Exercise: Creating a Custom Form

1. Start the form design session. You should have the SALES database window active.

Click the Form tab in the database window to invoke the Forms sheet.

CUSTOMER COLUMN Click to activate this form.

⬜ (icon)	Invoke the Form Design window.
File	Open the File menu.
Save As...	Invoke the Save As dialog box.
Type **CUSTOMER TABULAR FORM**	Enter the new name of the form.
(Enter)	Create the copy of the form. This is the form that we will be using for making changes. This name now appears in the title bar of the Form Design window.
⬜ (icon)	Maximize the Form Design window.

Notice the grid that appears on the form. Each dot represents the intersection of a column depicted along the top border of the form and a row depicted along the left side of the form (Figure 6.15). Each dot also represents a measurement of $\frac{1}{12}$ inch. When you are inserting or dragging a control, it snaps to the nearest dot location.

2. Delete the CUSTOMER DATA title from the Form Header band.

CUSTOMER DATA	Click the control if it is not already selected.
(Del)	Delete the first part of the control (the box).
CUSTOMER DATA	Click the control.
(Del)	Delete the second part of the control (the text).

3. Enter the new form heading in the Form Header band.

A (icon)	Click the Label button in the toolbox to invoke the Label tool. The pointer should turn into a crosshair and capital "A."
Click	Position the crosshair to the uppermost dot in the Form Header at the 2-inch mark and click the mouse to create a text box control.
Type **ABC COMPANY**	Enter the new text. Do not press Enter.
A (icon)	Click to invoke the Label tool.
Click	Position the crosshair to the 3-inch mark in the Form Header band at the fourth dot from the top and click to create a text box control.
Type **ACCOUNTS RECEIVABLE DATA ENTRY FORM**	Enter the new text. Do not press Enter.

4. Change the font size and center the form's first header.

ABC COMPANY	Click this control to select it.
⬌	Click and drag the middle-right handle to enlarge the box until the box reaches just to the left of the right margin (use Figure 6.15 as a guide).
⬌	Click and drag the middle-left handle to enlarge the box until the box reaches just to the right of the left margin.
⬜ (icon)	Click the down arrow of the Font Size box to invoke a selection box of available font sizes.

12	Select the font size. Notice that the text is now too large for the box.
▤	Click to center the text.
⇕	Click and drag the top-middle handle up one dot to enlarge the box. The text should now be readable.

5. Change the font size and center the form's second header.

ACCOUNTS RECEIVABLE...	Click this control to select it.
↔	Click and drag the middle-right handle to enlarge the box until the box reaches just to the left of the right margin.
↔	Click and drag the middle-left handle to enlarge the box until the box reaches just to the right of the left margin.
▣	Click the down arrow of the Font Size box to invoke a selection box of available font sizes.
12	Select the font size. Notice that the text is now too large for the box.
▤	Click to center the text.
⇕	Click and drag the bottom-middle handle down one dot to enlarge the box. The text should now be readable. Your Form Design window should now look like Figure 6.15.

6. Move the existing fields of the Detail band out of the way. Click and drag each field and label control to the bottom of the form. When you are finished, your form should look something like Figure 6.16.

Figure 6.15

The form with the new entries in the Form Header band.

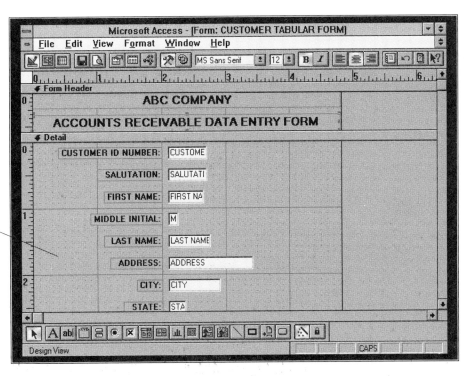

Figure 6.16

CUSTOMER TABULAR FORM with all controls moved to the bottom of the form.

Undo icon

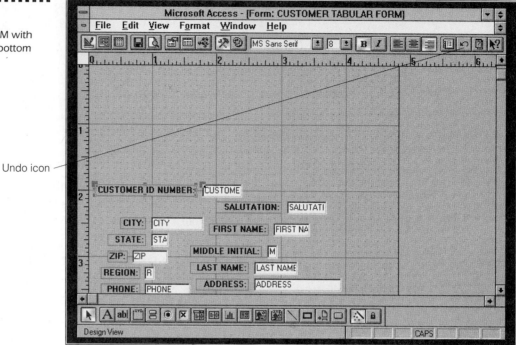

HINTS/HAZARDS   You may find that you have placed a field at the incorrect location. If this happens, you can drag it to the desired location. When you start the drag operation, the cursor turns into a hand.

7. Enter a section heading.

A	Click to invoke the Label tool.
Click	Position the crosshair to the uppermost dot in the Detail band at the 1½-inch mark and click to create a text box control. Use Figure 6.17 as a guide.
Type **Customer Information:**	Enter the new text. Do not press Enter.
Customer Information:	Click the section heading to select it.
⬇	Click the down arrow of the Font Size box to invoke a selection box of available font sizes.
10	Select the font size.
⬌	Click and drag the middle-right handle to enlarge the box until it is just large enough to contain the text.
▤	Click to left-justify the text.

HINTS/HAZARDS   If a field disappears while you are enlarging or shrinking it, click the Undo button on the toolbar (Figure 6.16).

8. Place the first label and change the text.

Click and drag   Click the CUSTOMER ID NUMBER field name and drag it under the heading just created. Refer to Figure 6.17.

9. Edit the label.

CUSTOMER   Click and drag to include the word "CUSTOMER" of the label. The text should now be in reverse video.

[Del]   Delete this word.

NUMBER: Click and drag to include the word "NUMBER:" of the label. Be sure to include the space in front of "NUMBER:". The text should now be in reverse video.

[Del]   Delete this word. The word "ID" is all that should remain in the label.

Type :   Enter the colon.

10. Shrink the label box.

    Click and drag the middle-right handle to shrink the box until it is just large enough to contain the text.

▤   Click to left-justify the text.

11. Move the field box.

Point, click, and drag   Position the pointer to the large square in the upper-left corner of the CUSTOMER ID NUMBER box (the hand pointer should have the index finger extended) and drag the box so that it is one dot ($\frac{1}{12}$ inch) to the right of the label.

12. Use the commands from steps 8 through 11 to position the first set of fields as shown in Figure 6.17. You may want to modify the labels before you move the boxes.

HINTS/HAZARDS   Click the Form View button on the toolbar at any time to see how the changed controls will appear on the form. When you are finished testing the appearance, click the Design View button to return to the Form Design window.

Figure 6.17

The first part of the data-entry
screen.

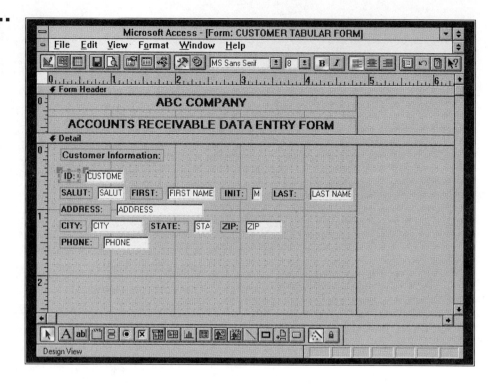

13. Enter the next section heading.

A	Click to invoke the Label tool.
Click	Position the crosshair to the third dot past the zero point on the horizontal ruler where it intersects with the $1\frac{3}{4}$-inch mark on the vertical ruler and click the mouse to create a text box control. Use Figure 6.18 as a guide for placement.
Type **Sales Information:**	Enter the new text. Do not press Enter.
Sales Information:	Click the title to select it.
(down arrow)	Click the down arrow of the Font Size box to invoke a selection box of available font sizes.
10	Select the font size.
⟷	Click and drag the middle-right handle to enlarge the box until the box is just large enough to contain the text.
(left-justify icon)	Click to left-justify the text.

14. Use the commands from steps 8 through 11 to position the second set of fields as shown in Figure 6.18. You may want to modify the labels before you move the boxes.

15. Test the form.

 Click this button on the toolbar to switch to Form view. Your screen should look like Figure 6.19. Use the Tab

Figure 6.18

The second part of the data-entry screen.

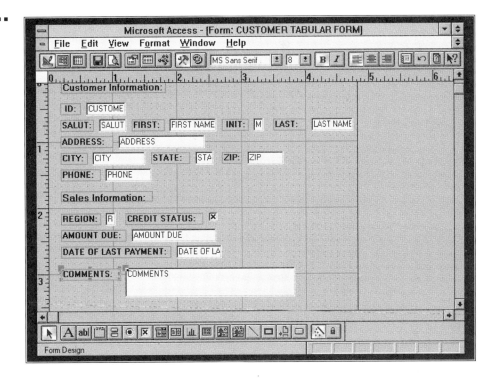

Figure 6.19

The data-entry form should look like this.

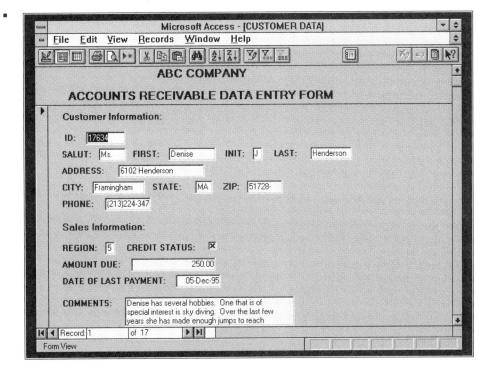

key to move from field to another; you will notice that the PHONE and CREDIT STATUS fields do not receive the focus in the proper order. This will be corrected in the next step.

 Return to the Form Design window.

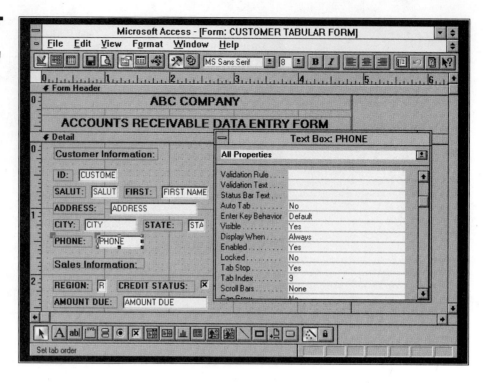

Figure 6.20

The Properties sheet for determining
the order of the phone field for
using Enter, Tab, and Shift + Tab.

16. Specify the order of the fields in the form for data entry. You have to do
    this, or Access will start with the ID field and go through the fields as they
    appear in the record's structure in the database (or however you initially
    established the order of the fields in the form) when you use Enter, Tab, or
    a Shift + Tab to position from one field to another.

PHONE	Click the field box for the PHONE field.
	Click to invoke the Properties sheet.
	Click the scroll arrow of the vertical scroll bar to view the Tab Index cell.
Tab Index	Click this cell. It should have the value 10.
Type **9**	Enter the new tab-order value. The succeeding fields have all been automatically updated by Access. Your Properties sheet for the PHONE field should now look like Figure 6.20.
CREDIT STATUS	Click the field box for the CREDIT STATUS field.
Tab Index	Click this cell. It should have the value 13.
Type **11**	Enter the new tab-order value. The succeeding fields have all been automatically updated by Access.
	Double-click the control-menu button of the Properties sheet to close it. The tab order of the fields is now appropriate for the form.

17. Save the form to disk.

    Save the form.

ADDING GRAPHICS

All that remains to be done is to add the graphics to the data-entry screen. You can add rectangular boxes to emphasize a single field or group of fields via the toolbox (see Figure 6.24). Then using the **Send to Back command**, you can send the graphic to the "back" of the form—behind other objects. The data-entry screen requires two boxes: one around the customer information data and one around the sales information. In the following steps, you will add these boxes.

Hands-On Exercise: Adding the Graphics

1. Change the background color of the form so the rectangles will appear in this color.

Click | Click anywhere in the dot grid in the Detail band. Make certain that you do not click a current control. The Detail band bar should now be dark gray.

Click this button on the toolbar to invoke the palette. The Back Color band should contain colors.

Back Color ☐ | Click the white square. The background of the form is now white (Figure 6.21).

Click the control-menu button to close the palette.

2. Include a box around the customer information.

Click this button in the toolbox. The pointer now turns into a crosshair with a rectangle.

Figure 6.21

The form with the palette open and the background color changed to white.

Detail band selected

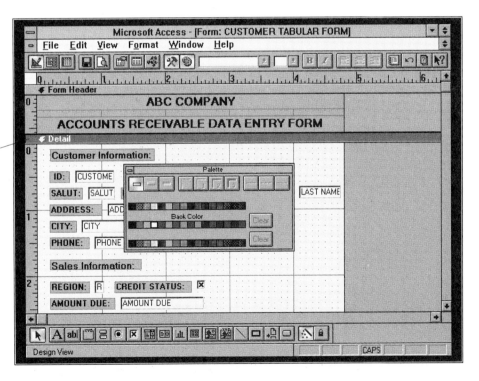

Figure 6.22

The form with the first box obscuring all of the previously entered fields and labels.

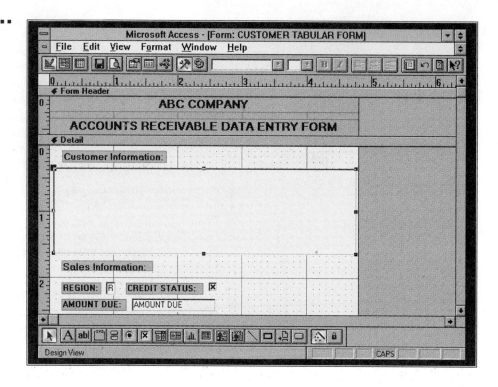

Click and drag   Position the crosshair to the first dot between the Customer Information heading and the ID heading. Click and drag to make a rectangle as shown in Figure 6.24. Your screen should now look Figure 6.22. Notice that this rectangle completely obscures all of the fields entered previously.

3. Send the box to the back of the form, behind the text.

Format   Open the Format menu.

Send to Back   Select this option. The top rectangle should now look like Figure 6.23.

4. Include a box around the sales information.

▢   Click this button in the toolbox. The pointer now turns into a crosshair with a rectangle.

Click and drag   Position the crosshair to the first dot between the Sales Information heading and the REGION heading. Click and drag to make a second rectangle as shown in Figure 6.24.

5. Send the box to the back of the form, behind the text.

Format   Open the Format menu.

Send to Back   Select this option. The bottom rectangle should now look like Figure 6.24.

Figure 6.23

The form with the fields visible in the first box.

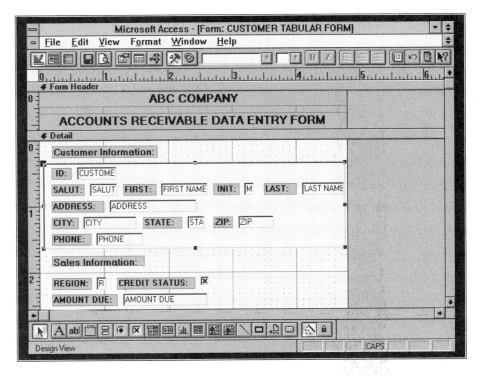

Figure 6.24

The form with both boxes added.

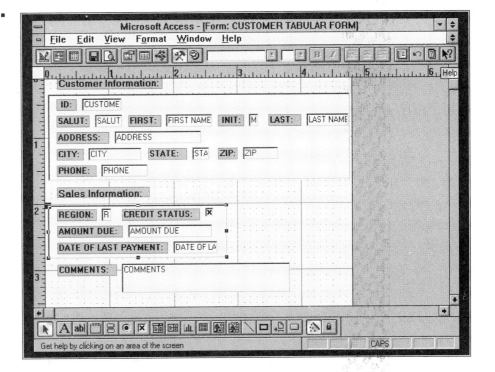

Figure 6.25

The form with all controls selected in the Detail band.

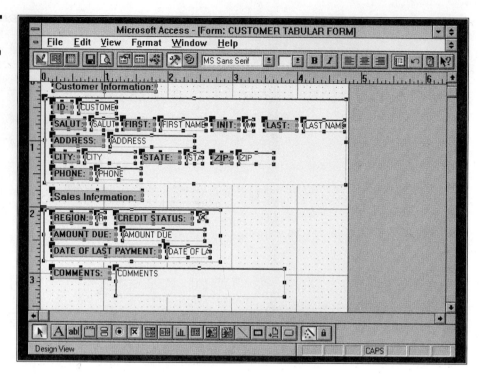

6. The form fields currently have a normal appearance. Create a "sunken" look for all fields in the Detail band. When you wish to include all fields, remember you must hold down the Shift key while you are performing the click-and-drag operation.

Shift + **click and drag**	Hold down Shift and position the pointer in the upper-left area of the Detail band to the left of all fields and labels. Click and drag the white rectangle to include all fields and labels in the Detail band. When you release the left mouse button, all fields are selected (Figure 6.25).
🎨	Invoke the palette (Figure 6.26).
⬜	Click this palette button to give the fields a sunken appearance.
➖	Close the palette.

7. Change the background back to gray.

Click	Click anywhere in the Detail band. The selected fields should now be deselected.
🎨	Invoke the palette.
Back Color ☐	Click the light gray box of the Back Color band. The background color should now change.
➖	Close the palette.

Figure 6.26

The form with the palette open.

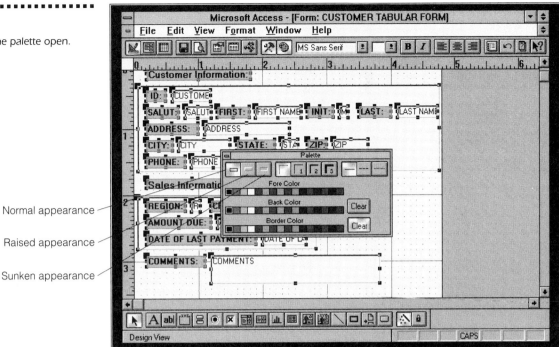

Normal appearance

Raised appearance

Sunken appearance

8. You are now ready to test the form to see whether it properly accesses data from the CUSTOMER DATA table.

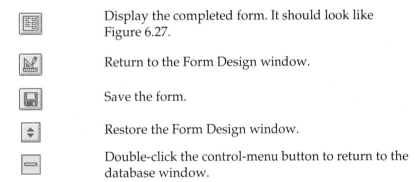

Display the completed form. It should look like Figure 6.27.

Return to the Form Design window.

Save the form.

Restore the Form Design window.

Double-click the control-menu button to return to the database window.

 USING THE FORM

To invoke the form in the database window, highlight the CUSTOMER TABULAR FORM entry in the Forms sheet.

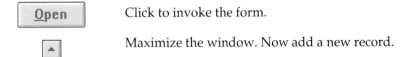

CUSTOMER TABULAR FORM   Click the form in the Forms sheet.

Open   Click to invoke the form.

Maximize the window. Now add a new record.

Figure 6.27

The completed form.

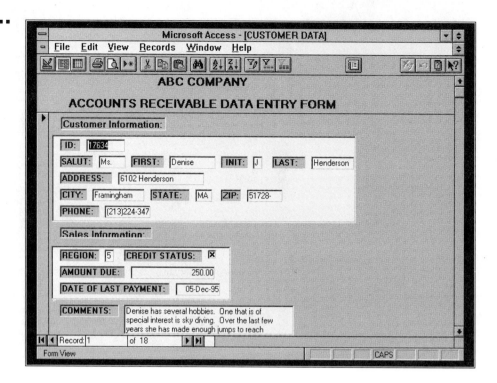

Click this button on the toolbar. Enter the following information. When you are finished, your screen should look like Figure 6.28. Press Enter or Tab after typing the information for each field. (Click the CREDIT STATUS field to obtain the ×.)

CUSTOMER ID NUMBER	33697
NAME	Mr. John W. Forsythe
ADDRESS	1617 W. Garden
LOCATION	Chicago, IL 60712
PHONE	(312)545-0923
REGION	3
CREDIT	Y
AMOUNT DUE	150
DATE OF LAST PAYMENT	12/14/95

Restore the Form Design window.

Double-click the control-menu button of the Form Design window.

Once you have saved the data-entry screen, use it anytime you want to append or edit records in the CUSTOMER DATA table.

HINTS/HAZARDS

You might want to experiment with the palette for controlling foreground, background, and border colors of various controls in the form. The palette can be used for changing colors of both label and field displays.

Figure 6.28
The form for the inserted record.

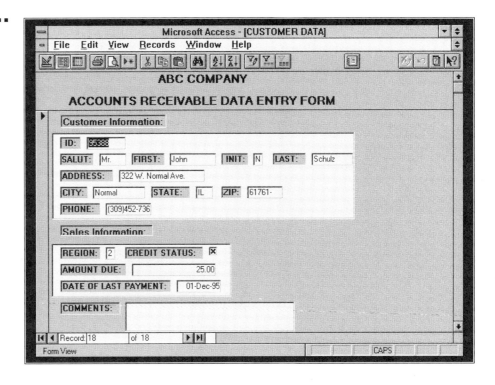

MACROS

Access makes frequently performed actions easier to do by placing the necessary commands in a **macro**. An Access macro contains Access Basic commands (the internal programming language of Access) which tell Access what actions need to be taken.

Macros are created, changed, and accessed from the Macros sheet of the database window. Macro instructions are entered in **macro datasheets** (Figure 6.29). The Action cell contains an icon which, when selected, displays a

Figure 6.29
The macro datasheet used for creating a macro.

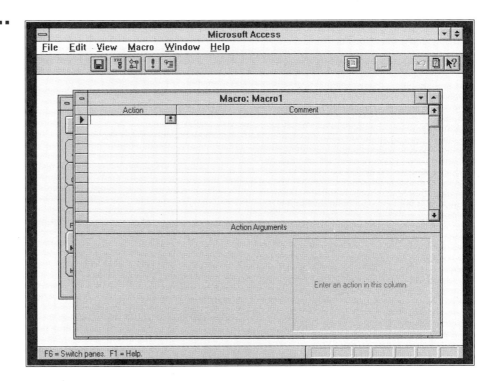

Figure 6.30

The macro Action cell selection box
allows you to select from a number
of Access actions.

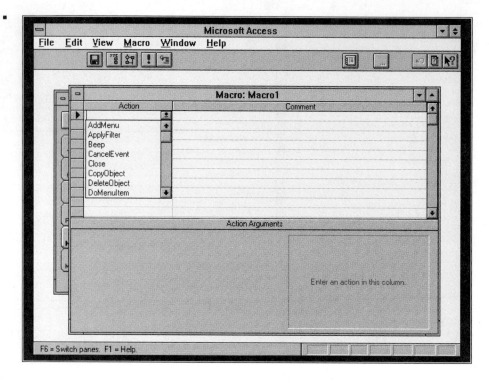

Figure 6.31

A macro Action cell entry results in
the Action Arguments box for that
command appearing at the bottom
of the macro datasheet.

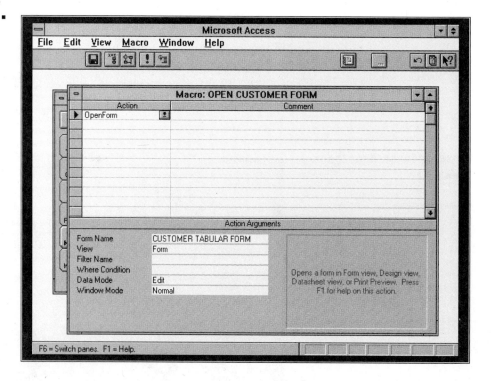

selection box containing a number of actions that can be used to tell Access
what it is supposed to do (Figure 6.30). When a command is selected, Access
displays a list of arguments for that command at the bottom of the macro
datasheet (Figure 6.31).

In addition to entering macros from macro datasheets, macros can also be
created for specific controls using the Control Wizards button in the toolbox of

the Form Design window. When macros are entered for controls via the toolbox, those controls become part of the Properties sheet.

CREATING MACROS FOR FORM CONTROLS

When macros are created by the Control Wizards, Access places the Basic statements for the macro in the Properties sheet. When the Control Wizards feature is invoked and you indicate to Access that you want to create a **command button** for placement in a form, the Control Wizards step you through several dialog boxes for indicating the task to be performed and the type of text/ graphic image to be placed on the face of the button.

In the following hands-on exercise, we will create command buttons that will be used for finding records, adding records to the table, positioning to the next record, positioning to the previous record, and closing the form.

In preparation for this exercise, the SALES database window should be onscreen.

 Hands-On Exercise: Adding Command Buttons to a Form

1. Activate the Form Design window for the form just created and save it to another name.

Click the Form tab of the database window to invoke the Forms sheet.

CUSTOMER TABULAR FORM
Select this form.

Click to invoke the Form Design Window.

File
Open the File menu.

Save As...
Invoke the Save As dialog box.

Type COMMAND BUTTON FORM
Enter the new form name.

Enter
Save the form using the new name. The title bar of the Form Design window should now reflect the new name.

HINTS/HAZARDS   When the Form Design window appears, the toolbox should also appear. It may be a separate window, or it may appear as a bar along the bottom of the window or in some other location. If you do not see the toolbox, issue the command sequence View, Toolbox to display the toolbox and its buttons.

2. Create the box to hold the command buttons and enter an appropriate title for the box.

Maximize the Form Design window.

Drag
Position the pointer to the right margin of the form and drag the margin to the 6¼-inch mark on the horizontal ruler (refer to Figure 6.32).

Figure 6.32

The box, along with an identifying title, created to hold the command buttons.

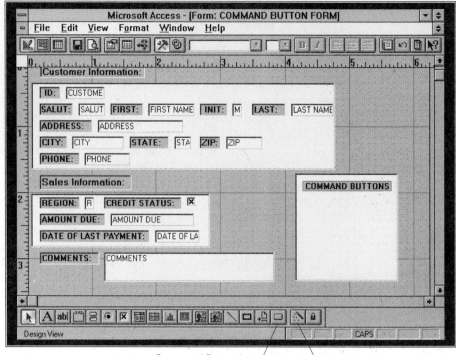

Command Button icon / Control Wizards button "off"

     Click the scroll arrow of the vertical scroll bar once to move the form up.

     Click this button in the toolbox. The pointer now turns into a crosshair and rectangle. Position the crosshair to around the 4¼-inch horizontal and 1¾-inch vertical location of the form. Click to establish the upper-left position of the rectangle and drag to the 5¾-inch horizontal and 3⅜-inch vertical location. Your form specification should now look like Figure 6.32 (we'll add the title in the next series of commands).

A   Invoke the Label tool. The pointer now turns into a crosshair and capital "A." Use Figure 6.32 as a guide for placement. Click close to the right margin of the box to establish the box location.

Type **COMMAND BUTTONS**   Enter the title. Click the box and drag it to the location shown in Figure 6.32. (Click outside the box and then click the title bar.)

3. Create the Find command button.

    Click the Control Wizards button to make the button appear "pressed." (Refer to Figure 6.32 and 6.33 for button comparisons.)

    Click the Command Button icon. The pointer turns into a crosshair with a box. Position the box to the upper-left area of the box (see Figure 6.36). Click the mouse, and a large button appears marked by handles. Access also displays the Command Button Wizard dialog box, shown in Figure 6.33, for indicating the type of button to be built.

Figure 6.33

The Command Button Wizard dialog box for determining the type of command button to be built.

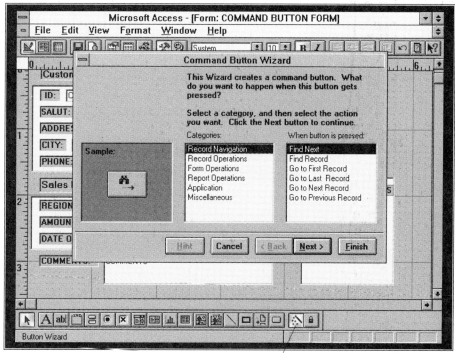

Control Wizards button "on"

Figure 6.34

The Command Button Wizard dialog box for determining whether text or a graphic will be used to label the button.

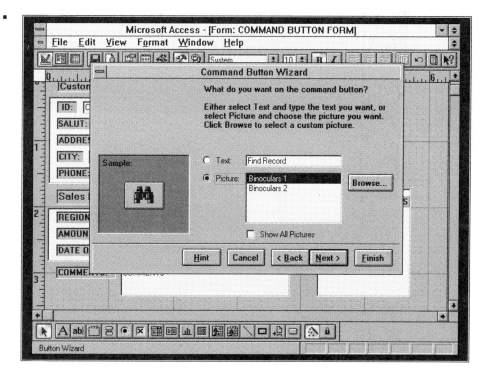

Record Navigation — Select this entry in the Categories selection box.

Find Record — Select this entry from the When button is pressed selection box.

Next > — The next dialog box appears (Figure 6.34), in which you choose text or a graphic image for the button face. We want the graphic image.

Next >	The next dialog box appears (Figure 6.35), in which you name the button.
Type **Find**	Enter the name of the button.
Finish	Access now places the button in the Command Buttons box (Figure 6.36).

Figure 6.35

The Command Button Wizard dialog box for indicating the name of the button.

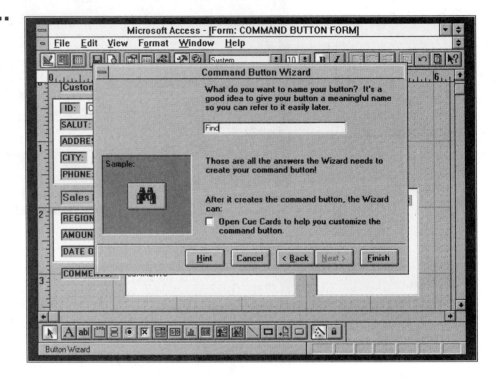

Figure 6.36

The Find button is placed in the Command Button box of the form.

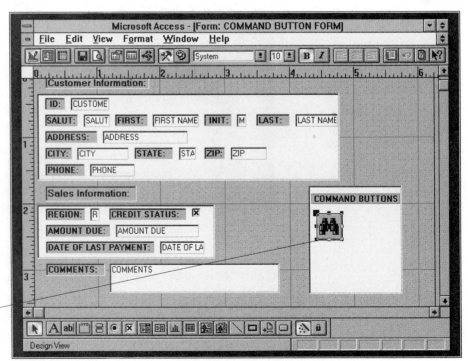

Find button created by the Control Wizards

Figure 6.37

The five command buttons added to the box.

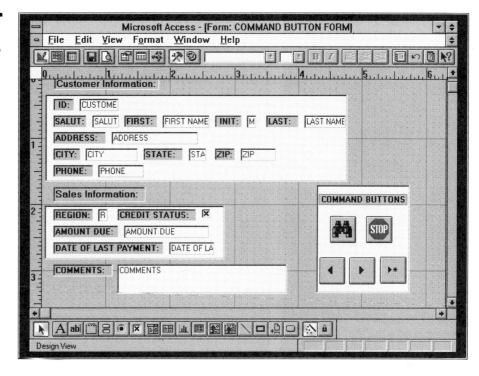

4. Create the Go To Previous Record command button.

    Click the Command Button icon. The pointer turns into a crosshair with a box. Position the box to the lower-left area of the box (see Figure 6.37). Click the mouse, and a button appears marked by handles. Access also displays the Command Button Wizard dialog box (Figure 6.33).

Record Navigation   Select this entry in the Categories selection box.

Go to Previous Record   Select this entry from the When button is pressed selection box.

Next >   The next dialog box appears, in which you choose text or a graphic image for the button face. We want the graphic image.

Next >   The next dialog box appears, in which you name the button.

Type **Previous Record**   Enter the name of the button.

Finish   Access now places the button in the Command Buttons box (Figure 6.37).

5. Create the Go To Next Record command button.

Click the Command Button icon. Position to the bottom center of the box (see Figure 6.37). Click the mouse, and a button appears marked by handles. Access also displays the Command Button Wizard dialog box.

Record Navigation   Select this entry in the Categories selection box.

Go to Next Record Select this entry from the When button is pressed selection box.

Next > Choose text or a graphic image for the button face. We want the graphic image.

Next > Name the button.

Type **Next Record** Enter the name of the button.

Finish Access now places the button in the Command Buttons box (Figure 6.37).

6. Create the Add New Record command button.

Click Command Button icon. Position to the lower-right area of the box and click. The Command Button Wizard dialog box appears.

Record Operations Select this entry in the Categories selection box.

Add New Record Select this entry from the When button is pressed selection box.

Next > Choose text or a graphic image for the button face. We want the graphic image.

Next > Name the button.

Type **Add Record** Enter the name of the button.

Finish Access now places the button in the Command Buttons box.

7. Create the Close Form command button.

Click Command Button icon. Position to the upper-right area of the box and click. The Command Button Wizard dialog box appears.

Form Operations Select this entry in the Categories selection box.

Close Form Select this entry from the When button is pressed selection box.

Next > Choose text or a graphic image for the button face. We want the stop sign graphic image.

Stop Sign Select this entry.

Next > Name the button.

Type **Stop** Enter the name of the button.

Finish Access now places the button in the Command Buttons box. You may have to drag your buttons to arrange them as shown in Figure 6.37.

8. Create a red background for the title bar.

COMMAND BUTTONS   Click the title bar to select it.

Invoke the palette.

Back Color ▦   Click the red box in the Back Color band.

Close the palette.

9. Save and test the form.

Save the completed form.

View the completed form (Figure 6.38). Experiment with various command buttons but do not use the Stop button.

10. Return to Design view.

Click to return to the Form Design window.

 Double-click the Stop command button to invoke the Properties sheet for this control. Notice that the name contained in the title bar is the same that we entered to name the button.

Click and hold until the On Click cell appears.

On Click   Select this entry. The message [Event Procedure] appears in the cell, indicating that there is Access code controlling this procedure.

Figure 6.38

The completed form with the Command Buttons box.

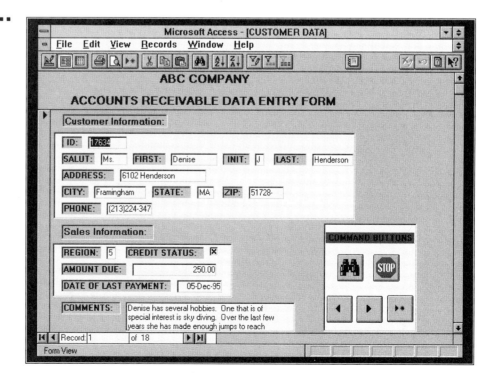

Figure 6.39

The Module window with the macro instructions in Access Basic code created by the Control Wizards.

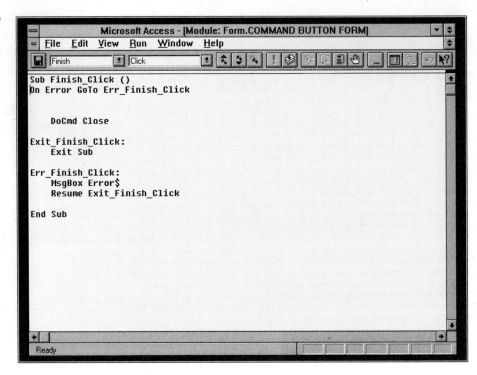

```
Sub Finish_Click ()
On Error GoTo Err_Finish_Click


    DoCmd Close

Exit_Finish_Click:
    Exit Sub

Err_Finish_Click:
    MsgBox Error$
    Resume Exit_Finish_Click

End Sub
```

Click the Build button on the toolbar. A Module window like that shown in Figure 6.39 appears with the Access Basic code instructions that were created by the Control Wizards.

Double-click the control-menu button of the Module window to return to the Properties sheet.

Double-click the control-menu button of the Properties sheet to return to the form specification.

11. Return to the database window.

Restore the Form Design window.

Double-click the control-menu button to return to the database window.

CREATING A MACRO THAT USES THE MACRO DATASHEETS

The macros that we created in the previous exercise were part of a form and were executed when we clicked a command button. The macro that we are going to create now will use the macro datasheets discussed previously and will be accessible from the Macros sheet of the database window. This macro will automatically open our COMMAND BUTTON FORM, maximize the form window, and make certain that we are positioned to the first record.

The SALES database window should be onscreen.

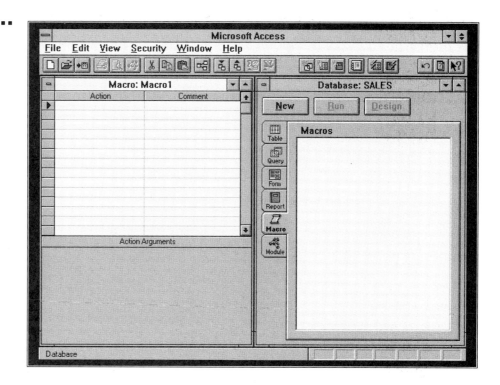

Figure 6.40

The tiled database and macro datasheet windows.

1. Start creating the macro.

Macro   Click the Macro tab of the database window to invoke the Macros sheet.

New   Activate the Macro datasheet.

Window   Open the Window menu.

Tile   Select this option. You should now have two windows onscreen, as shown in Figure 6.40.

Form   Click the Form tab of the database window to invoke the Forms sheet.

COMMAND BUTTON FORM   Click and drag this name to the first Action cell of the macro datasheet.

▼   Minimize the database window.

▲   Maximize the macro datasheet. Your screen should now look like Figure 6.41. Notice that Access automatically placed the correct command in the Action cell and also filled in the needed arguments at the bottom of the form for this Action cell. If we had not used the drag operation, we would have had to make these entries manually.

2. Enter the second command.

⬇   Click the next Action cell in the right corner to activate the list box of possible commands.

Figure 6.41

The macro datasheet with the first entry in the Action cell and additional arguments automatically entered via the drag operation.

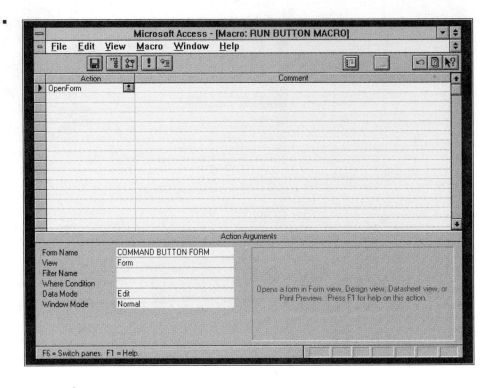

Click	Click below the slider until the Maximize command appears.
Maximize	Select this command. It now appears in the cell, and the selection box is closed.

3. Enter the command to position to the first record of the table.

▼	Click the next Action cell in the right corner to activate the list box of possible commands.
Click	Click below the slider until the GoToRecord command appears.
GoToRecord	Select this command. It now appears in the cell, and the selection box is closed. The action arguments for this command are also visible at the bottom of the datasheet.
Record	Click the Record cell of the Action Arguments box in the right corner to activate the list box of possible commands.
First	Select this command. It now appears in the cell, and the selection box is closed. We are now finished with the macro.

4. Save the macro.

File	Open the File menu.
Save As...	Invoke the Save As dialog box.
Type **RUN BUTTON FORM**	Enter the macro name.

Enter   Save the macro.

$\Leftrightarrow$ Restore the macro datasheet.

⊟   Double-click the control-menu button to close the macro datasheet.

Database SALES   Double-click this entry to activate the database window.

5. Run the macro.

    Click the Macro tab to invoke the Macros sheet.

RUN BUTTON MACRO   Select this macro.

Run   Execute the macro. The button-controlled form as a maximized window now appears onscreen, indicating that the macro is working.

STOP   Click the Stop command button to close the form and return to the maximized SALES database window.

CHAPTER REVIEW

Access lets you generate self-documenting screens that resemble a paper form. You can use these screens for inputting or changing data via the Forms sheet of the database window.

Access provides Form Wizards that allow you to create a form with a minimum of effort by specifying, via Form Wizards dialog boxes, such things as the file to use, the type of form to create, the style desired for the form, and the title to use.

Before a data-entry screen can be created, you must specify a table to tie input fields with the fields that appear onscreen. You must identify and load to the form the fields that will actively participate in the inputting or changing of data.

The Form Design window automatically divides a form into three parts: the Form Header, Detail, and Form Footer bands. As you incorporate fields into the form, or as Access automatically builds the form using a Form Wizard and incorporates fields, each field is entered as two parts. The first part is a label composed of the field name. The second part is the field box also containing the field name. Using selection handles, you can move both parts independently or at the same time.

The toolbox contains commands that let you draw lines and boxes onscreen by positioning the pointer to the beginning corner, clicking, and dragging the pointer to the ending (diagonally opposite) corner, and then releasing the mouse button. Access then automatically draws the line or box.

Access also allows you to incorporate macros. These can be placed in the Macros sheet of the database window or they can be incorporated in a form as command buttons with the macro commands stored to the On Click cell of the Properties sheet of the control. The Control Wizards in the toolbox make it easy to create such embedded macros by stepping you through a series of dialog boxes.

All macros contain what is known as Access Basic commands. Access Basic is Access's internal programming language.

A macro created using the Macros sheet is placed in a macro datasheet. The statements in the datasheet can be entered manually or by using a drag operation to indicate to Access what operation, for instance, should be started.

KEY TERMS AND CONCEPTS

AutoForm Form Wizard
command button
controls
field box
Form Wizards
Graph Form Wizard
hand icon
index finger icon
macro

macro datasheet
Main/Subform Form Wizard
resizing a control
selecting multiple controls
Send to Back command
Single-Column Form Wizard
Tabular Form Wizard
toolbox

CHAPTER QUIZ

Multiple Choice

1. Which of the following statements is true with respect to data-entry screens?
   a. They are more self-documenting than edit screens.
   b. They allow little control over the order in which data are entered.
   c. They do not allow automatic integration of a data-screen field with a database field.
   d. None of the above statements is true.

2. Which of the following is not a valid Form Wizard?
   a. Tabular
   b. Graph
   c. Hybrid
   d. AutoForm

3. The process of moving a field is referred to as:
   a. moving
   b. transferring
   c. copying
   d. dragging

4. Which of the following Properties sheet cells controls the order accessed via the Tab key.
   a. Tab Stop
   b. Tab Order
   c. Tab Index
   d. Tab Number

5. The _____ message in a Properties sheet cell indicates that macro instructions have been embedded in a control.
   a. [Event Procedure]
   b. [Macro]
   c. [Macro Functions]
   d. [Module Event]

True/False

6. The Single-Column and AutoForm Form Wizards generate the same type of form.

7. Once a line has been drawn, it can be deleted by selecting that control and pressing the Del key.

8. When the pointer is shaped like a hand with its index finger extended, you are allowed to move only the selected control of a matched pair of controls.

9. The Control Wizards button is found on the toolbar.

10. Macro datasheets may require entries in both an Action cell and the Action Arguments box.

Answers

1. a   2. c   3. d   4. c   5. a   6. t   7. t   8. t   9. f   10. t

Exercises

1. The _____ Form Wizard places the field names and data fields in one column in the form.

2. The _____ button of a Form Wizards dialog box allows you to include all fields from a table within the form.

3. The object or entity on a form is called a(n) _____.

4. The _____ bar of the form contains the table name when that form is generated via a Form Wizard.

5. The squares around a selected control are called _____.

6. A field entry on a form is composed of _____ parts.

7. When the pointer is shaped like a _____, all parts of the field move at once in a drag operation.

8. When you want to move just one part of a field specification, you must point to the large square in the _____-_____ corner of the selected control.

9. The _____ key is used to include multiple controls in a drag operation.

10. Every control in an Access form has a _____ sheet.

11. The form can be tested at any time by clicking the _____ button on the toolbar.

12. Use the _____ button in the toolbox for creating a graphic rectangle on a form.

13. When fields are moved to a different location on the form, you may have to change the _____ _____ cell of the Properties sheet before the Tab key properly moves from field to field in form order.

14. The _____ button on the toolbar is used to change colors within the form.

15. Macros contain embedded instructions in Access's built-in _____ _____ language.

16. Use the _____ _____ in the toolbox to create macro-driven buttons on a form.

17. The Send to _____ command is used to make objects under a rectangle visible.

18. When a command button is created, you can choose between text and _____ being displayed on the button face.

19. Macro tasks are specified on the macro _____.

20. The lower portion of the macro datasheet contains the _____ _____.

COMPUTER EXERCISES

1. Design and create a data-entry form for your PAYMAST table. Embed command buttons in this form like we did in the chapter.

2. Append two records to the PAYROLL NAME AND ADDRESS table.

APPENDIX: ACCESS 2.0 FOR WINDOWS COMMAND SUMMARY

Datasheet Toolbar Buttons

Button	Name	Function
	New Database	Opens a pop-up window from which you can choose a new database to create.
	Open Database	Displays the Open Database dialog box, which you use to activate the desired database.
	Attach Table	Attaches a table from another database to the current table.
	Print	Prints the active document.
	Print Preview	Shows how a report, form, datasheet, or module will appear when printed.
	Code	Displays an Access Basic form module or report module where you can view, edit, create, or run procedures.
	Cut	Cuts selected text/data and moves it to the Windows Clipboard.
	Copy	Copies selected text/data to the Windows Clipboard.
	Paste	Pastes the contents of the Windows Clipboard at the cursor location.
	Relationships	Displays this window to view or edit existing relationships or to define new ones between tables and queries.
	Import	Imports data from a text file, spreadsheet, or database table into an Access table.
	Export	Copies information from an Access table into another Microsoft application.
	Merge It	Starts or switches to Microsoft Word Merge Wizard.
	MS Excel	Saves the contents of the current object to an Excel worksheet and starts Excel.
	New Query	Creates a query for the table or object currently open.
	New Form	Creates a form based on the active table or query.
	New Report	Creates a report based on the active table or query.
	Database Window	Displays the database window.
	AutoForm	Creates a form that displays all fields and records of the selected table or query.
	AutoReport	Creates a report that displays all fields and records of the selected table or query.
	Cue Cards	Displays the Cue Cards main menu.
	Help	Invokes on-line help for the next item that you click.

Positioning Commands in the Datasheet Window

Key(s) or Button	Action
[◄◄]	Moves to the first record.
[►►]	Moves to the last record.
Home	Moves to the first column.
End	Moves to the last column.
Tab or Enter	Moves to the next column.
Shift + Tab	Moves to the previous column.
↑ or [◄]	Moves to the previous record.
↓ or [►]	Moves to the next record.
Ctrl + Home or [◄◄]	Moves to the first record, first column.
Ctrl + End	Moves to the last record, last column.
[►►]	Moves to the beginning of the last record.
Pg Up	Moves to up 26 rows.
Pg Dn	Moves to down 26 rows.

Field Editing Commands

Key(s)	Action
F2	Switches from navigation mode to edit mode when using the cursor keys to move among fields/records.
→	Moves right one character.
←	Moves left one character.
Ctrl + →	Moves right one word.
Ctrl + ←	Moves left one word.
Home	Moves to the beginning of the field.
End	Moves to the end of the field.
Ctrl + End	Moves to the end of a multiple-line field.
Ctrl + Home	Moves to the beginning of a multiple-line field.
Ctrl + C	Copies to the Clipboard.
Ctrl + V	Pastes contents of Clipboard at the insertion point.
Ctrl + X	Cuts and copies to the Clipboard.

Input Mask Characters

Character	Description
0	Requires a digit (0–9) entry; no plus (+) or minus (–) signs allowed.
9	Digit or space entry required; plus and minus signs not allowed.
#	Digit or space entry not required; blank positions are converted to spaces; plus and minus signs are allowed.
L	Letter (A–Z), entry required.
?	Letter (A–Z), entry optional.
A	Letter or digit, entry required.
a	Letter or digit, entry optional.
C	Any character or space, entry optional.
&	Any character or space, entry required.
. , : ; - /	Decimal placeholder and thousand, date, and time separators. (The characters depend on the settings in the International section of the Microsoft Windows Control Panel.)
<	Causes all characters that follow to be converted to lowercase.
>	Causes all characters that follow to be converted to uppercase.
!	Causes input mask to fill from right to left, rather than from left to right, when characters on the left side of the input mask are optional. You can include the exclamation point anywhere in the input mask.
\	Causes the character that follows to be displayed as the literal character (for example, \A is displayed as A).

Report Design Window Toolbar Buttons

Button	Name	Function
	Design View	Displays the report in Design view.
	Print Preview	Displays the document in Print Preview to see how it will look when printed.
	Sample Preview	Displays a quick preview with sample data.
	Save	Saves the report specifications to disk.
	Sorting and Grouping	Adds, deletes, or changes group levels using the Sorting and Grouping dialog box.
	Properties	Opens or closes the Properties sheet for the selected item.
	Field List	Opens or closes a list of fields for the underlying table that can be included in the report or form via a drag operation.
	Code	Opens the Module window to enter SQL statements to further manipulate the database.
	Toolbox	Opens or closes the toolbox used to create controls.
	Palette	Opens or closes the palette used to control the appearance of fields and lines used in a report.
	Bold	Boldfaces text in a selected field.
	Italic	Italicizes text in a selected field.
	Left-Align Text	Left-aligns text within a selected field or control.
	Center-Align Text	Centers text within a selected field or control.
	Right-Align Text	Right-aligns text with a selected field or control.
	Database Window	Shows the database window.
	Undo	Undoes the most recent change.
	Cue Cards	Displays the on-line coach to help you with a specific task.
	Help	Activates context-sensitive Help when you click a specific area of the screen.

Toolbox Buttons

Button	Name	Function
	Pointer	Deselects an active tool and returns the pointer to its original shape and function. This is the default when the toolbox is displayed.
	Label	Creates a box that contains constant text.
	Text Box	Creates a box that allows you to display and edit text data.
	Option Group	Creates an adjustable frame that can be used to hold toggle buttons, option buttons, or check boxes. Only one object may be selected and active at a time.
	Toggle Button	Creates a button that changes from on to off when clicked with the mouse. The on equals -1; the off equals 0.
	Option Button	Creates a round button that behaves the same as a toggle button.
	Check Box	Creates a check box that toggles on and off.
	Combo Box	Creates a drop-down combo box with a list from which you can select an item or enter a value in a text box.
	List Box	Creates a drop-down list box from which you can select. A list box is a combo box without the editable text box.
	Graph	Launches the Graph Wizard to create a graph object based on a query or table.
	Subform/Subreport	Adds a subform or subreport to a main form or report. The subform or subreport must exist before this control is used.
	Unbound Object	Adds an OLE object to a form or report.
	Bound Object	Displays the contents of an OLE field if that field contains a graphic object. Otherwise, an icon appears at that location.
	Line	Draws a straight line that can be sized and relocated. The size and color of the line can be controlled via the palette.
	Rectangle	Creates a rectangle that can be sized and relocated. Various display attributes are controlled via the palette.
	Page Break	Causes the printer to start a new page at this location in the report.
	Command Button	Creates a command button that, when selected, triggers an event that can execute an Access macro.
	Control Wizards	Toggles the Control Wizards on or off. These wizards can assist you in creating option groups, list boxes, and combo boxes.
	Tool Lock	Maintains the currently selected tool as the active tool until you select another tool, click the Tool Lock button again, or click the Pointer button. Without the lock, Access reselects the pointer tool after you use a tool.

Relational Operators

Operator	Description
<	Less than
<=	Less than or equal to
=	Equal to
>=	Greater than or equal to
>	Greater than
<>	Not equal to

Logical Operators

Operator	Description
Not	The opposite of this expression must occur for this action to take place.
And	This condition requires that both conditions be true before any action will be taken.
Or	This condition requires that only one of the conditions be true for the action to be taken.
()	Parentheses group relations together. If nested parentheses are used, Access evaluates an expression by starting with the innermost set and working outward.

SQL Aggregate Functions

Function	Description
Group By	Specifies the field on which to sort and develop the level break.
Sum	Totals the values in a field.
Avg	Averages the values of a field.
Min	Determines the smallest value in a field.
Max	Determines the greatest value in a field.
Count	Determines the number of values in a field (no null values included).
StDev	Determines the statistical standard deviation of the values in a field.
Var	Determines the statistical variation of the values in a field.
First	Determines the value of the field of the first record.
Last	Determines the value of the field of the last record.

Query Toolbar Buttons

Button	Name	Function
	Design View	Switches to Design View of a query.
	SQL View	Opens the Query window in SQL view and displays the SQL statement for the current query.
	Datasheet View	Switches to the Datasheet view of the query.
	Save	Saves the design of the query to disk.
	Run	Runs the query displayed and shows the results in the Datasheet window.
	Properties	Shows or hides the Properties sheet for the selected item.
	Add Table	Chooses tables or queries whose field lists you want to add to the active query.
	Totals	Shows or hides the Total row in the QBE grid of the Query Design window.
	Table Names	Displays or hides the table names in the QBE grid.
	Select Query	Makes the active query a select query.
	Crosstab Query	Makes the active query a crosstab query.
	Make-Table Query	Makes the active query a make-table query.
	Update Query	Makes the active query an update query.
	Append Query	Makes the active query an append query.
	Delete Query	Makes the active query a delete query.
	New Query	Creates a query based on the active table or query.
	New Form	Creates a form based on the active query.
	New Report	Creates a report based on the active query.
	Database Window	Displays the database window.
	Build	Performs a task or creates an expression using the Expression Builder.
	Undo	Undoes the most recent action.
	Cue Cards	Displays the Cue Cards main menu.
	Help	Invokes Help when you click this button and then the feature about which you wish to obtain help.

Access Basic commands   An Access macro contains Access Basic commands (the internal programming language of Access) which tell Access what actions need to be taken.

action query   Does something with the data after it is obtained.

adding new records   If you want to add new records to a table in the Datasheet window, position the pointer to the last row (the one with the asterisk in the gray border column). You can also click the New Record button on the toolbar, and Access will place in the new record line of the table.

alphanumeric   Combination of the words "alphabetic" and "numeric." A set of alphanumeric characters usually includes special characters such as the dollar sign and comma.

alphanumeric keys   Keys that contain a letter of the alphabet, a number, or a special character.

Alt   Key label for the Alternate key.

Alternate key   Key used to create a second set of function keys in some application programs, to enter the ASCII character code directly from the keyboard, and (together with letters) to enter BASIC commands.

Archive Query   Creates a query that copies records from an existing table into a new table.

arrow keys   Keys (down, up, right, and left) found on the numeric keypad or separately, and typically used to move a pointer or cursor.

AutoReport   A report similar to the Single-Column report is generated. Any intermediate dialog boxes are bypassed, and the report is displayed via the Print Preview window.

Avg command   The Access command that calculates the average for all records containing the specified field.

Backspace key   Key used to erase the last character typed. It is labeled with an arrow that points toward the left.

Between   Access operator that determines whether a numeric value lies within a range of values (for example, Between 1 and 6).

Caps Lock key   Key used to switch the case of letters A through Z on the keyboard. This key does not affect numbers and special characters.

character   Any graphic symbol that has a specific meaning to people. Letters (both upper- and lowercase), numbers, and various symbols (such as punctuation marks) are all characters.

column   Vertical line of text.

common field   A field that has the same name and contents and appears in more than one file.

concatenate   To join two character strings, usually accomplished through the use of the & sign.

concatenation formula   Fields are concatenated in a report layout by joining the fields together with an ampersand (&). When you concatenate text fields, most of them have lower-order spaces (spaces in the right-hand portion of the field). These spaces must be removed before the fields can be joined. The ampersand is Access's way of forc-ing string concatenation of two operands (fields). When a field is being joined to another field via the & command, a space usually has to be included between the fields to make the data readable.

constant text   Information that remains the same from one document to the next.

Control key   General-purpose key whose uses include invoking breaks, pauses, system resets, clear screens, print echos, and various edit commands. In instructions, the Control key is often represented as a caret (^T).

Control Wizards   The Control Wizards in the toolbox make it easy to create embedded macros by stepping you through a series of dialog boxes.

counter field   Used if you want to number the records as they appear in a table, query, and so forth. This type of field cannot be updated.

Create   Access command that lets you build a database and describe the fields and the data type of each field.

Criteria cell   Where you enter any selection criteria for including records in the dynaset for a specified field. After you finish entering the expression and press the Enter key, Access examines it and displays the expression using standard Access syntax.

Crosstab Query   Displays data in a compact, spreadsheet-like format.

Ctrl   Key label for the Control key.

Cue Cards   Special Access help screens that provide text-based information on how to perform a specific task. They can be made up of multiple screens that step you through how to perform a specific task. You can access this feature by entering the command Help, Cue Cards.

currency field   Used to contain money-related data to be used in calculations. It does a better job of rounding for dollars and cents than the Number format. Once the currency data type has been specified, you usually have to indicate how the data is to be displayed and stored in the Properties box for that field.

cursor movement   Operation of moving the cursor through the text.

cursor-movement key   One of the four arrow keys on the numeric keypad, used to move the cursor left, right, up, or down.

data (datum)   Information of any kind.

data type   To be stored in a field, determines the type of field: text, number, yes/no, memo, date/time, currency, counter, and OLE object.

database   A set of information related to a specific application. In the context of Access 2.0, "database" can be viewed as a large repository (like a file cabinet) in which tables, reports, queries, and other objects are stored.

database management   The ability to input, store, report, and manipulate data.

Datasheet window   Access's main method of displaying the records of an invoked (active) table. You can use this window to make any desired changes to a table.

date/time field   Contains eight positions and automatically has the slashes (/) in their correct locations; an empty date field appears as _/_/_.

default   Original (or initial) setting of a software package.

Default Value cell   As the name implies, allows you to specify the default value for a field or control. This default value is entered in a field when a new record is created.

Del   Key label for the Delete key.

Delete key   Key used to erase the character or record at the current cursor position.

delimited parameter   Access command that lets you place specific characters around fields to be copied.

delimiter   Character that indicates to the computer where one part of a command ends and another part begins. Typical delimiters are the space, the period, and the comma.

Detail band   Contains the actual data from the records in the database. Text boxes that allow you to display fields from records are placed in this band.

display   *(noun)* Any sort of output device for a computer, usually a video screen; *(verb)* Placing information on such a screen.

dynaset table When you execute the query, a result set, or dynaset table, is generated that provides a view, or partial picture, of the data contained in one or more database tables. Access allows you to use a dynaset just as you would a database table to display, enter, and edit data. The difference is that instead of dealing with only one table in the Datasheet window, you may be dealing with a number of fields from several different tables that appear in the dynaset.

edit Process by which the format of data is modified for output by inserting dollar signs, blanks, and so on. Used as a verb, it means to validate and rearrange input data.

Enter/Return key The key that is pressed to indicate that you have finished entering an instruction or a paragraph.

error message Message informing you that you typed something the program cannot process or that some other system failure has occurred.

execute To perform the intent of a command or instruction; to run a program or a portion of a program.

extension One- to three-character portion of a filename. Extensions are typically used to indicate families of files, such as backups (.BK!), regular database files (.MDB), and worksheets (.WK1).

field Subdivision of a record that holds one piece of data about a transaction.

field list Displays a field list of the underlying table. The field(s) used in creating the primary key appear in boldface. Fields can be dragged from the list box to the desired location in the report specification.

Field Properties box Besides giving the field name and data type when you are defining the fields of a record, you also want to determine the optimal field length as well as possibly control how the data are to be entered. Field length, alignment, fill characters, color, and other features are controlled via the Field Properties box for each field.

file Collection of data or programs that serves a single purpose. A file is stored on a disk and given a name so you can recall it.

filename Unique identifier of a file, composed of one to eight characters. If an optional one- to three-character extension is used, there must be a period between the filename and the filename extension.

filename extension The three-character portion of a filename that lets you create families of files. If used, a period must be included.

Find Access command used to locate records in a file.

Find Duplicates Query Creates a query that finds duplicate records in a single table or query.

Find First command button Finds the first occurrence of the search string.

Find Next button Used to find subsequent occurrences of the search string.

Find Unmatched Query   Finds records in one table that have now-related records in another table.

For parameter   Access command that lets you specify which records are to be included in a command.

Format cell   Allows you to use a predefined format for a data type as well as to design your own display format.

Forms sheet   Access database window sheet that lets you create a form.

functions   Formulas or processes built into a software package. Functions save a tremendous amount of effort and tedium.

Goto First Record command   Access command that positions the pointer at the first record.

Goto Last Record command   Access command that positions the pointer at the last record.

gridlines   Access automatically includes gridlines around each cell of the table displayed in the Datasheet window. For most people, these gridlines increase the readability of the table by helping the eye track along the appropriate line/record.

Group Footer band   Holds any identifying text and subtotals that have been generated by Access for a group of records.

Group Header band   Contains information such as a group name or text that you want to have printed at the beginning of a group of records. This header is added automatically when the group field is defined to Access.

Groups/Totals report   Table fields are grouped together and totals are generated for each grouping. This is a common style of report.

Handles   When you select a field or its field name, the entry clicked is surrounded by a rectangle made up of little boxes. Each of these boxes is called a handle and can be used in a drag operation to increase or decrease the size of the box.

hard copy   Printed document on paper.

Hide Columns command   Access command that allows you to hide fields so that you can get desired fields together on one screen to make the information from a table more readable. This is accomplished by selecting a column or columns and then issuing the Format, Hide Columns command.

In   Determines whether or not a string value is in a list of values (for example, In("IL", "IA", "MN", "IN")).

Index command   Access command used to order information logically within a file without physically reordering the records themselves. Indexes may be single- or multiple-field.

Input Mask cell   Specifies how data is entered and displayed in the text box. If you do not want to enter the input mask manually, Access allows you to click the wizard button and offers to build the mask for you via the Input Mask Wizard.

Ins   Key label for the Insert key.

Insert key   Key used to tell the computer program that you want to insert characters to the left of the cursor. The Insert mode remains in effect until you press the key again or until you press another special key (arrow keys, Del, End), indicating that you want to go on to a different editing operation.

Is Null operator   Used to determine whether a value is Null or Not Null (whether a field is empty or not empty).

key   Data item (field) that identifies a record.

Last Record   Access command that enables you to position the pointer at the end of the file.

Like   Determines whether a string value begins with one or more specified characters. You must use the wildcards * and ? for this to work properly (for example, Blo*).

lock key   Key used to cause subsequent key operations to be interpreted in a specific manner by the computer. Lock keys are toggle keys; they include Caps Lock, Num Lock, and Scroll Lock.

locking a field   Access command that enables you to make certain that some identifying fields of each record always appear onscreen. This is accomplished by using the Freeze Columns option of the Format menu.

logical operator   The Access operators .AND., .OR., and .NOT.

macro datasheet   Macro instructions are entered in macro datasheets. The Action cell contains an icon which, when selected, displays a selection box with a number of actions that can be used to tell Access what it is supposed to do.

Macros sheet   Access database window sheet that lets you create a macro.

Mailing Label report   Mailing labels are created. Each group of fields constitutes a cell (label) which will be printed according to the design of the stock Avery labels you are using.

memo field   Can hold large documents (up to 64,000 bytes or characters of data). Memo fields can be used when you want narrative descriptive information stored about the entity being represented by the record. For instance, you might want to make annotations about a customer's hobbies, children's names, likes/dislikes, and so forth.

menu   List of commands available to a user of a software package.

multiple-field index   An index created by concatenating two fields of data.

multiple-field sorts   Must be specified to Access via the Filter dialog box.

naming conventions   Access naming conventions include table names and field names. Access allows you to use up to 64 characters. These can include letters, numbers, spaces, and special characters except the period (.), exclamation mark (!), backquote (`), and brackets ({ }).

nested function   Function that resides inside another function. The innermost function must be executed before any outer ones.

Next command   Access command that moves the pointer forward or backward in a file.

Num Lock   Key label for the Numeric Lock key.

number field   Restricted to the sign (+ or –), numerals, and the decimal point(.); the decimal point must be counted as part of the field length. This data type is used anytime you want to be able to perform calculations using the contents of the field.

numeric entry   Process of entering numbers into the computer. The numeric keypad can be set into numeric-entry mode via the Num Lock key; after this has been done, numbers and number symbols (decimal, minus, plus) can be entered.

numeric keypad   Section of the keyboard containing numeric entry and editing keys.

Numeric Lock key   Key used to switch the numeric keypad back and forth between numeric entry and editing.

OLE object field   Can be used to store objects from other Windows applications that support object linking and embedding (OLE). When you display a record that contains an OLE field, you can view the OLE object (graphic image, graph, worksheet, and so forth) by double-clicking the field. Windows then launches the parent application against the OLE object.

output   Computer-generated data whose destination is the screen, disk, printer, or some other output device.

Page Footer band   Contains the text or data that are placed at the bottom of each page. The page number is automatically placed in this band by a Report Wizard.

Page Header band   Defines the area at the top of each page of the report. It contains information such as page numbers, dates, and titles (company name, report name, and column headings).

Page Down key   Key that is sometimes used to cause text onscreen to move up. Text at the top of the screen moves offscreen while text is added at the bottom.

Page Up key   Key that is sometimes used to cause text onscreen to move down. Text at the bottom of the screen moves offscreen while text is added at the top.

palette   Used to add color and the appearance of depth, as well as to change the appearance of borders and lines in forms and reports.

PgDn   Key label for the Page Down key.

PgUp   Key label for the Page Up key.

precedence   Order in which calculations are executed.

"Press any key to continue"   Message often displayed by a program when the computer is waiting for you to do something (read text or load a diskette, for example) and does not know when you will be done. Some keys are generally inactive and do not cause the program to continue when they are pressed; these include Alt, Shift, Ctrl, Scroll Lock, Num Lock, and Caps Lock.

primary key   In Access, the record number; in sorting, the major sort field. The unique identifier for a particular record, most often a unique identifier such as customer number or Social Security number. When a database is in primary-key order, the records may appear in the table in order by the contents of the field used to build the primary key, but no two records can have the same key value.

primary-key index   The unique identifier of a record in a table. Every record within a table must have a different value in a field that has been designated as the primary key.

primary memory   Internal memory used by the computer for a number of different functions. It can contain data, program instructions, or intermediate results of calculations.

printer   Device used to make a paper copy of any output.

procedures   Written instructions on how to use hardware or software.

Properties sheet   Shows the rules governing how a section or control is being displayed.

QBE grid   The query QBE grid can be used to specify the following items about the environment: one or more tables for use, fields and calculated fields, sets or characteristics of records to include, or the order of the records.

query   A set of instructions that specifies how Access should organize or change your data. You use the Query Design window to build a model of the information you want, specifying the tables and desired fields.

record   Entity that contains information about a specific business happening or transaction.

record number   Identification used by Access as the primary key for a record. Also the physical location in the file for a given record.

record pointer   Used to keep track of where the pointer is within a table. The record number that appears on the status bar when you are in the Datasheet window is the current location of the pointer.

relational structure   Structural arrangement consisting of one or more tables. Data are stored in the form of relations in these tables.

Replace command   Makes changes to a specific record or to all records within a table. Unlike the Datasheet window, the Replace command does not display a record before it is changed.

Report   Access command that creates or accesses a parameter file, modifying how a specific printed report is to be generated.

Report Footer band   Holds text and data that you want to have printed at the bottom of the last page of a report. A grand total number would, for instance, appear in this band.

Report Header band   Contains information that you want to appear only on the first page of a report.

report template   An Access entity that contains all the commands needed for generating a report.

Reports sheet   Access database window sheet that lets you create a report template containing the settings to be used in generating a printed report.

resizing a control   You select a control in a form by clicking the mouse on it. The control is now surrounded by a border with eight handles, which allow you to resize the control. Resizing might be needed if you have increased the size of the font being used for text contained in a control. In such a situation, you would grab the right-corner square and drag it downward and to the right until the box is big enough to hold the text of the control.

Row Height command   Used to display the Row Height dialog box and enter a new row height. Access then displays the resized table rows in the Datasheet window.

ruler ribbon   Below the title bar of the Report Design window. As you position objects in the report, their location is shown in a dark shading on the ruler.

scroll   Function that moves all the text onscreen (usually upward) to make room for more text (usually at the bottom).

secondary key   Defined by information from one or more fields within the database. Used to arrange the database in some other order. There may be multiple occurences of a key value.

select query   Gets data from a table but does not do anything with it except display it.

selecting multiple controls   This is accomplished by holding down the Shift key while using a click-and-drag operation to include other controls.

Shift key   Key used to select the upper character on keys that have two characters or to reverse the case of letters A through Z, depending on the status of the Caps Lock key.

Show cell   Used to determine whether or not a field/column is to be displayed in the dynaset. Fields with an × appear in the dynaset generated by the query whereas fields with a blank show box do not appear. Both types of fields can be used to control the records that appear in the dynaset.

Single-Column report   All table fields are placed in one column as text, and the contents of each field are placed in a text box.

single-field index   An index created by Access using the contents of a single field.

status bar   Appears at the bottom of the screen. It displays helpful information while you are using Access.

subroutine   Segment of a program that can be executed by a single call. Subroutines perform the same sequence of instructions at many different places in a single program.

Sum   Access command used to total the contents of a field for all records within a file.

Summary report   Made up of totals for groups of records.

syntax   Structure of instructions in a language. If you make a mistake in entering an instruction and garble the syntax, the computer sometimes responds with the message "Syntax Error".

table structure   A set of instructions regarding the arrangement of information within each record, the type of characters (numeric or alphanumeric, for example) used to store each field, and the number of characters required by each field.

Tabular report   Has each record on one row, similar to the appearance of the Datasheet window display.

target drive   Disk to which files will be copied.

testing   Process by which a program or worksheet is examined and tried out to make certain that it generates the proper results.

text characters   Letters and numbers, usually in English.

text field   Holds any alphanumeric character (number, letter, or special character).

toggle key   Key with two states, on and off, that causes subsequent key operations to be processed in a predetermined manner. Toggle keys include Caps Lock, Num Lock, and Scroll Lock.

toolbar   The toolbar permits you to click on buttons here instead of entering commands via the Access menu structure. The buttons on the toolbar vary with which Access features you have active.

toolbox   The toolbox is a floating toolbar that is displayed whenever the Design view of a form or report is invoked. Clicking one of the toolbox buttons activates that feature, and the pointer then changes to the picture on the tool.

Update command   Access command that lets you use the contents of one file to update another file.

uppercase   Set of upper characters on two-character keys and capital letters (A to Z). Any uppercase character can be typed by holding down the Shift key while pressing the desired key.

Validation Rule cell   Allows you to enter the algebraic or logical expression that is to be evaluated when data are entered for this field. You can enter an algebraic expression manually or use the wizard button to invoke the Expression Builder.

Validation Text cell   Specifies text that is part of the alert dialog box that appears onscreen if the data entered in the field do not conform to the expression entered in the Validation Rule cell.

wizards   Access wizards provide interactive help. Rather than just providing information about a task like Cue Cards do, they ask you questions about the task to be performed and then do most of the work for you. As you start performing various tasks, Access prompts you about whether or not you want to use a wizard.

yes/no field   Will be marked Y (yes) or N (no) and is always only one position in length. A yes is stored as a −1 whereas a no is stored as a 0.

INDEX

Access dialog box, DB.94

Access window, DB.6–DB.11

Action cell selection box for macros, DB.262

Action queries, DB.180

Activating a database, DB.19–DB.21, DB.32–DB.33

Add-ins option, File menu, DB.8, DB.10

Add Table dialog box, DB.18

Alert dialog box example, DB.93

Ampersand (&) as concatenation character,
DB.140–DB.142

Archive query, DB.180

Ascending sorts, DB.65

Asterisk (*), DB.31
as query wildcard, DB.196
as search wildcard, DB.64

AutoForm Form Wizard, DB.240

AutoReports, DB.104
Print Preview window for, DB.198

Avery labels, DB.158
dialog box displaying types of, DB.161
reports, DB.104

Background color of form, DB.255

Backquotes, DB.22

BACKUP command, DB.204

Backup copies of tables via queries, DB.204–DB.210

Between operator, DB.182

Boxes in forms, DB.255–DB.259

Brackets (), DB.22

Buttons
Control Wizards button, DB.262–DB.263
Form View button, DB.251
New Form button, DB.14
New Record button, DB.58
Program button, DB.6
Run button, DB.186

Calculations
embedded in report, DB.151–DB.157
linking tables including, DB.218–DB.221
query calculations on groups of records, DB.199
Case sensitivity with Find command, DB.62

Characters
concatenation character, DB.140–DB.142
input mask, DB.91
table names, DB.22–DB.23

Columns
freezing columns, DB.57–DB.58
hiding columns, DB.54–DB.57

Column Width dialog box, DB.50

Command buttons, DB.13–DB.14

Command Button Wizard dialog box, DB.265–DB.266

Concatenating fields
for index, DB.75
for merge operation, DB.167
in multiple-line reports, DB.140–DB.142

Constant text in report template, DB.163

Control-break processing, DB.130

Controlling data entry and display, DB.89–DB.100

Controls for forms. See Form controls

Control Wizards button, DB.262–DB.263

Copies of tables, exercise for creating, DB.206–DB.208

Copyright screen, DB.6

Counter fields, DB.22

Criteria cell for query fields, DB.185

Crosstab query, DB.180

Cue Cards
defined, DB.18
help window, DB.13
window, DB.7

Currency
data type, DB.25, DB.26
fields, DB.22

Database
creating a, DB.19–DB.21
defined, DB.4
on drive A, DB.24

Datasheet window, DB.30, DB.46–DB.58
changing field display width, DB.48–DB.52
cursor movement in, DB.47
dynasets in, DB.188
with frozen columns, DB.57–DB.58
gridlines in, DB.48
maximized Datasheet window, DB.47
row height, changing the, DB.52–DB.54

Data types, DB.22, DB.23
Date/time fields, DB.22
Default drive, resetting the, DB.46
Default value cell, DB.92–DB.93
Deleting
    cell contents, DB.35
    gridlines in Datasheet window, DB.48
    indexes, DB.75–DB.76
    records, DB.101
    in SpeedMenu, DB.29
Del key, DB.35
Descending sorts, DB.65
Design command, DB.86
Designing fields, DB.4–DB.5
Design view
    for calculations in report, DB.154
    for mailing labels, DB.163
    for multiple-line report, DB.146
    for Report Design window, DB.108–DB.110
    for Report Design window reports, DB.117
    for subtotals report, DB.135
Detail band, DB.110. see also Properties sheet
    form with controls selected in, DB.258
    for merge letter, DB.166
    for multiple-line report, DB.148, DB.149
Dot matrix printers for labels, DB.158
Dragging
    columns, DB.48–DB.49
    resizing records by, DB.54
Drives list box, Open Database dialog box, DB.20
Dynasets, DB.180–DB.182
    in Datasheet window, DB.188

Editing
    field editing commands, DB.35
    help window for, DB.17
    records in table, DB.34–DB.37
Ellipses (...), DB.8
Embedding calculations in report template,
    DB.151–DB.157
Entering data in tables, DB.30–DB.32
Equal sign (=), DB.181
Errors in table structure, DB.28
Exclamation mark (!), DB.22
Exiting Access 2 for Windows, DB.10
Expression Builder, DB.93
    completion of, DB.97

concatenating fields with, DB.140–DB.142
    for merge operation, DB.165–DB.166
Expressions, DB.140

Field cell, DB.184–DB.185
Field list of Report Design window, DB.110
Field Properties, DB.94
    data type selection box, DB.24
Fields. see also specific types
    adding fields to record structure, DB.86–DB.89
    concatenating fields for index, DB.75
    defined, DB.4
    designing fields, DB.4–DB.5
    editing commands for, DB.35
    formats for, DB.89–DB.90
    hiding fields, DB.54–DB.57
    lengths, DB.23
    moving fields, DB.54
    names, DB.23
    naming conventions, DB.22–DB.23
    null values in, DB.94
    position, changing the, DB.100
    properties of, DB.23–DB.24
    in query, DB.184–DB.185
    resizing fields, DB.25, DB.50–DB.52
    selected fields, tables including, DB.208–DB.210
    sunken appearance for fields in forms, DB.258
File, Convert Database command, DB.18
File maintenance via queries, DB.204–DB.210
File menu, DB.8
Filename extensions for tables, DB.22
Filters. see also Sorting
    dialog box, DB.67, DB.77
    for selected records, DB.76–DB.78
    in sorts, DB.66
Find command
    alert dialog box for, DB.63
    continuing search with, DB.64
    dialog box, DB.60, DB.61
in Form Design window, DB.243–DB.244
    help window for, DB.16
    options of, DB.61–DB.62
    records, location of, DB.60–DB.64
    using Find command, exercise for, DB.62–DB.64
    wildcard in search operation, DB.64
Find duplicates query, DB.180
Find First command, DB.62

Find unmatched query, DB.180

Five-up labels, DB.158

FLTR indicator, DB.66

Fonts for forms, DB.248–DB.249

Format cell, DB.89–DB.90

Form controls

    for custom forms, DB.245–DB.246

    for Form Wizards, DB.239, DB.242

    macros for, DB.263–DB.270

    multiple controls, DB.246

    properties for, DB.246–DB.247

    resizing controls, DB.246

    toolbox for, DB.247

Form Design window, DB.239

    speedbar in, DB.242

    toolbox for, DB.263

Form Header band, DB.249

Forms. *see also* Form controls; Form Wizards

    command button in form, exercise for creating, DB.263–DB.270

    custom data-entry forms, DB.245–DB.254

    graphics added to, DB.255–DB.259

    for inserted records, DB.261

    resizing controls, DB.246

    toolbox for controls, DB.247

    using the forms, DB.259–DB.261

Form View icon, DB.251

Form Wizards, DB.236–DB.254

    creating forms, exercise for, DB.240–DB.245

    dialog boxes, DB.237–DB.239

    types of, DB.240

Freeze Columns option, DB.57–DB.58

Glossary, DB.284–DB.289

Go To submenu, DB.59, DB.60

Grand totals, exercise for generating, DB.202–DB.204

Graphics

    in forms, DB.255–DB.259

    in reports, DB.169–DB.172

Graph Wizard, DB.169–DB.172

    Graph Form Wizard, DB.240

Gridlines in Datasheet window, DB.48

Group Footer band, DB.110

Group Header band, DB.109

Groups/Totals reports, DB.104

Groups/Totals Report Wizard, DB.130, DB.131

Hardware limitations for Access 2.0 for Windows, DB.5

Help, Contents command, DB.13

Help facility, DB.11–DB.14. *see also* Cue Cards; Wizards

    exercise for obtaining help, DB.14–DB.18

    Search window of, DB.15

    in SpeedMenu, DB.29

Hide Columns command, DB.54–DB.57

Hiding fields, DB.54–DB.57

Indexes, DB.70–DB.76

    concatenating fields for index, DB.75

    deleting, DB.75–DB.76

    multiple-field indexes, DB.75

    number of, DB.75

    primary-key indexes, DB.70–DB.71

    single-field indexes, DB.71–DB.75

Indexes window, DB.71

In operator, DB.182

Input mask, DB.91–DB.92

    characters, DB.91

Input Mask Wizard, DB.91

Insert Row command, DB.86–DB.89

Is Null operator, DB.94, DB.182

Keyboard Shortcuts, DB.17

Keys, DB.4

Labels, DB.158–DB.163. *see also* Avery labels; Mailing labels

Laser printers for labels, DB.158

Letters, merge operations for, DB.163–DB.168

Level-break processing, DB.130

Like operator, DB.182

Limits of Access 2.0 for Windows, DB.5

Linking tables, DB.210–DB.221

    with calculations included, DB.218–DB.221

    four tables, exercise for linking, DB.214–DB.218

Locking fields, DB.57–DB.58

Logical operators for queries, DB.181

Macro datasheets, DB.261

    creating macros using, DB.270–DB.273

Macros, DB.261–DB.273. *see also* Macro datasheets

    Action cell selection box for, DB.262

    for form controls, DB.263–DB.270

    module window with instructions for, DB.270

Mailing labels, DB.158–DB.163

reports, DB.104

Mailing Label Wizard, DB.158–DB.163

dialog box, DB.159, DB.160

Main/Subform Form Wizard, DB.240

Make-Table Query dialog box, DB.204–DB.205

Margins in subtotal report, DB.138–DB.139

Maximized Datasheet window, DB.47

.MDB files, DB.4

Memo fields, DB.22

entering data in, DB.35–DB.37

Menu bar

in Access window, DB.6, DB.8

of Report Design window, DB.108

Menu-driven interface, DB.5

Menus, moving through, DB.8

Merge operations, DB.163–DB.168

Modes for Access 2.0, DB.5

Module window with macro instructions, DB.270

Mouse, DB.5. *see also* Record pointer

Expression Builder requiring, DB.140

resizing columns with, DB.48–DB.49

selecting column by pointing with, DB.49–DB.50

Moving

in Datasheet window, DB.47

fields, DB.54

through menus, DB.8

Multiple columns, selection of, DB.49

Multiple-field indexes, DB.75

Multiple-field sorts, DB.66–DB.70

Multiple-line reports, DB.139–DB.151

Names

field names, DB.23

naming conventions, DB.22–DB.23

Navigation buttons, DB.59

New button in Query Design window, DB.182

New Form dialog box, DB.236, DB.237

New Form button, DB.14

New Record button, DB.58

New Report dialog box, DB.102

New Table dialog box, DB.25

Null values, DB.94

Number fields, DB.22

Numerical data, DB.31

OLE object fields, DB.22

One-up labels, DB.158

Open Database option

dialog box, DB.10, DB.20

help screen for, DB.12

Output to option in SpeedMenu, DB.29

Page Footer band, DB.110

Page Header band, DB.109, DB.118

Palette, DB.112, DB.113

for forms, DB.255, DB.260

Parent tables, DB.222

Pencil, DB.31

Periods (.), DB.22

PgUp/PgDn, saving with, DB.32

Pointer. *See* Record pointer

Predefined formats, DB.89–DB.90

Primary keys, DB.4

indexes, DB.70–DB.71

Print dialog box, DB.37

Printers

for labels, DB.158

for merge operations, DB.163

Printing

labels, DB.158–DB.163

reports, DB.36–DB.38

Report Wizard reports, DB.106

in SpeedMenu, DB.29

Print Preview, DB.38

for AutoReport, DB.198

for calculations in report, DB.153, DB.157

help about, DB.11, DB.12

for multiple-line report, DB.145, DB.150

for Report Design window reports, DB.116, DB.121

for Report Wizard report, DB.107

for subtotals report, DB.134, DB.138

for three-up labels, DB.162

Program icon, DB.6

Program mode, DB.5

Properties sheet, DB.112, DB.121
    for controls, DB.246–DB.247
    for custom data-entry form, DB.254
    for merge letter, DB.166

Queries, DB.180. *see also* Linking tables
    complex queries, exercise for, DB.191–DB.198
    copies of tables, exercise for creating,
      DB.206–DB.208
    creating queries, exercise for, DB.189–DB.190
    fields in, DB.184–DB.185
    grand totals, exercise for generating,
      DB.202–DB.204
    selected fields, tables including, DB.208–DB.210
    specifications, creation of, DB.182–DB.188
    string searches, DB.196
    subtotals, generation of, DB.199–DB.202
    summary queries, DB.199–DB.202
    table maintenance via, DB.204–DB.210
    table used by, DB.182
    updating tables with, DB.222–DB.227
Queries sheet, DB.181
    recalling queries with, DB.182
Query, Update, Run command, DB.222
Query By Example (QBE) grid, DB.180, DB.182,
    DB.184
    completed grid, example of, DB.186
    dragging fields into, DB.217
    with extension field inserted, DB.219
    for grand total query, DB.203
    for linking tables, DB.213–DB.214
    for updating tables, DB.225
Query Design window, DB.184
    New button in, DB.182
    toolbar, DB.187
    for updating tables, DB.223
Query Properties dialog box, DB.205
Query Wizards, DB.180
Question mark (?)
    as query wildcard, DB.196
    as search wildcard, DB.64

RAM limitations for Access 2.0 for windows, DB.5
Record pointer, DB.58–DB.60
    column selection with, DB.49–DB.50
    manipulation of, DB.58–DB.60

Records
    adding records to table, DB.33
    defined, DB.4
    deleting records, DB.101
    editing records in table, DB.34–DB.37
    navigating through, DB.30–DB.32
    new records, DB.58
    printout of, DB.37–DB.38
Rectangular boxes in forms, DB.255–DB.259
Relational operators for queries, DB.181
Rename option in SpeedMenu, DB.29
Replace command, DB.100
Replace dialog box, DB.100
Report Design window, DB.108–DB.122
    for calculations in report, DB.155, DB.156
    components of, DB.108–DB.112
    exercise for building reports, DB.113–DB.122
    merge template in, DB.164
    order of records for report, DB.115
    toolbar of, DB.108, DB.109
    toolbox of, DB.110, DB.111
Report Footer band, DB.110
Report Header band, DB.108
    centered data in, DB.120
    company name in, DB.119
    graph generated in, DB.171
    for multiple-line report, DB.146–DB.147
    for subtotals report, DB.135
Reports, DB.101–DB.102
    calculations embedded in, DB.151–DB.157
    graphing data in, DB.169–DB.172
    multiple-line reports, DB.139–DB.151
    printing reports, DB.37–DB.38
    with Report Design window, DB.108–DB.122
    with Report Wizard, DB.103–DB.108
    subtotals in, DB.130–DB.139
Reports sheet, DB.101
Report template, DB.101
Report Wizards
    building reports with, DB.103–DB.108
    embedding calculations in reports with,
      DB.152–DB.157
    Groups/Totals Report Wizard, DB.130, DB.131
    Mailing Label command, DB.158–DB.163
    for multiple-line reports, DB.142–DB.151
    subtotals with, DB.130–DB.139

title changes for reports with, DB.107
types of reports with, DB.104
Resizing
columns in Datasheet window, DB.48–DB.52
fields, DB.25, DB.50–DB.52
form controls, DB.246
records, DB.54
Result set, DB.180
Row height, changing the, DB.52–DB.54
Row Height dialog box, DB.53
Ruler ribbon of Report Design window, DB.108
Run icon, DB.186

Save As dialog box, DB.28
Saving
with PgUp/PgDn, DB.32
table structure, DB.28–DB.29
Scroll bars in Report Design window, DB.112
Searching. *see also* Find command
Help facility, Search window of, DB.15
Replace command, DB.100
wildcards in search, DB.64
Secondary keys, DB.4
Select queries, DB.180
for tables, DB.205
Select Query window, DB.182
Send option in SpeedMenu, DB.29
Send to Back command, DB.255
Set Primary Key button, DB.70
Show cell for query fields, DB.185
Show Columns, DB.54
dialog box, DB.56
Single-Column Form Wizard, DB.240
Single-column reports, DB.104
Single-field indexes, DB.71–DB.75
Sort cell for query fields, DB.185
Sorting. *see also* Filters
multiple-field sorts, DB.66–DB.70
on one field, DB.65–DB.66
selected records, filters for, DB.76–DB.78
Specifications for Access 2.0 for Windows, DB.5
SpeedMenus, DB.10–DB.11
options in, DB.29
SQL aggregate functions, DB.199, DB.200
Starting Access 2.0 for Windows, DB.6

Status bar in Access window, DB.11
String concatenations, DB.140–DB.142
String searches, DB.196
Structure. *See* Table structure
Subtotals, queries generating, DB.199–DB.202
Summary reports, DB.104
Sunken appearance for fields in forms, DB.258

Table Design window, 26
indexes from, DB.66
invoking, DB.86
Table Editor, DB.33
Tables. *see also* Dynasets; Indexes; Linking tables;
Table structure
adding records to, DB.33
copies of tables, exercise for creating,
DB.206–DB.208
creating tables, DB.22–DB.30
defined, DB.4
editing records in table, DB.34–DB.37
entering data in, DB.30–DB.32
maintenance via queries, DB.204–DB.210
naming conventions, DB.22–DB.23
queries using, DB.182
record structure for, DB.27
selected fields, tables including, DB.208–DB.210
updating tables with queries, DB.222–DB.227
Table structure, DB.4
adding fields to, DB.86–DB.89
controlling data entry, DB.89–DB.100
creating the structure, DB.24–DB.27
defining table structure, exercise for, DB.27–DB.29
modification of, DB.86–DB.100
notes on creating, DB.28
Tabular Form Wizard, DB.240
Tabular reports, DB.104, DB.105
Tabular Report Wizard dialog box, DB.114, DB.143
Text fields, DB.22
Three-up labels, DB.158, DB.162
Title bar in Access window, DB.6
Toolbar
of Access window, DB.9
buttons, list of, DB.9
of Query Design window, DB.187
of Report Design window, DB.108, DB.109

Toolbox
  for controls to forms, DB.247
  of Form Design window, DB.263
  of Report Design window, DB.110, DB.111

Update command, DB.222
Updating tables with queries, DB.222–DB.227

Validation Rule cell, DB.93–DB.94
Validation Text cell, DB.93–DB.94
Variable text in report template, DB.163–DB.164

Where selection box options, DB.61
Wildcards

in queries, DB.196
in search operation, DB.64
Wizards, DB.18. *see also* Form Wizards; Query
  Wizards; Report Wizards
  Command Button Wizard dialog box,
    DB.265–DB.266
  Control Wizards button, DB.262–DB.263
  Graph Wizard, DB.169–DB.172
  Input Mask Wizard, DB.91

Yes/no fields, DB.22

Zoom command, DB.35–DB.36, DB.186
  for query calculation, DB.220